Philosophical Aspects of the Mind-Body Problem

Philosophical Aspects of the Mind-Body Problem

edited and with an introduction by
Chung-ying Cheng

The University Press of Hawaii
Honolulu

Filmset in Hong Kong by Asco Trade Typesetting Ltd.

Manufactured in the United States of America
Designed by Penny L. Faron

Library of Congress Cataloging in Publication Data

Conference on the Philosophy of Mind and Psychology,
    University of Hawaii, 1968.
    Philosophical aspects of the mind-body problem.

    Includes bibliographies and index.
    1. Mind and body—Congresses. I. Cheng, Chung-ying,
1934–   II. Title.
BF161.C68   1968   150'.19   75–17914
ISBN 0–8248–0342–6

Contents

Preface

THE PRESENT volume contains the proceedings of a most stimulating conference (The Conference on the Philosophy of Mind and Psychology) that was held at the University of Hawaii in March 1968. It provided a splendid opportunity for an exchange and comparison of ideas on one of the central issues of modern and current philosophy: the cluster of problems regarding the relations of mind and body. There is little doubt that this vital issue had been temporarily suppressed (if not repressed!) especially by the philosophical behaviorists, by the positivists—and that it was "solved" in a highly problematic and controversial way by various materialists, physicalists, emergentists, identity theorists, dualistic interactionists, parallelists, or epiphenomenalists.

While the most important contributions toward the dénouement of (what Schopenhauer called) the *Weltknoten* (the world knot) are to be expected, and are indeed most promisingly forthcoming from neuro-psychophysiology, the indispensable task of the philosophers should not be underestimated. Philosophers notoriously disagree even on the formulation of the problem(s), and still more strongly on the proposed solutions. Nevertheless, a large majority of them are convinced that there are *conceptual* questions that need to be answered if an all-around satisfactory resolution of the issues is to be attained.

To this end, it seemed extremely worthwhile for a group of American philosophers to convene with two of Australia's most outstanding philosophers of science, and in several days of intensive discussion to thrash out at least some aspects of the perennially vexing mind-body problems. Hawaii seemed a most desirable and plausible mid-point for such a meeting. Judging by the enthusiasm with which the participants engaged in the search for greater clarity, the present book should prove very interesting, perhaps exciting, to its readers.

It can hardly be expected that a conference of a few days and the subsequent reflections would produce any "final" settlement of the crucial questions. But it is our hope that we have contributed in a fruitful way toward at least the clarification of the basic ideas in this domain.

The participants wish to express their sincere gratitude to the University of Hawaii, and especially to Professor Winfield E. Nagley, chairman of the University of Hawaii's philosophy department, for making splendid arrangements; to the Minnesota Center for Philosophy of Science (University of Minnesota), and the Carnegie Corporation of New York, as well as the Rand Corporation of Santa Monica, California, for generously supporting our conference.

HERBERT FEIGL

Minneapolis, 1972

Introduction:
Understanding the Identity
Theory and Its Problems

Chung-ying Cheng

THE PROBLEM of mind-body relationship would be a pseudoproblem if no precise and meaningful formulation of the problem and no intelligible discussions of solutions were possible.[1] In the past twenty years Herbert Feigl has rescued the problem from charges of scientific nontestability and has effectively shown that both the problem and its solution can be precisely and significantly articulated. He has pointed out that the problem can be divided into three basic problems— of *sentience*, of *sapience*, and of *self-hood*—and that each can be separately related to logical and neuro-physiological considerations of empirical import.[2]

On the basis of Feigl's distinction, the problem of mind-body relationship has been vividly and fruitfully discussed in contemporary philosophy. On the proposed solution side, if we confine our attention to the problem of relating the mental to the physical on the level of sentience, there is a spectrum of positions ranging from Cartesian-type dualism to thorough-going physicalistic monism. According to the former, the mental and the physical are absolutely separate and distinct principles which must not be reduced to each other. On the other hand, reductive materialism such as represented by J. J. C. Smart holds that data of perception and feeling have no reality in themselves, but are completely explainable in terms of scientific principles of basic physical sciences. Between these two extremes, of course, there are positions described as interactionism, epiphenomenalism, and emergentism, all of which permit a certain degree of autonomy for the mental, and yet at the same time attempt to explain the mental as fundamentally related to various primary dimensions of the physical. The existence of these positions clearly demonstrates that the problem of relationship between the mental and the physical is eminently significant and philosophically interesting.

With this brief account of contemporary perspectives on the mind-body problem, we are confronted with the task of explaining the most relevant issues in current discussions of this problem. Fortunately, Feigl's article, "Some

Crucial Issues of Mind–Body Monism," reprinted in this volume, seems to best serve our purpose of elucidation.[3]

In his article, Feigl points out the importance of recognizing the status and role of immediate experience in a philosophical account of mind-body relationship. He recognizes the data of immediate experience as radically different from things-in-themselves, which he considers fully knowable. The knowledge which we possess of things-in-themselves, according to Feigl, is known by description. In contrast, it might be expected that Feigl would identify knowledge of any of the data of immediate experience with knowledge by acquaintance. He calls data of immediate experience "nomological danglers" which are first-personal and private and which can be known by description from a third-person point of view. In this sense, the strict sense of knowledge as objectively and scientifically verifiable is maintained and regarded as sufficient for the explanation of human behavior. Given this concept of knowledge, one might ask what significance could be attached to the understanding of the data of immediate experience. A simple reply to his question, in light of Feigl's discussion, is that these data are beginning points for confirmation of theories, for identification of features of cerebral processes, as well as for the presupposed references of moral imperatives. All these do not require that they are incorrigible, for statements of them could be revised in the light of further observations and theorizing. Furthermore, they do not exist by themselves, but are always "suffused" with "interpretations, remnants of memory, expectations, etc." and are therefore Gestalt patterns and configurations of experience. Given these Gestalten, an isomorphism can be seen to hold between these and certain features of brain processes. What is made clear by these points is that the data of immediate experience are not absolutely fixed and are not to be understood or identified out of interpretative contexts. When appropriately understood, they are to be regarded as a reflection of various brain processes.[4]

Although Feigl does not push for this point, the suggestiveness contained in it should give reasons for avoiding certain dualistic objections to the identity theory of mind and body. Feigl also seems to regard introspective avowals of "raw feels" as direct evidence of knowing them. In other words, if I could say "I have a pain," I could say "I know that I have a pain."[5]

There are now two further points which essentially bear upon the identification of the phenomenal experience. First, Feigl regards reference to a person's own immediate experience as "the prototype of all designations of objects, properties or relations by the words of our language." This suggests that reference to one's own immediate experience is the basis and starting point of reference to objects, and so forth. How this might be true should be made clear. In referring to an object, one explicitly or implicitly uses indexical expressions such as "this," "that," "now," "there," or "here." All have a built-in reference to "I," which can be held to be understandable only when statements like "I am in pain" and "I am afraid" are understandable.

Second, Feigl distinguishes between the truth condition and the confirming evidence of a knowledge-claim. In personal statements of immediate experience, he says, if we regard the truth condition of such a statement as what objectively will be identified as the central state of the brain for a state of immediate data, and the confirming evidence as avowals of such immediate experience, then their truth conditions could be identified with their confirming evidence. Perhaps in saying that truth conditions can be identified with confirming evidence, Feigl means that the mental and the physical can be identified in a powerful theory of corresponding specification of brain states. The implication is that the truth condition of such a statement *interprets* and explains the confirming evidence, even though the person who has the confirming evidence in his direct experience may not *know* the truth condition of his statement of direct experience.

The crux of Feigl's position regarding the data of immediate experience perhaps can be summarized as follows:

1. Statements of immediate experience are not incorrigible.
2. They are to be understood in interpretative contexts.
3. By introspection, one knows the truth of statements of immediate experience.
4. Reference to one's own immediate experience is the prototype of all designations of objects, properties, and relations.
5. Statements of immediate experience can be interpreted as signifying types of central states of brain and therefore are basically explainable by reference to them.

These points represent a monism of mind and body which is not a reduction of the mental to behaviorial patterns, or elements of sensation to aspects of stimulus, but to physical central states of the brain in empirically well-defined neurophysiological contexts. Even if one grants that statements of immediate experience can be interpreted or explained as basically referring to central states of mind in neurophysiological contexts, it does not follow that, knowing one's reference to an immediate experience of introspection, one comes to know the brain state corresponding to the experience. To know this, one needs bridge laws or correspondence rules in a theory which, however, should be empirically testable. From this point of view it is clear that the identity of the mental and the physical has to be understood from a nonpersonal scientific perspective, whereas the reference to the mental has to be understood from a personal introspective perspective. The distinction between the physical and the mental therefore becomes a distinction between the nonpersonal and the egocentric perspectives (or categories). What perhaps cannot be reduced is the egocentric perspective in terms of the nonegocentric scientific perspective and vice versa. Even though the scientific perspective and egocentric perspectives cannot be mutually reduced, they need not be considered incompatible, nor need they be considered incompatible with the identity thesis of mind and body. In fact, they can be considered complementary in light of the actual procedures of constructing bridge laws or correspondence rules between them and the possible procedures of anchoring referential concepts and observables in a theoretical network.[6]

The egocentric perspective provides, and in a sense selects, the data of immediate experience as referential points (referents) to which scientific concepts can apply. Without such provision science will not be experientially anchored and will remain an empty structure devoid of substance. On the other hand, it is the scientific theory which gives interpretative meanings to the data immediately experienced and relates them in a structure for rational understanding. Given this view, Feigl's "nomological danglers" have a special place in the system of science. He says, "The 'anchoring' of a theory in data of experience is precisely what distinguishes physics from pure mathematics."[7] In other words, whereas mathematics is structural and can be considered with no reference to experience, physical science is a structure with reference to experience. If we follow this line of construal of scientific knowledge, the identity theory of the physical and the mental can be defended without abolishing the belief that the data of immediate experience are available to an individual. For what is privately available to an individual can be presumably explained by scientific concepts without changing the identifying reference of the sense experience. In fact, the sense experience serves as an index where scientific concepts could apply. All possible differences in subjective experiences of sense can be also looked upon as differences in associated interpretations of the experiences, whereas all such experiences share the universal referential forces for identifying objects for scientific description.[8]

If science itself is categorical and intersubjective in its structural description of reality, then science as a structural description of reality must be invariant to all possible varieties of sense modalities. It follows from this that (1) any Martian being with the intelligence of the human being, even with different immediate experience, generally could arrive at the same concepts and the same theories in describing reality, and that (2) he could arrive at descriptive knowledge of human sensations and psychological life, including data of immediate experience of human beings, on the basis of scientific knowledge as accessible through his own sense modalities.[9]

This amounts to saying that scientific knowledge applies to all modalities of sense which are referential points of this knowledge. But in order to argue for the identity of mind and body, we have also to consider the possibility of describing the mental in terms of the physical, even though the physical as demonstrated in a system of scientific concepts is referentially related to the mental experience (or data of immediate experience). If we consider mental predicates (M) as descriptive and not only referential (or indexical), then the identity of mind and body implies the replacement of M in terms of a set of physical predicates (P), or a reinterpretation of M in terms of P. Even though there is no absolute reason why M must be replaced by P or reinterpreted in P, the systematic structure provided by neurophysiology and behaviorial sciences should be a sufficient reason for providing the description of the mental in terms of the physical. Thus the identity thesis of mind and body can be largely explained as describing the mental in terms of the physical, while maintaining the referential power of the mental. If there is a better system which can be applied to the description of the mental, then it should replace the original given system for achieving a better description of the mental. In light of these possible replacements of one set of concepts by a successor set, the identity of mind and body becomes more precisely describable as conforming to whatever scientific theories are accepted at a given time. The ultimate question of the mind-body identity is how the mental can be precisely and objectively and propositionally identified in a system of concepts which apply to all things in the universe other than what is referred to the mind.[10]

In regard to this identity thesis of mind and body, what Feigl has formulated as a thesis of cross-categorial identification can be restated. It is held by Feigl that concepts designating qualities of immediate experience and concepts referring to entities in the physical world are of different semantical types. Thus the monism of mind and body resulting from identification of mentalistic phenomena with the neurophysiological events and processes is a case of cross-categorial identification. To be more precise, the cross-categorial identification is one of identifying description of the physical with the description of the mental. But in light of what we have said earlier, this identification is best understood as consisting of two steps: (1) identifying what has been identified by immediate experiences as points of reference for physical descriptions, and (2) replacing phenomenal descriptions of the data of immediate experience by physicalistic descriptions in contexts of intersubjective scientific framework. In this sense cross-categorial identification can be described as mutual replacement of two sets of concepts with regard to the same set of objects of reference.[11]

One might even suggest that Quine's canonical extensional language can be used to express the scientific intersubjective descriptions of the mental in which egocentric particulars ("I," "now," "here," etc.) and egocentric universals ("being hot," "being painful," etc.) will disappear. In their place, there are merely scientific universals and definite descriptions and bound variables. But this does not imply an elimination of the egocentric perspective. Nor is this logically incompatible with the existence of such a perspective. It might even be suggested that some bound variables of the Quinean type of canonical language will range over egocentric particulars as produced by the egocentric perspective, and some intersubjective concepts of the Quinean type of canonical language will be equivalent to some mentalistic descriptions (egocentric universals) from the egocentric point of view.

Feigl has noted a number of controversial questions on the arguments for the iden†ity theory. Two seem to be important for a possible refutation of the identity thesis.

First, there is the argument on "the difference in 'grain' between the phenomenal continuity (for example, of a smooth color expanse, or the homogeneity of a musical tone) and the atomic structure of the 'corresponding' brain process." Although there is no ready explanation for such difference, it is possible to construct a logical argument that could point to the fact that the difference in question does not make a difference. Granted that what we perceive is a continuous color expanse and that we can say that we have a percept of continuity, and granted that our brain process is describable only in terms of quantum discontinua of neurons, then we have two different models (the percept of the mental and the concept of the brain) of the same thing, one continuous and one discontinuous. But it is logically possible that the theory of perceptual continua can have a model in the domain of denumerable objects (by the Löwenheim-Skolem theorem), if it has an intended nondenumerable model. In light of this logical argument it is clear that the grain argument need not be an obstacle in establishing the identity thesis. What the grain argument means is simply that, given that the mental reference and the physical reference are identical, there could be two nonequivalent models for the description of the mind-body reference. The grain argument implies at most that at present the physicalistic description, being noncategorial in regard to some phenomena, is logically incomplete. This does not imply that the identity thesis is refuted or false.

There is a second serious argument against monism of mind and body, namely, that parallelism or epiphenomenalism is as good as the identity thesis. The identity thesis has no specific ground for recommending its acceptance other than that for the acceptance of parallelism and epiphenomenalism. Feigl does not consider this a simple case of using Occam's razor. He points out that if we mean by "physical" the structural type of conception and by "mental" the phenomenal experience, then "the physical (in the sense just defined) may well designate (or codesignate) those small parts of the world which are phenomenal as well." In other words, the identity of mind and body is not so much an identity of the mental and physical descriptions, but the description of the phenomenal experiences as identified by the mental in terms of the physical. If there is any reason for doing this, there is reason for the statement of the identity of the structure of the phenomenally given with the structure of aspects of cerebral processes. Whereas parallelism and epiphenomenalism have to posit two sets of references, the identity theory permits positing only one identifiable set of references (namely, those identified by immediate experience) and the possibility of replacement between systems of concepts of description as explained above. The case is clearly not one of logical simplicity, but one involving empirical certification to the effect that, whereas the egocentric (the mental) does serve to identify a reference, the intersubjective (the physical) perspective yields only structural descriptions of things as identified by perception or extended perception.[12]

Against this conceptual background, the essays in this volume were developed out of a conference specifically devoted to the consideration of the identity theory of mind and body. This volume presents a variety of viewpoints and approaches to problems surrounding the theory. There are in the main three types of positions.

One type of position argues that the identity between mind and body can be maintained for both logical and empirical reasons. Another type of position shows the incompleteness of the physicalist theory of the mental, while granting the validity of such a theory. The third type criticizes the identity theory in order to demonstrate why such a theory is logically impossible and empirically unnecessary. Apart from these, one contribution in this volume comes from an experimental psychologist. James T. Townsend's article deals with the psychophysical equation between perceptual responses and external stimuli, which can be regarded as neutral to the issue of the identity theory. Even though Townsend asserts that his paper shows the unity of mind and body, the experimental results can be nevertheless construed as manifesting an empirical lawlike correlation between the mental and the physical, which is susceptible of an identity interpretation as much as of a parallelistic or epiphenomenalistic interpretation.

Representing the first type of position mentioned above are contributions by Pepper, Smart, Lewis, Maxwell, and Cheng. Representing the second are contributions by Ellis, Cheng, and Gunderson. Criticism of the identity theory itself is made in the two contributions by Watanabe.

Stephen Pepper in his essay, "A Split in the Identity Theory," has resolutely rejected the parallelism of mind and body in favor of the identity theory. As he sees it, there are far more difficulties than are recognized in explaining the mental in the parallelistic thesis. He points out further that there are other important reasons than those of parsimony for a defense of the identity thesis. Among these reasons the causal (representative) theory of perception counts as a strong support for the identity thesis for Pepper. The causal (representative) theory of perception is the view that perception is explained in terms of stimuli from external objects, neural responses of the organism as well as the physical media receiving the stimuli and eliciting the responses. On the basis of this view, the difference in perceptual content of a physiologist's observation of a person's brain and his introspective report correlated with it could be expected and yet accounted for. The identity theorist would consider what is referred to as the brain state of the percipient of a sensation as identical with what is referred to as the introspective report of the percipient. One need not and could not identify the mental state of the percipient with what is referred to as the mental state of the third-person inspector, just as one cannot and should not identify the mental state of an individual with the physical object actually perceived. Furthermore,

Pepper points out, a physiologist can read what he perceived in light of his theory. This means that one can be taught to replace the language and concepts of private experience with the language and concepts of neurophysiology in describing the introspective experience of sense perception.

Pepper has distinguished three types of identity theories of mind and body: the double-language theory, the physical-identity theory, and the qualitative-identity theory. The double-language theory is attributed to Feigl in his early papers. It is the view that the *same* events are described by the physicalistic language of natural science and the phenomenalistic language of introspection. This leaves many objections unanswered, such as the question as to what is the more basic language for describing the common object. The two remaining theories attempt to answer these questions.

The physical-identity theory as presented by J. J. C. Smart attempts to explain all qualitative sense experiences in terms of behavioralistic and ultimately neurophysiological descriptions and holds that there is no loss, but rather gain, of precision and scope in such an attempt. The physical-identity theorist would then conclude that the so-called *qualia* are but disguised brain processes. The difficulty with this theory is that there is uncertainty about the full reduction of the meaning of phenomenalistic language describing felt qualia to physicalistic terms. This difficulty of the physical-identity theory is then taken up in the qualitative-identity theory as represented by Feigl in his more recent writings. According to this view, the actually felt qualitative events of immediate experience are identical with brain processes in the conceptual physical description of these events. The phenomenal event is known by acquaintance and the physical event is known by description. What is thus known as knowledge by acquaintance is nonstructural and nonrelational, whereas what is thus known as knowledge by description is structural and relational. The phenomenal event and the physical event are identical and yet known in different ways. Feigl also maintains that both ways of knowing are not incorrigible. The difference between this theory and the double-language theory is that the felt qualia of experience are known in different ways and yet these ways of knowing are supplementary and need not overlap, nor are they mutually substitutable. Both belong to an integral knowledge of the event designated as the mental in the phenomenal report.

Pepper points out that, as a street map is related to actual streets, there should be perfectly isomorphic relationships between characters of the map describing an intersection and relevant features in the actual experience of the person reading the map. On the strength of this analogy, Pepper also seeks to account for the "grain" difficulty mentioned in our discussion of Feigl's article— the difference of "grain" between raw feel of homogeneity and continuity vs. atomized discreteness, thus between the physical description and the phenomenal description. But the difference in question can be regarded as similar to the difference between a detailed description in the map and a less detailed perception of the street at an intersection. Pepper admits that one has to introduce other factors to account fully for this discrepancy. In general, for this exposition of the qualitative-identity theory, which Pepper proposes to refer to as "qualitative neural identification theory," it is not made clear whether the phenomenal language will be abolished in the actual description of the phenomenal. As his map analogy suggests, both physical and phenomenal languages must be used, as they are to be regarded as complementary, one for identification and the other for description.

David Lewis' article, "Psychophysical and Theoretical Identifications," proposes a new argument for the identity theory of mind and body. In this argument, Lewis appears to hold an identity theory of Pepper's physicalistic kind.

Lewis, like Pepper, holds that psychophysical identities are not posited for the sake of parsimony, but can be conceived as implied consequences of a suitable physiological theory. The essence of Lewis' argument is as follows:

Mental state M = the occupant of causal role R
def

Neural state N = the occupant of causal role R
def

Therefore M = N

Apparently the central importance of this argument is reserved for the causal role R supposedly occupied by both M and N. R thus functions as a middle term in a syllogism. Lewis suggests that R could be conceived as defined in a suitable theory T. Then the mental states could be regarded as T-terms (theoretical terms) and given meaning by T, for they are regarded as occupants of the causal roles specified by T. Later if we find that the neural states M realize T (i.e., T as an open sentence is true of N), we could, with reference to a functional definition of M which specifies its causal roles in T, logically infer the identity of M and N. There is no difficulty of general logic in this account, but there could be several substantive difficulties regarding the inference of the psychophysical identity. First, one has to assume that a well-defined theory of mental states has been developed; this also should include warranted assertions regarding causal connections of M to behaviors (stimuli and motor responses) and among themselves. One has also to assume that meanings of our M terms are actually given by such T. These assumptions are to be proven if they are to hold as premises for the psychophysical identity. Lewis himself could accept them only as a "good myth," however. Thus there is the possibility that the first premises are not satisfied or satisfiable.

Second, even granted the existence of a satisfactory theory of mental states T, it is an open question how we come to discover neural states as playing the same causal roles defined by T. We could develop a theory T′ of neural states and then prove that T and T are isomorphic. However, it is also possible that descriptions of the neural states merely accidentally coincided with descriptions of T, while in fact remaining separate and distinct from M. Descriptions of a murderer could fit more than one person. One could, as Lewis does, require that the description be uniquely realizable. But this does not automatically apply to the mind and body case, for the theory of mental states as an incomplete theory may be exemplified in more than one model. The requirement that $t = (\gamma x) T (x)$ therefore becomes gratuitous.[13] In the murder case mentioned in Lewis' article, the true murderers could be three totally different persons. Thus the second premise of Lewis' syllogism could be called into question.

Finally, even granting the validity of Lewis' argument, the only conclusion that one can draw is that $M = N$ relative to T or to the causal roles which they both uniquely play. But given a different theory T ', M and N may be regarded as playing different roles and hence are distinct entities. There could be a theory T ' such that M satisifies T ' but N does not, and vice versa. This can be best illustrated by the Mr. Hyde and Dr. Jekyll case. Are Dr. Jekyll and Mr. Hyde one person or two different persons? "They" play different roles in different contexts. In one, a murderer is identified as Dr. Jekyll, in another a good Samaritan is identified as Mr. Hyde. There is no reason to object to conceiving of Jekyll and Hyde as in fact two different persons. The criticism intended here is that Lewis' argument establishes only a relative and hypothetical identity.[14]

Assuming satisfaction of his premises regarding the mental and the physical, the original intent of Lewis' identity theory is to argue for the identity as consisting in explaining the *causal roles* of mind, independently of a well-defined theory of mind.[15]

Smart, in his essay "On Some Criticisms of a Physicalist Theory of Colors," suggests a modification of his theory of colors. In his book *Philosophy and Scientific Realism*, he originally defined colors as dispositions of physical objects to evoke characteristic patterns of discriminatory color behaviors by normal human percipients in normal circumstances. But colors of things can change systematically without entailing changes in patterns of discriminatory behavioral responses as evoked by physical objects. To acknowledge such changes and to avoid circularity, one has to bring in color experiences in human beings which should not be defined in terms of objective properties of things. But if this is the case, one has to give up the entire physicalist theory which Smart seeks to establish. To remedy the situation, Smart accepts the view (as originally proposed by David Lewis) that colors are physical states of the surfaces of objects which normally explain patterns of discriminatory reactions of normal human percipients. The question is how to characterize these physical states of the surfaces of objects. Do we characterize them by referring to our patterns of discriminatory behaviors? But there could be many mixtures of properties (e.g., wave lengths of light), which give rise to the same color reactions in a normal percipient. If there is no simple formula for describing these properties (e.g., greenness), they have to be conceived as "disjunctive and idiosyncratic properties." But one does not know from recognizing the simple patterns of discriminatory color behaviors whether the properties which cause them are disjunctive or simple. Because they could be disjunctive, one has to allow that two different physical states can cause the same patterns of color behavior. A and B can be different, and yet each can explain the same phenomenon C. Thus one need not appeal to color experiences for explanations of color changes. They are explained by physical states of things and the brain states of the normal percipients. To generalize, one might apply similar arguments to produce explanations of other types of discriminatory behavior of human beings and consolidate a physicalist picture of the world without any mention of the mental experiences as explanans. The overall question of this physical identity theory, then, is whether qualitative experiences of differences of colors in the above color-change situation really mean an objective difference after all. A collateral question is how we come to discover different causes of our same discriminatory behavior without giving a report of difference in color experiences. In other words, even granted that different physical properties may cause the same patterns of color behavior, assuming different sense experiences of color, there is the question of explaining different color experiences in terms of the same or similar (different physical) properties.

The question of an adequate explanation of different sense experiences by the same physicalistic properties is taken up in Brian Ellis' article, "Physicalism and the Content of Sense Experience." Ellis maintains that, as no physicalist theory could account for the existence of qualia (contents) of sense experience, no physicalist theory is complete since there will always be "nomological danglers" in the theory.

Ellis' argument for such a thesis is as follows: Given two different taste experiences, Ea and Eb, which one best fits description D? Since a highly developed physicalist theory of taste experience is capable of explaining (or predicting) every fact about a taste experience that one is capable of describing, T will explain and predict D. But then it could not explain or predict why there was one taste experience rather than the other. In other words, T will predict Ea just as well as Eb. Thus, if $N_t A$ is a neural state occurring at t, and $M_t(E_y)$ is a corresponding mental state occurring at t, and E is best described by D, then

$$N_t(A) \supset (\exists E) (M_t(E) \cdot D(E))$$

Both Ea and Eb could instantiate E to make the prediction true.

According to Ellis, this means that there are irreducible and logically distinct qualia of sense experiences which are descriptively identical. In order to identify a specific sense experience Ea, one has to add an extratheoretical singular statement to the effect $N(R_a) = M(E_a)$. For this cannot be derived from T and indeed cannot even be known until E_a is experienced. Thus T is incomplete with regard to the types of statements of contingent identities. By the same token, Ellis holds that T also cannot explain any contingent occurrence of events which are not confined to those of sense experience, and hence are incomplete with regard to these types of statements as well. The generalized form of argument along this line, according to Ellis, consists of recognizing that no matter how highly developed T is, T could be realized or instantiated in more than one instance. This is comparable to [the case of] an axiomatic system, for which it is always possible to have more than one physical interpretation. Granting this argument, it is clear that the incompleteness of a theory is in its noncategorialness. This again is explained ultimately in terms of the different indexical instantiations of the same given description.

With this logical sense of incompleteness understood, the neurophysiological theory could be regarded as incomplete and in its nature unable to predict any unique occurrence of an instance of an event. For T is made to explain single occurrences of sense experiences when they are already identified. In this sense, then, there is no harm in the incompleteness of a theory. For if sense experiences are identified merely for explanation, there is no need for explaining these identifications. The nomological danglers can be regarded simply as indexical identifications of sense experience explained by T. They can be thus regarded as instantiating principles for instantiating neurophysiological laws. In this sense it is generally right, as Ellis points out, that "nomological danglers" are not confined to sense experiences of human beings, but could extend to cover all things in so far as they can be indexically identified for explanations.

Even though Ellis is correct in insisting on the relevance of instantiating principles for an account of specific experiences, he goes a little far in suggesting that we could not explain two distinct sense experiences which fit one best description. For he maintains that we could discriminate between two distinct sense experiences, but may not be able to describe them differently. If this is true in theory, then sense experiences become simply "ineffable." The two sense qualia which Ellis supposes cannot be separated by description could be numerically different or qualitatively different. Apparently when we regard the difference as due to indexical reference, the difference becomes merely numerical. But even in this weak sense of numerical difference, one can still create different descriptions by taking into consideration contexts in which the two sense experiences are found or identified. Some describable difference could be found in the contexts (temporal, spatial, and qualitative), and thus by reference to such contexts one could reach different descriptions to avoid the charge of nonexplicability of sense qualia. Sense qualia, not *qua* qualia, but *qua* items in contexts, are descriptively different and thus differently explainable by T. The net result is that the more we know about a context of a sense experience the more we know of the qualia in that context, and the more able we are to present a "complete" account of sense experiences. This knowledge of contexts corresponds to what Maxwell refers to as structural knowledge of sense experiences. From this point of view, the most we can say about incompleteness of a theory is that it does not instantiate or identify by direct experiences similar indexical sense experiences. There is no reason for Ellis to consider a theory incomplete otherwise.

Chung-ying Cheng's "Mind and Body: Aspects of Identity" discusses another problem of completeness of a universal physicalistic theory. It is a problem directed toward assessing in what sense of completeness that which Sellars has called a complete scientific image can be complete. Clearly one criterion for this intended completeness is that the theory should be capable of explaining the "cross-categorial" identity between the mental and the physical, as well as the theory or the system of the phenomenal or the mental experience. Two senses of explanation by this theory are distinguished: the weak sense of explaining the phenomenal and the mental by deriving and predicting what the theory of the mental predicts or describes without the theorist presupposing any knowledge of the mental system T_m. An example might be the Martian scientist who learns and predicts all human behavior on the basis of his microtheories without his knowing any mental terms based on introspective experience. The strong sense of explaining, on the other hand, consists in producing the weak explanation plus knowledge that what is explained in physicalist terms is in some cases equivalent to what is identified and experienced as the phenomenal and the mental. On the basis of this distinction, a theory is called complete in a weak sense if it provides a weak explanation, and is called complete in the strong sense if it produces a strong explanation. But there is a paradox in the case of strong explanation. If one has to identify what is derived from T in physicalistic terms with actually experienced sense experiences, then one has to know the phenomenal and the mental independently of the universal physicalistic theory T. This would immediately destroy the intended completeness of T unless such knowledge is also accounted for in T. The answer to this predicament is to admit that such knowledge is both genuine and accountable in T. To make this possible it must be admitted that when a universal physicalistic theorist predicts and derives knowledge of the neural states of his brain corresponding to his feelings of pain, he will actually experience the pain as pain and be able to identify what he knows as experienced pain with what he knows as the neural state of his brain. This means simply that a complete physicalist theory must somehow be exemplified in actual experiences in order to be strongly explanatory. The manifest image of those experiences and of knowing is hence not given away in the scientific complete image, but instead acquires an objective place in the physicalist theory. It becomes a matter of interpretation of the sense experience in T, not a simple reduction.

A further requirement along this line is obvious in regard to the universal physicalist theory as something known as a theory to the universal physicalistic theorist. If knowledge is considered a matter of mental awareness, the theory has to assign a corresponding brain state for such knowledge in the universal scientist. The scientist will have to know his knowledge as a brain state of a complicated structure. This process of knowing one's knowledge *as* a brain state will have to be a consequence of the theory known as a brain state. The infinite regress here is not harmful in so far as this principle of self-referential explanatoriness is recognized. This principle of self-referential explanatoriness is to identify knowledge of the theory as knowledge of a brain state which should be a part of what is described in the theory. It is a form of identification that the theory has to introduce. It can be called epistemic identification. To recognize that the physical is recognized in some cases as the mental by the theory is another instance of epistemic identification. For a complete physicalist theory, both self-referential epistemic identification and nonself-referential epistemic identification must be introduced and recognized as experienced by the universal theorist. This general principle of (self-referential and nonself-referential) epistemic identifications is equivalent to the identification of the weak explanatoriness with the strong explanatoriness of the theory in the theory.

Cheng has argued that there are many aspects of identity of the mental and the physical in the identity theory. The above epistemic identity in a physicalist theory is an identity often neglected in understanding the (complete) implication of an identity-theoretic depiction of the world. Two other reasons for the identity theory are recognized and argued for in Cheng's article. It argues that the mental and the physical should be identified with each other for both logical and methodological reasons, and thus that the identity theory is both logically and methodologically superior to parallelism. The logical strength of identification comes from the descriptive and ontological simplicity which it could achieve. It is specifically referred to as a kind of axiomatic decision made by the identity theorist. But there are empirical and methodological reasons for the identity theory as well. In a pragmatic context of extended testing and inquiry, the identity theory is a hypothesis which leads to more fruitful testing than parallelism, and in the end to better factual integration of theoretical knowledge. Specifically, Cheng has reached the view that the primariness and privacy of introspective data of immediate experience need not controvert the scientific process of physicalistic description or explanation, for the primariness and privacy of such data can be regarded as demonstrating actual instances of the scientific terms and are therefore providing essentially occasions for intersubjective verification of a scientific theory. They are not to be left out and their constitutive role must be properly recognized.

Keith Gunderson's "Asymmetries and Mind–Body Perplexities", provides another view of the problem of completeness in a physicalist identity theory. Gunderson has divided the problem of the identity theory into the problem of investigational asymmetry and the problem of characterization. He asserts that, before one can start to characterize the mental in terms of the physical, one has to realize that there is an investigational asymmetry in one's effort to make characterization; yet it is to be recognized that this investigational asymmetry is not damaging to the physicalist characterizations of the mental. So-called investigational asymmetry is the situation in which one can perceive objects in the world, but one cannot literally perceive one's perceiving or one's perceptive organs. Thus one cannot see one's own eyes and one can not examine one's self in the way in which one examines things outside oneself. Put more generally, one's perspective of perception in having a perceptive experience will never be perceived in terms of neurophysiology. "Anyone else's original experiences, for example, which include a perspective of the world, will never be made available to me through behavioral or neurological observation," Gunderson writes. But this does not mean that there is anything nonphysical in anyone's visual experiences. Gunderson suggests that, even though my perspective of looking at things may not be able to apply to my brain or my eyes, my brain and my eyes are open to perception from other perspectives of other people. Thus the essential investigational asymmetry from one given perspective is compensated by adoption of other conjugate perspectives. There is indeed no reason why different perspectives may not yield physicalist observations which cover all perceiving subjects in the field. Thus, even though the initial investigational asymmetry could make the physicalist account essentially incomplete (as it has to exclude investigational knowledge of oneself), there is little reason to suppose that the accumulated knowledge of self from other perspectives is any more restraining.

In this connection, I believe that some principles which relate to the phenomena of investigational asymmetry need to be made explicit. The first principle is that all perspectives inherent in human experiences and all perspectives present in different human beings are equally asymmetric and self-excluding in investigational scope. We could call this the principle of *perspectival parity*. The second is the principle that all perspectives are complementary and could collectively yield physiological information applicable to individual perspectives. This we may call the principle of *perspectival duality* or *conjugation*. Gunderson has set the stage for the formulation of these two important principles for avoiding the perplexities of investigational asymmetries and also for providing a basis for drawing a physicalistic picture of the mental without suffering from the incompleteness of one single perspectival asymmetry.

Gunderson's view seems to be neutral with regard to the physical-identity theory and the qualitative-identity theory as suggested by Pepper. But the investigational problem for the mind-body identity could be understood to have something as prejudged for the characterization problem. For the asymmetry situation points to the fact that although ordinarily one cannot see one's own eyes and brain state in the way in which one sees others' eyes and brain state of seeing, one can report his own visual experience in phenomenal terms, because he is directly acquainted with his own sense experience. One might regard his own perspective as providing a direct manifestation of his own sense experience, as well as providing an occasion for objective observation from other perspectives. The irreflexivity of perspective perception, however, provides a basis for and a unique way of identifying and characterizing one's own experiences.

In his article, "Russell on Perception and Mind-Body: A Study in Philosophical Method," Grover Maxwell formulates a neat view regarding the identity theory of mind and body by considering two different and distinct ways of knowing based on Russell. In developing essentially the later philosophy of Russell, Maxwell points out that we are directly acquainted with our sense experiences; our other knowledge of things with which we are not directly acquainted is merely structural and basically embedded in terms of the logic of definite and indefinite descriptions. Maxwell argues for this point on the general grounds that we must recognize a methodology of reasoning and discovery in a broader scope than induction or simple confirmation theory, which is based on a realistic estimate of competing hypotheses as shown in actual science. This point is more clearly elaborated in his other paper, "Theories, Perception and Structural Realism,"[16] than in the present one. But the argument remains the same: unless we adopt the right methodology, we would meet difficulties in justifying our scientific outlook, and specifically the identity theory of mind and body.

On the basis of his constructive methodology, Maxwell has come to advocate and defend a version of what Pepper calls the qualitative-identity theory of mind and body which is similar to Feigl's position. What becomes clear in his account is the fact that our knowledge in neurophysiology about our brain states is hypothetical-inferential (not just hypothetical-deductive) and is based on our knowledge of our direct experience of first-order properties of things. It becomes clear that our sense experiences of first-order properties of things are both the basis and the "referee" of our knowledge of the structural properties of things.[17] Without direct knowledge of intrinsic properties of things we are not able to infer their structural properties. From another point of view, our knowledge of structural properties of things is exemplified in our direct knowledge by acquaintance and experience. Granted this methodology, it is also clear that our knowledge of things could be eventually represented by quantified existential statements (called Ramsey sentences). Some statements are exemplified in our direct experiences, and this means that our direct experiences could be regarded as actual instances (or conditions) of instantiation of these statements. But in the network of objective statements of a theory the mental events nevertheless receive a causal account. Thus it is Maxwell's view that the identity theory of mind and body will follow from a physicalist theory of the world as a network of events with spatial-temporal locations; that is, a mental event is a physical event exemplified in our direct experiences of knowing by acquaintance.

Maxwell does not discuss the difficulty of this view (for one is directly aware only of a sense experience, not its corresponding brain-state), that of recognizing such a physical event as a mental event. This difficulty should lead to consideration of the problem of completeness of a physicalist theory of mind as discussed by Ellis, Cheng, and Gunderson.

Finally we come to the two anti-identity-theory articles by Satosi Watanabe.

In his article "Logic of the Empirical World," Watanabe raised his objection to the identity theory by pointing out that one cannot assume a 1–1 correspondence between the mentalistic language (or perhaps description) and the physicalistic language (or description), or between a mental state and a physiological state. Watanabe implies that there must be a many-to-many correspondence between a mental state and a brain state. But this objection does not seem to apply to all versions of identity theories or in arguments for the identity theory presented in earlier papers. In the first place, there could be one-to-many, many-to-one, or many-to-many correspondences between a mental state and a brain state. In discussing Smart's and Ellis' articles, we have come to see that different physical properties may cause the same color sensation, and differently identified sense experiences (of taste) could be explained by the same physical theory.

Given this fact of many-to-many relationship between the mental and the physical, it does not follow that the mental state is not describable (or best describable) in terms of a brain state, or that both of them do not specifically refer to the same referent. Our explication of the identity theory should provide ample reasons for such a belief. But one principle for specific identification of a mental state in terms of a brain state should be made clear: indexically identifiable mental events could be described in contexts which provide clues for specific identification and, vice versa, for identification of neural events in the brain. What constitutes identification of a mental or a neural event depends on various configurations of events in which the mental or the neural is found or identified. Thus, by enlarging the network of knowledge of causal relationships or structural properties of things, we could in effect produce a model of the mind-body identity in which one type of mental event will always correspond to one type of neural event under restraining contextual conditions.

Watanabe's second contribution, "Can Cognitive Process Be Totally Mechanized?" argues for the impossibility of fully mechanizing or mechanically simulating human mental capacities such as deduction (theorem proving), induction, aesthetic evaluation of theories, and adaptation and learning. Watanabe has gone beyond the sphere of sentience and in fact has entered the sphere of sapience in showing the implausibility of the identity theory. If we indeed identify the physical with the mechanical computer, the impossibility of mechanizing our sapient capacity might be a reason for dismissing the identity thesis. If, on the other hand, we conceive neurophysiology and even microphysics as far more subtle than computer circuits, and as themselves admitting no mechanization, then there is still the logical possibility that even in the sphere of sapience the physical and the mental do coincide and can be theoretically identified with each other on good empirical and logical grounds. Nothing said earlier in this introduction is incompatible with this possibility.

NOTES

1. The early logical positivists have regarded the problem of mind-body relationship and other metaphysical problems as pseudoproblems because, by the positivists' verificational theory of meaning, the problems are not verifiably meaningful.

2. For a thorough bibliography, see Herbert Feigl, *The 'Mental' and the 'Physical'. The Essay and a Postscript* (Minneapolis: University of Minnesota Press, 1967).

3. Indeed, one may regard Feigl's article as the best introduction to current issues in philosophy of mind-body problems. It pinpoints the essential problem areas of mind-body relationship, and lays out the most promising exit from the difficulties of the problem. See also Herbert Feigl, "Body Monism," *Synthese* 11 (1970): 1–18.

4. Feigl also indicated that the very understanding of moral imperatives requires references to direct experiences ("Body Monism," p. 4).

5. Feigl does not make clear whether he is to regard the former in some sense as entailing the latter. He makes his point in opposition to many Oxford linguistic analysts.

6. Feigl writes: "Bridge laws or correspondence rules are in any case indispensable if a scientific theory is to be understood as an empirically testable set of postulates. Just where we place the 'bridge-heads,' i.e., the concepts in the theoretical network and the observables, is to some extent a matter of decision, and depends mainly on the aims of clarification and logical reconstruction." See chapter 1 of this volume.

7. Feigl continues: "The concepts of the physical sciences are invariant with respect to the different sense modalities in which they may be (ostensively) 'anchored.'" See chapter 1.

8. See chapter 6 of this volume.

9. See chapter 1.

10. "Whatever genuine knowledge we can attain is *propositional,*" Feigl writes. "It reflects, for example, the similarities, dissimilarities (and degrees thereof) of the immediately experienced qualities." (See chapter 1.) The propositional characterization of sense qualia could be phenomenological. But the identity thesis relative to a physical theory would hold that these must be mapped into some structural features of cerebral processes which are to be characterized physicalistically.

11. Even though here the main emphasis is on replacing mentalistic concepts by physicalistic concepts, there is no logical reason why a system of mentalistic concepts may not be used to replace a system of physicalistic concepts. Many idealistic philosophers have attempted to carry out essentially this project. But the mentalistic language is not intersubjective, but subjective or egocentric and hence it resists public verification and communication. The identity theory is in effect equivalent to the view that there is no ultimate private description of the mental except the identifying pure reference as such. A broader view regarding the cross-categorial identification is to regard any system of concepts replacing another system of concepts as an instance of cross-categorial identification.

12. With this explanation, Feigl is apt to point out that the efficacy of the mental, and the interaction between the brain or the mind, are no puzzles anymore. For what is referred to as the mental must be as efficacious (in causing actions) as the physical. Both refer to the same thing and serve as two different perspectival models for the same thing. The interaction between the mental and the physical can be described in mentalistic or in purely physicalistic terms.

13. The requirement that the neural statements uniquely realize T could be also controverted on the grounds that there could be other entities that satisfy T.

14. See Peter Geach, "Identity," *Review of Metaphysics* 21, no. 1 (September 1967): 3–12.

15. Furthermore, Lewis' argument here seems to be compatible with the double-language theory, the physical-identity theory, and the qualitative-identity theory. But assuming that the causal relations are better understood in physical relations, the argument in question provides reduction of the mental to the physical. It becomes, therefore, a form of physical-identity theory. It does not take the role of qualitative experience of perception and other mental events as essential for understanding the identity theory, because Lewis does not consider the phenomenon of instantiation in immediate experience as essential for the formulation of such an identity theory.

16. Maxwell's other paper is included in R. Colodny, ed., *The Nature and Function of Scientific Theories: Essays in Contemporary Science and Philosophy*, University of Pittsburgh Series in the Philosophy of Science, vol. 4 (University of Pittsburgh Press, 1970), pp. 3–34.

17. Maxwell reads "to infer P from our percepts" as "to propose P as the theory (and/or hypothesis) that best explains our percepts."

I

Some Crucial Issues
of Mind-Body Monism

Herbert Feigl

THE FOLLOWING considerations concern exclusively one of the (at least) three components of the traditionally as well as currently discussed mind-body problems. It is the *sentience* aspect rather than the aspects of sapience or selfhood that I wish to review in brief compass. Although I admit that the obvious interconnections of these three strands make it hazardous to separate them and thus to concentrate only on sentience (traditionally: consciousness, awareness, direct acquaintance, the phenomenally given, etc.), it nevertheless seems timely, even urgent, to attempt once again to clarify and reappraise what is right and what is wrong with physicalism (or the new materialism) as well as with some antiphysicalistic points of view.

My remarks are made within a framework of assumptions or presuppositions that may be best characterized as those of a scientifically oriented critical realism, and a tentative (physicalistic) reductionism. Since this position has been amply argued for in numerous publications (e.g., by R. Carnap; P. Oppenheim and H. Putnam; J. J. C. Smart; D. M. Armstrong; myself; and many others) I shall review now very succinctly only the points relevant for the important qualifications which differentiate my own views from those of the others.

Having originally taken my cues from the (by now "classical") critical realism of the early Moritz Schlick and the later Bertrand Russell, as well as having favored the somewhat similar views of the American monistic "naturalists" (especially R. W. Sellars, but also C. A. Strong and Durant Drake), I assume that there is—*epistemologically*—an important distinction to be made between the data of immediate experience and the world of "things-in-themselves." But in radical disagreement with the agnostic doctrine of Kant (and in complete agreement with Schlick and Russell) I consider the things-in-themselves knowable. And I hasten to add that such scientific knowledge as we possess of them, and keep expanding, is "structural," i.e., it is knowledge by description (in B. Russell's sense, recently explicated more formally by R. B. Braithwaite, R. Carnap, and G. Maxwell with the help of the Ramsey-sentence approach). While very few of the deep-rooted beliefs of common sense—as for example those philosophically formulated in "direct realism"—survive epistemological and scientific criticism, some of the basic tenets of common sense remain (relatively) unscathed. If the well-known disastrous slide into phenomenalism (or instrumentalism) and ultimately into a solipsism of the present moment is to be avoided, Berkeley's *esse est percipi* must be rejected from the start, and the *existence* (independently of perception) of the "external world" assumed.

The much-discussed quantum-mechanical, partial dependence of the observed or measured situation upon the act of observation or measurement can be safely disregarded in the present context. The influence of observation on observed objects maintained by a majority of present-day physicists is in any case negligible in regard to macroobjects. ("It does not hurt the moon to look at it," even if electrons do get a "kick" out of being looked at.) As to whether the finer details of neural processes (e.g., in the synapses of the central nervous system) require considerations of complementarity and indeterminacy is, however, a relevant question in regard to the identification (individuation) of neural events. Moreover, it seems quite questionable as to whether the "subjectivistic" interpretation of quantum mechanics is really called for.

For our purposes, and with some simplification, we can regard the assumptions of critical realism as among the premises of a hypothetico-deductive system. But just as the theories of the factual sciences generally, so also even these frame assumptions must be testable (in principle, and no matter how indirectly) by the data of immediate observation. This minimum of empiricism is in any case indispensable if the obvious fundamental difference of pure logic and mathematics from factual knowledge is to be properly understood.

One other assumption of common sense survives: It is the identity of mental states, events or processes (sensations, thoughts, intentions, desires, volitions, moods, sentiments, etc.) referred to by persons who "have" them and other persons who come to know about them on the basis of behavioral (including, of course, linguistic) or neurophysiological evidence. To illustrate: My doctor knows that he is causing me the experience of a pain when he lances an abscess on my arm; and I *feel* that pain and can report (or "avow") it. This much seems clear, and is indeed insisted upon by the philosophers of ordinary language (Wittgenstein, Austin, Strawson, Malcolm, et al.). Despite their opposition to the idea of a private language (or perhaps because of that opposition!) they do not countenance the notion that the word "pain" has different meanings in first person experiential reports and in ascriptions to other persons (or by other persons to me).

This point, however, requires a crucially important reexamination. I maintain (again in agreement with Russell) that without analogical conception and reasoning by analogy the identity (in the sense of synonymy) of first-person (self-ascribed, reported, avowed, or otherwise indicated) experience with experience ascribed to that (first) person by other persons can be understood only in the very different sense made widely familiar by the (logical) behaviorists, physicalists, or the Australian materialists. This other sense is quite clear: it retains essentially the point of view of the "psychology of the other one." Anxious to make psychology an honest natural science, the behaviorists—from Watson to Skinner—have consistently dealt with mental phenomena within the frame of an intersubjective account of the world. This trend of thought began with the crude identification of mind with behavior (J. B. Watson, E. A. Singer), and became more sophisticated in the views of R. Carnap, G. Ryle, and B. F. Skinner. These two philosophers and that brilliant psychologist attempted (in different ways) to show that assumptions of a publicly (intersubjectively) inaccessible mental life are either outright meaningless (though pictorially and/or emotionally significant) or, in any case, redundant for the aims of scientific description and explanation of human behavior.

There are two reasons—and I trust not merely *argumenta ad hominem*—which have for a long time convinced me of the indispensability of a subjectivistically understood conception of immediate (first person) experience. There is, first, the epistemic primacy of the data of immediate experience. Lest I be accused of attempting to resurrect the doctrine of "incorrigible" sense-data-statements, let me say right now that the empiricism to which I subscribe requires neither infallible "protocol" or "basic" statements; nor does it assume an atomistic ("pointillistic") structure of the phenomenally given. Moreover I would not only admit, but insist that sense-data as traditionally understood are the products (really "destructs") of a very special sort of analysis. Ordinary, normal adult direct experience is perhaps best described as the life-world (*Lebenswelt*) of the phenomenologists and existentialists. That is to say that ordinary immediate experience is suffused with interpretation, remnants of memory, expectations, associations, etc. But even if by a wrench of abstraction we succeed in stripping off this overlay, what remains are hardly ever elementary ("atomic") sense data but *Gestalten* (i.e., patterns, configurations, etc.). Experimental psychophysiology has for some time suggested that the much discussed isomorphism holds between these Gestalten and certain global features of cerebral processes. (I shall return to this important point later.)

In the pursuit of a logico-epistemological reconstruction of our knowledge-claims regarding the external or physical world we are—in the last analysis—driven back to the phenomenally given as the ultimate testing ground. Consider such confirmations as, for example, of astrophysical hypotheses by means of telescopic, spectroscopic or other observations. Feyerabend's contentions to the contrary notwithstanding, the astronomer ultimately has got to *see* (or if he is blind, to hear or touch) something. Of course I admit that what is thus sensed would make no sense without some presupposed theory (as e.g., of optics, photography or the like). But those theories in turn have been (let us assume successfully) tested by previous observations. "Incorrigibility" is not required. Even basic statements may have to be revised in the light of further observations and theories.

In this age of electronic computers, robots, etc., it has been argued that the human observer and his immediate experience could be replaced by machines that do the "observing." The reply to this objection is quite simple: How would we human beings ascertain the reliability of observation machines; and is it not epistemology for human beings (and neither for gods nor machines) that we are trying to work out?

The second point (that again I do not consider an *argumentum ad hominem*— let alone a sentimental and fallacious piece of reasoning) is that the very understanding of moral imperatives requires indispensably references—literally—to direct experience. "Thou shalt not wantonly inflict pains on humans or animals" will serve as a simple example. The word *pain* here has a surplus (factual, not purely emotive!) meaning over and above the one that radical behaviorists, physicalists or materialists countenance. I trust that I am not taken to be moralizing in this context. What I am saying is that there is a cognitive presupposition in ethical imperatives. Even someone who holds a purely noncognitive (emotivist) position in moral philosophy can, I hope, understand and agree.

Having been a member of the Vienna Circle (ca. 1924–1930), I realize that logical positivists (empiricists) or radical physicalists will shake their collective heads and accuse me of apostasy. But I have been a renegade from that movement and became a critical (or hypercritical) realist at least thirty years ago. Along with others I have tried to liberalize the empiricist meaning criterion in a manner that still excludes the "pernicious" transcendence of certain types of metaphysics and theology, and yet allows for analogical conception and inference. If a theologian wishes to construe his beliefs in this manner, I will not tell him that what he is asserting is meaningless. I shall merely ask him by what sort of reasons he can justify his beliefs. Far-out scientific hypotheses, such as those of current nuclear theory or of cosmology, are merely precariously transcendent. Hence I think that empiricists should consider theological (or metaphysical) assertions as meaningful provided they are at least incompletely and indirectly testable.

Considered superficially, analogical conception and inference of other minds appear to share the features of perniciously transcendent metaphysics and theology. To use the well-known Peirce-James formulation, there seems to be "no difference that makes a difference" in regard to all conceivable evidence. But I submit that our "private," "privileged" access (each must speak for himself in this matter) to our own immediate experience *is* a cognitive matter. The arguments of the Wittgensteinians (especially of Norman Malcolm) are utterly implausible to me. Introspective reports or avowals are either true or false. (I have already admitted that they are not incorrigible. They may conflict with other basic statements, with background knowledge or well-established theories.) Reference to one's own immediate experience is the (epistemological!) prototype of all designations of objects, properties or relations by the words of our language. Never mind how we come to use language. Very likely, reinforcement along with the existent (innate) set of our (brain-mind) capacities accounts for that. Carnap was historically the first (anticipating both Ryle and Skinner) to point out how the use of introspective phrases (e.g., "I am glad," "I am tired," "I am afraid," "I hope...," "I am thinking of...," etc.) is acquired; i.e., how the child learns, in the context of environmental circumstances, "taught" by his elders, the uses of those subjective expressions. Of course the physicalists are right in regarding avowals as caused by central states. But to the extent that whatever human beings do or say is in principle open to causal analysis (within the possible limits implied by quantum mechanical indeterminacy), this is entirely compatible with a semiotic account (i.e., by syntax, semantics and pragmatics). This renders it possible to apply the metaconcepts of designation (representation) and of truth and falsity. In opposition to many of the Oxford linguistic philosophers (and also to Malcolm) I think it makes perfectly good sense to say "I know that I have a pain," "I know that I am glad," etc. But if the finesses of lexicography should speak against such uses of "I know that...," I shall not be adamant on this point, and simply choose some other locution.

As I see it, the neo-Wittgensteinian approach to the notorious vexations of the "other minds" problems is still positivistic. The "beetle in the box" is just as ascertainable as the brain in the skull. But, I admit, the ascertainment of the "raw feels" (E. C. Tolman's term for immediate awareness or the phenomenal qualities) cannot be achieved in the simple manner of independently verifying the conclusion of an analogical inference. Obviously this has been the bugbear of the positivists. For similar reasons statements about the historical past should have caused them the same sort of misgivings but, strangely enough, hardly anything of the sort appears in the positivistic literature.

From the point of view of the liberalized criterion of factual meaningfulness we don't have to restrict the meaning of mental state ascriptions to the behavioral "criteria." The criteria of which the neo-Wittgensteinians speak are allegedly quite different from symptoms. Nor are they to be understood as logically equivalent to, or entailing, the ascriptions in question. They can serve as (empirically?) necessary and sufficient conditions of those ascriptions only under 'normal' circumstances. Perhaps this can be accepted as a fairly adequate analysis of the way we actually ascribe—in ordinary situations and in terms of the commonly used language—mental states to other persons. But is there then really that essential difference between (fairly reliable) *symptoms* and *criteria*?

For the consistent physicalists, as well as those behaviorists who at least admit that there are central states (i.e., who do not insist on the "black box" or "empty organism" outlook) peripheral behavior, including linguistic utterances, facial expressions, etc., serves as a probabilistic indicator of central states induced by stimuli and/or apt to (causally) produce overt responses.

Quite generally, and especially ever since the developments in pure semantics (Tarski, Carnap, et al.) it is now quite legitimate and simple to distinguish the truth conditions from the confirming evidence of a given knowledge-claim. The ascription of mental states, no matter (for the present purpose) whether understood phenomenally or in terms of brain states, is clearly and radically different from statements about the behavioral evidence. Only in the case of first-person direct-observation (phenomenal, experiential) statements is it plausible to identify their truth conditions with their confirming evidence. If the term "self-evident" had not suffered traditionally so much from misuses and ambiguities, I would not hesitate to characterize statements about the phenomenally given as self-evident.

Along with other proponents of the mind-brain identity thesis, I have never asserted an identity of mental states with actual or possible peripheral behavior. It should be understood without elaboration that I also repudiate as fallacious the identification of mental qualities with aspects of the stimuli. Obviously a color sensation, for example, is not identical with the radiation (of a certain intensity and frequency pattern) that elicits that sensation. And, as indicated above, I also reject the phenomenalistic identification of physical objects with complexes of "elements" (Mach) of direct perception or configurations of sensation. What in more modern parlance is termed the translatability thesis of physical into phenomenal language is untenable. If the errors of these types of reductionism are to be eliminated, then all the relationships mentioned, far from being identities, had better be viewed as lawful (causal) relationships between distinguishable states or events.

There is, however, one type of identification that recommends itself to our favorable attention. This is the reduction of one sort of entity to another as it occurs in the context of scientific explanation. This sort of reductive identification is often (but not always or necessarily) a macro-micro reduction. Much used examples are the kinetic theory of heat; the electron-gas theory of electric currents; the identification of table salt with sodium chloride; of genes with DNA helical molecules; of (short term) memory traces with reverberating neural circuits; etc., etc. The identification of gravitational fields with a Riemannian (i.e., non-Euclidean) structure of space-time in the general theory of relativity provides an example in which no microreduction is utilized. As I have emphatically pointed out in previous publications, these identifications (i.e., the ascertainment of such reductive identities) are empirical in nature. It requires empirical evidence to substantiate them. They are thus fundamentally different from identities in logic or pure mathematics.

As a first approximation in the logical reconstruction of scientific explanation this way of analyzing theoretical reductions still seems to me plausible and fruitful. But taking into account the forceful arguments of P. K. Feyerabend, a more adequate and precise way of explicating those reductions would be in terms of replacement or supplantation. This is required wherever the reducing theory is logically inconsistent with the reduced theories or empirical laws. In that case we do not have identities but replacement by "successor concepts." But since, against Feyerabend, I maintain that the successor concepts coincide in many cases at least for a certain range of the relevant variables (and approximately) with the replaced original concepts, I shall allow myself for our purposes the simpler locutions of "identity" and "identification."

Physical theories that have attained a fairly high degree of completeness characteristically provide the premises for the derivation of empirical laws. Most importantly, these empirical laws include statements about the functioning of pertinent measuring instruments, such as e.g., thermometers, ammeters, photometers, etc. Thus the expansion of the thermometric substance in a thermometer is derivable (at least with very high probability) from the kinetic theory of heat (in statistical-molecular mechanics). This still does not render the equivalence of thermometrically measured temperature with the average kinetic energy a matter of analytic synonymy. First of all the postulates of the microtheory that furnishes the premises are synthetic and empirical. Secondly, the simple relation between thermometric indications and the corresponding set of microconditions is part of the confirming evidence of the theory. Redefining "temperature" in terms of the microtheory can and has been done, but this sort of conventionalistic device merely conceals the empirical character of the "bridge law" which certainly cannot be denied, especially if classical (phenomenological) thermodynamics is compared with statistical mechanics.

Bridge laws or correspondence rules are in any case indispensable if a scientific theory is to be understood as an empirically testable set of postulates. Just where we place the bridgeheads, i.e., the concepts in the theoretical network and the observables, is to some extent a matter of decision, and depends mainly on the aims of clarification and logical reconstruction. Thus there is, for example, some leeway as to what should be selected as the observables in the Ramsey-sentence approach.

I admit that if a given physical theory has achieved the identifications, reductions, or replacements, then one is tempted to think that there is no need for bridge laws (or nomological danglers) because the theory is then—in a sense(!) —complete. This, however, is an illusion. The "anchoring" of a theory in data of experience is precisely what distinguishes physics from pure mathematics.

I shall now try to show that the "nomological danglers" can be understood in a way that is entirely unobjectionable. They do not violate any principle of parsimony (often referred to as Occam's razor). Of course I agree that parsimony in the sense of factual simplicity is one of the guiding principles of scientific theorizing. According to Newton's first *regula philosophandi* we should not assume more causes than are necessary for the explanation of given phenomena. But in the case of the mind-body problem whatever parsimony or simplicity can be achieved should result from a proper epistemological analysis of the differences and the relations between physical and psychological concepts. In other words, parsimony should be achieved as a byproduct of a clarification rather than from a wilful application of Occam's razor.

The first thing to do then is to reflect on the differences between the concepts of the physical sciences and the concepts that designate immediately the phenomenally given events and their qualities and relations. To put it very briefly: the concepts of the physical sciences are invariant with respect to the different sense modalities in which they may be (ostensively) "anchored." To illustrate: although it would be more difficult for a congenitally blind person to arrive at physical or astronomical knowledge, it is not impossible in principle. For the blind person could be equipped with photoelectric cells which react to incoming light rays from spectroscopes, telescopes or microscopes, etc. The photoelectric cells might then be connected through amplifiers with radio sets or other devices which through their emitted sounds, etc., would furnish discernible kinds of information in the auditory or tactual modalities. If this seems at first glance a bit fantastic, it should be remembered that our knowledge of stars that emit only either ultraviolet or else radio waves is just as indirect. And so is our knowledge of the structure of atomic nuclei, of the spin of subatomic particles, etc.

I contend, consequently, that a being with something like human intelligence (i.e., capacities for inference, theory construction, critical reasoning, etc.) might have a repertoire of sense modalities, and of immediate experience generally, that is utterly different from that of us earthlings; and that such a being (say, a Martian) might well arrive at the same concepts and theories as we do in the physical sciences. And if mind-body monism holds, the Martian could (in principle) also achieve complete knowledge (by description) of the psychology of human beings, including, of course, their sensations, perceptions, thoughts, emotions, moods, volitions, intentions, etc.—all that on the basis of such behavioral and neurophysiological evidence as is accessible through his (the Martian's) sense modalities.

The piece of science fiction naturally leads to the question: If that is the nature of physical knowledge, can the physical sciences ever include the private, purely subjective aspects of mental events? I shall try to answer yes, if the question is understood in one way, and no, if understood in another way. The answer customarily given in traditional philosophy is negative because it is felt that the qualities of immediate experience are "homeless" in the physical account of the universe. Some thinkers (e.g., Bergson, Poincaré, Eddington, Schlick, et al.) have in their various ways maintained a doctrine of the ineffability, inexpressibility or incommunicability of the "content" of direct experience. Only the structure, so they say, is intersubjectively knowable and communicable. But on closer analysis this contention boils down to the obvious truth contained in the distinction between *having* (or living through, enjoying or suffering) an immediate experience (and thus being able to achieve "knowledge by acquaintance" of experienced qualities) and knowing *about* it ("by description").

The—at present—utopian kind of physical knowledge can give an account of introspection, self-knowledge, avowals, etc. We may (somewhat speculatively) say that some part of the cerebral cortex "scans" the processes in some other part of the brain. And since the scanning part would be the one connected to the motoric nerves of the speech organs, we can thus sketch—at least by way of a "promissory note"—what the scientific account of private mental states (and their avowals) would be like. It is this sort of speculation that makes (especially the Australian) materialists so confident that a physicalistic central state theory of mind is possible, and that it need not be incomplete. Indeed, in the frame of intersubjective science nothing need be left out—except the "feel" of the raw-feels.

This is why we must admit something *is* omitted in the intersubjective, scientific account. But what are omitted are not ineffable qualia or the like, for even in their introspective description we deal with their *structural* features. Whatever genuine knowledge we can attain is *propositional*. It reflects, for example, the similarities, dissimilarities (and degrees thereof) of the immediately experienced qualities. Propositional characterizations of these qualities would then isomorphically correspond to some structural features of cerebral processes —all this, of course, only if physicalism is assumed.

I think what is omitted or left out in the physicalistic (intersubjective) account of the world is not any event, process or feature. It is—rather obviously —the *egocentric* perspective which the intersubjective world view quite deliberately displaces and replaces. It is in the egocentric perspective (prominently stressed by Descartes, Berkeley, Hume and the positivists) that we label the qualia of immediate experience directly. (The "successor" concept in the physicalist account is the scanning process mentioned above.) Now, the customary (and often ambiguous) uses of ordinary language to the contrary notwithstanding, it is surely a "category mistake" (of a special kind) to combine egocentric-subjective language with the intersubjective-physicalistic one. Most of the philosophical puzzles of the mind-body problem can be shown to originate from this sort of mixing of terms belonging to two categorially different conceptual systems. The *phenomenal* (visual, tactual, kinesthetic, etc.) spatialities of the ego-centric account are to be emphatically distinguished from the nonpictorial, unvisualizable concept of *physical* space. Similar distinctions have already been suggested above for the categorial differences between experienced qualities and the properties of physical objects.

In short, concepts which directly designate qualities of immediate experience and concepts whose meaning is largely independent of the specific (ostensive) anchoring in one or another of the sense modalities, and which only by probabilistic indication refer to entities, events or processes in what we (somewhat misleadingly) call the physical world, are of an entirely different semantical type.

Hence, if we wish to formulate a mind-brain identity thesis that involves more than the reduction of behavioral to neurophysiological concepts, a further step needs to be made. The identification of mentalistic (subjective, egocentric, private) phenomena with neurophysiological events or processes is then (as James Cornman put it) a "cross-categorial" one. In fact, I should think this is the only cross-categorial identification required if we wish to relate the egocentric to the physicalistic accounts. All the other reductive identifications (as in physics, chemistry, and biology) are not really cross-categorial as long as we replace the naive realism (or direct realism) of common sense with a clarified critical realism. But even from the point of view of common sense, as Keith Gunderson has convincingly shown, we can clear up some of the perplexities of the mind-body puzzles by reflecting upon the epistemic asymmetries that obtain between one's knowledge of one's own mental states and one's knowledge of the external world as well as the mental states of others. Just as one cannot see one's own eyes (without the help of mirrors, etc.) so one cannot in the purely egocentric perspective perceive oneself entirely as a part of the physical world. Just as one's eyes are not a part of one's visual field (Wittgenstein, *Tractatus*), so is one's brain (without the aid of an auto-cerebroscope) not part of the world perceived. Thus even within the "manifest image" (W. Sellars) of the world it is well-nigh impossible to escape the egocentric orientation. But this is remedied in the inter-subjective scientific conception. Here the individual self becomes an organism among other organisms and all the rest of things and events that constitute the universe. Linguistically this "great transformation" manifests itself by the disappearance of the egocentric particulars "now," "here," and "I," along with all their cognate expressions. They are replaced by proper names, coordinates, definite descriptions, etc. The "existentially poignant uniqueness" of the self of which we have heard so much in recent philosophy can be understood only within the frame of the egocentric perspective. Once the "democratization" so characteristic of the intersubjective frame is achieved, whatever uniqueness may remain is the usual empirical one of differentiating and individuating properties and relations. The directly experienced uniqueness is indeed inexpressible within the categorial frame of science.

Notes on Controversial Questions

1. The arguments for the identity theory here suggested are primarily based on logical and epistemological considerations. While I think that the empirical evidence of psychophysiology makes it plausible that most forms of dualism and interactionism (along with the older forms of animism and vitalism) can be disregarded, the question of evolutionary emergence is still open. Equally unsettled is the question as to whether emergentism (if it could only be clearly formulated; the essay by Meehl and Sellars is a notable attempt in that direction) is compatible with some form of monism. Personally I believe that the accumu-

lating evidence points increasingly toward a (qualified) reductionism in biology and behavioral pyschology.

2. The identity theory that I favor does of course not require and could not accommodate nomological danglers in the intersubjective (scientific) theory of the world. But in the cross-categorial identification there remains the brute fact of the isomorphism of phenomenal with physical *Gestalten*. There does not seem any ready explanation of the difference in "grain" between the phenomenal continuity (for example, of a smooth color expanse, or the homogeneity of a musical tone) and the atomic structure of the corresponding brain processes. It should be clear that the identity formulation (whose ascertainment depends upon empirical confirmation) holds only in extensional contexts. Like any other logically contingent identity it cannot be expected to hold *salva veritate* in all intensional contexts. Thus, to *know* that you are experiencing a certain mental event does not entail that you *know* with which brain process it is identical. (This is analogous to the case of the child who knows that the milk is warm without knowing anything about the mean velocities of the molecules of which the milk is composed.)

3. The unconscious mental processes as assumed in psychoanalytic theories can be viewed as quite legitimately postulated by means of explanatory theoretical concepts. These concepts are to be understood as analogues to familiar concepts designating conscious phenomena and/or as behaviorally indicated central processes whose neurophysiological nature is still largely unknown. Methodologically the situation here is somewhat similar to that of thermodynamics before the development of the kinetic theory of heat, or of chemistry before the introduction of the atomic theory. Philosophers who maintain that the idea of unconscious mental processes is inconsistent, merely reveal that they stick to an (unfruitful) terminological decision according to which "mental" is defined as "phenomenal" or "conscious."

4. Does the identity theory suggest a panpsychistic metaphysics? No, if we conform to the rules of analogical inference, the differences between lifeless matter and the living organisms (and especially those equipped with central nervous systems) are too enormous for assuming similarities of their respective "inner natures." Nevertheless a pan-quality-ism (S. C. Pepper's term) is not unreasonable provided that the intrinsic qualities of inorganic things or systems are conceived as incomparably more "colorless" than the qualities of human experience. It should be evident without further discussion that any similarities of my identity theory with the metaphysical solutions of Spinoza's attribute theory or of Leibniz's monadology are only very superficial and largely coincidental.

5. If a metaphysician is dissatisfied with the purely structural characterization of independently existing physical entities, i.e., if he wishes for something more than definite descriptions or Ramsey sentences, perhaps he can be consoled by being permitted to "introject" the intuitive notion of existence. This notion,

of course, has no place (makes no sense) in the intersubjective scientific conception of the world. But since Descartes was surely not talking outright nonsense when (in the famous *cogito ergo sum*) he ascribed existence to himself, we may grant that this intuitive and subjective idea of existence is significant in the egocentric perspective. But, of course, it makes no difference that amounts to an intersubjectively testable difference in the scientific world perspective.

6. The cross-categorial identity thesis should also be helpful for a better understanding of the causal account of perception. It enables us to relate in greater detail the egocentric (phenomenal or phenomenological) account of knowledge to the scientific one. In the intersubjective (scientific) account of perception, we view (as we can and do already in everyday life) the knowing subject (person, organism) and the incoming stimuli as it were from the side. In this lateral perspective it is clear even to untutored common sense that and why a blindfolded person cannot see environmental objects, and why, once the blindfold is removed, he can perceive them. This triviality can serve as an excellent antidote to the exclusively egocentric epistemologies of Berkeley and his positivist followers. Once the identity thesis is adopted, the main (philosophical) puzzles of the causal theory of perception resolve themselves. The detailed psychophysiology of perception is, of course, still far from complete.

7. Now to answer the perennial question: why not parallelism or epiphenomenalism instead of identity? As stated above, I don't think Occam's razor alone furnishes the answer. It is the mistaken conception of the *physical* (much more than that of the mental) that is largely responsible for such dualistic theories as parallelism or epiphenomenalism. I propose we mean by "physical" the (structural) type of conception and/or whatever physical concepts (in this sense) designate or denote. And by "mental" (but only for the purpose of the present essay) we mean what had better be called phenomenal. To recapitulate: as was already seen quite clearly by Schlick and Russell, the physical (in the sense just defined) may well designate (or codesignate) those small parts of the world that are phenomenal as well. If so, one of the great mysteries of modern philosophy has been (largely) dispelled. There *is* an identity of properties if we abandon picture thinking (naive and direct realism) about physical objects. The identity is that of the *structure* of the phenomenally given with the *structure* of certain global aspects (Gestalten) of the processes in the cerebral cortex. The identity theory thus understood takes care of the traditional puzzles regarding the efficacy of the mental (as in deliberation, attention, intention, volition, desires, pleasure, displeasure, etc.). Mental processes (being cross-categorially identical with brain processes) are of course among the most important causes of our behavior. And surely there is interaction—namely, between the brain (as well as other parts of the nervous system) and the rest of the organism.

8. It seems that analogies and homologies remain favorite devices not only in science but also in philosophical speculation and analysis. I found the application (made by N. Brody and P. Oppenheim) of Bohr's doctrine of com-

plementarity to the mind-body problem interesting and suggestive. But on closer analysis all I am able to accept is the categorial difference, and therefore (syntactical) noncombinability (incompatibility or noncompatibility seem to me inappropriate here) of the egocentric and the intersubjective conceptual frames. My differences from the outlook of the brilliant and sophisticated Australian materialism (of Smart, Armstrong, Medlin, Kekes, et al.) should by now be evident. When radical physicalists argue for the completeness of their world view, I object—not on the usual (and to them acceptable) grounds, i.e., that science can never be known to be finished-in-principle. Fully aware of the introduction of new entities throughout the history of science, they, of course, allow for such additions and modifications. (We all agree that science may well be, and probably *is*, an endless quest.) No, I am objecting to the physicalists' deliberate blindness in regard to something that admittedly does not amount to a *surplus* in the scientific-intersubjective frame. Hence I consider their arguments against the ψ-ϕ nomological danglers as an *ignoratio elenchi*. It should be clear by now that the physicalists' assertion of the (potential) completeness of a physicalistic account of the world amounts to the truism (indeed, the tautology) that there can be nothing within the intersubjective-physicalistic account of the world that is not intersubjective-physicalistic. An enormous amount of confused and fruitless disputes could be avoided once we recognize the game of the radical physicalists for what it is! These admittedly keen and clear-headed philosophers consistently (and, alas, often unwittingly) apply the "HYLAS TOUCH"! No wonder then, that whatever they deal with turns out to be physical!

9. Just a few words on the fashionable topics of intentionality, and the action vs. movement distinction. As in my previous publications I still think that (Brentano's notion of) intentionality is best explicated in terms of the semantical concept of designation. No matter as to whether mental imagery or imageless thoughts or words are on the subject side of the relation, the object (existent or nonexistent) is the referent (symbolically) designated. Hence, despite first impressions, this part of the problem of sapience is not part of the genuine mind-body problem, but can be resolved within the context of the relation of the *psychological* (or physiological, or computerological, or robotological) to the *logical*. The fallacies of psychologism are in any case to be avoided.

The colossal literature on intention (in the other sense, in which it is connected with action) seems to me largely fruitless and exhibits glaringly the futility of the ordinary language approach in philosophy. Surely, there is a perfectly good meaning to *causal* explanations of intentional, purposive, goal-directed behavior. Desires, ends-in-view, etc., furnish (like most explanation in terms of motivation) only the trivialities that even nursemaids and fishwives know very well, and that are still quite distant from genuine scientific explanation. To make a little clearer what was already known for centuries may be lexicographically useful, but it does not solve any philosophical problems.

10. What sort of bearing my view has on the methodology of theory con-

struction in psychology is clearly indicated in my essay "Philosophical Embarrassments of Psychology" now republished in Duane P. Schultz (ed.) *The Science of Psychology: Critical Reflections*, New York: Appleton-Century-Crofts, 1970. My major previous publications on the mind-body problems are listed below.

Selected Bibliography

Armstrong, D. M. *A Materialist Theory of the Mind*. New York: The Humanities Press, 1968.

Aune, Bruce. *Knowledge, Mind and Nature*. New York: Random House, 1967.

Borst, C. V., ed. *The Mind/Brain Identity Theory*. New York: Macmillan; London: St. Martin's, 1970.

Brody, Nathan, and Oppenheim, Paul. "Application of Bohr's Principle of Complementarity to the Mind-Body Problem," *Journal of Philosophy* 66 (1969): 97–113.

Carnap, Rudolf. "Psychology in Physical Language." In A.J. Ayer, ed., *Logical Positivim*. New York: The Free Press, 1962.

———. *Philosophical Foundations of Physics*. New York: Basic Books, 1966.

Cornman, James. "The Identity of Mind and Body." In C. V. Borst, ed., *The Mind/Brain Identity Theory*. New York: Macmillan; London: St. Martin's, 1970.

Feigl, Herbert. "The Mind-Body Problem in the Development of Logical Empiricism." In H. Feigl and M. Brodbeck, eds., *Readings in the Philosophy of Science*. New York: Appleton-Century-Crofts, 1953.

———. "Physicalism, Unity of Science and the Foundations of Psychology." In P. A. Schilpp, ed., *The Philosophy of Rudolf Carnap*. La Salle, Ill.: Open Court Publ. Co., 1963.

———. *The "Mental" and the "Physical": The Essay and A Postscript*. Minneapolis: University of Minnesota Press, 1967.

Feigl, Herbert, and Meehl, Paul E. "Popper on Free Will and Body-Mind Problems." In P. A. Schilpp, ed., *The Philosophy of Karl Popper*. La Salle, Ill.: Open Court Publ. Co., 1973.

Feyerabend, P. K. "Problems of Empiricism." In R. G. Colodny, ed., *Beyond the Edge of Certainty*. Englewood Cliffs, N.J.: Prentice-Hall, 1965.

Feyerabend, P. K., and Maxwell, G., eds. *Mind, Matter and Method*. Minneapolis: University of Minnesota Press, 1966.

Gunderson, Keith. "Asymmetries and Mind-Body Perplexities." In M. Radner and S. Winokur, eds., *Minnesota Studies in the Philosophy of Science*, Vol. 4. Minneapolis: University of Minnesota Press, 1970.

Hampshire, Stuart, ed., *Philosophy of Mind*. London and New York: Harper and Row, 1966.

Hook, S., ed. *Dimensions of Mind*. New York: New York University Press, 1960.

Kekes, John. "Theoretical Identity." *Southern Journal of Philosophy* 8 (1970): 25–36.

———. "Physicalism, the Identity Theory and the Doctrine of Emergence." *Philosophy of Science* 33 (1966): 360–375.

Malcolm, Norman. "Scientific Materialism and the Identity Theory." In C. V.

Borst, ed., *The Mind-Brain Identity Theory*. New York: Macmillan; London, St. Martin's, 1970.

Maxwell, G. "Scientific Methodology and the Causal Theory of Perception." In I. Lakatos and A. Musgrave, eds. *Problems in the Philosophy of Science*. Amsterdam: North Holland Publ. Co., 1968.

————. "Reply [to Professors Quine, Ayer, Popper, and Kneale]," ibid., especially p. 174.

————. "Theories, Perception, and Structural Realism." In R. Colodny, ed., *The Nature and Function of Scientific Theories: Essays in Contemporary Science and Philosophy*, Vol. 4, University of Pittsburgh Series in the Philosophy of Science. Pittsburgh: University of Pittsburgh Press, 1970.

————. "Structural Realism and the Meaning of Theoretical Terms." In M. Radner and S. Winokur, eds., *Minnesota Studies in the Philosophy of Science*, Vol. 4. Minneapolis: University of Minnesota Press, 1970.

————. Review of Bruce Aune's *Knowledge, Mind and Nature*. *Philosophical Review* 78 (1969): 392–397.

Medlin, Brian. "Ryle and the Mechanical Hypothesis." In C. F. Presley, ed., *The Identity Theory of Mind*. St. Lucia: University of Queensland Press, 1967.

Meehl, P. E. "The Compleat Autocerebroscopist." In P. K. Feyerabend and G. Maxwell, eds., *Mind, Matter and Method*. Minneapolis: University of Minnesota Press, 1966.

————. "Psychological Determinism and Human Rationality." In M. Radner and S. Winokur, eds., *Minnesota Studies in the Philosophy of Science*, Vol. 4. Minneapolis: University of Minnesota Press, 1970.

Meehl, P. E., and W. Sellars. "The Concept of Emergence." In H. Feigl and M. Scriven, eds., *Minnesota Studies in the Philosophy of Science*, Vol. 1. Minneapolis: University of Minnesota Press, 1956.

Pepper, S.C. *Concept and Quality*. LaSalle, Ill.: Open Court Publ. Co., 1967.

Presley, C. F., ed., *The Identity Theory of Mind*. St. Lucia: University of Queensland Press, 1967.

Russell, Bertrand. *Human Knowledge*. New York: Simon & Schuster, 1948.

Schaffner, Kenneth. "Approaches to Reduction." *Philosophy of Science* 34 (1967): 137–147.

Schilpp, P. A., ed. *The Philosophy of Rudolf Carnap*. LaSalle, Ill.: Open Court Publ. Co., 1963.

Schlick, Moritz. *Allgemeine Erkenntnislehre*. Berlin: Springer, 1925. (English translation by A. E. Blumberg, Vienna-New York: Springer, 1972).

Smart, J. J. C. *Philosophy and Scientific Realism*. London: Routledge & Kegan Paul; New York: Humanities Press, 1963.

————. *Between Science and Philosophy*. New York: Random House, 1968.

Wann, T. W., ed., *Behaviorism and Phenomenology*. Chicago: University of Chicago Press, 1964.

Note: There are two very ample lists of pertinent references in my slender book of 1967, *The "Mental" and the "Physical"* (see above).

2

A Split
in the Identity Theory

Stephen C. Pepper

RICHARD BRANDT and Jaegwon Kim, in a recent article, "The Logic of the Identity Theory,"[1] lay out the skeleton of the argument with clarity but, I feel, with some serious omissions. Their exposition deals solely with the question of the correlation between phenomenal and physical properties in brain events, and the possible substitution of identity for correlation as an applicable relationship.

It is true that these correlations produce the initial empirical evidence for the mind-body problem. But there are many other evidential considerations that have given impetus to some form of identity theory. Brandt and Kim, in their summary of the logic of the theory, conclude that its sole legitimate appeal is that of parsimony, its claim to reduce the number of ontological entities in the world. On a broader view, however, they seriously question whether in practice and in terms of total structure an identity theory is any more economical than the usual forms of psychophysical correspondence theories.

This conclusion seems oversimplified on two counts. First, it overlooks a great deal of evidence for a closer, or at least more complicated, connection than simple correlation between phenomenal and physical characters. Second, it fails to appreciate the particularly anomalous nature of the complexity produced by the psychophysical parallelism hypothesis. As Feigl has aphoristically remarked, the phenomenal entities are "nomological danglers." They are presented as superfluous to the physical system. The comparison between a parallelism theory and an identity theory in terms of economy is not like that between a Ptolemaic and a Copernican theory of astronomy. In the latter, the orbits of the planets are mutually integrated in both hypotheses. There are no danglers stringing off completely foreign to the system.

Furthermore, the phenomenal danglers are commonly exhibited as emerging *ex nihilo* on the occurrence of a certain physical neural structure in the course of biological generative processes. There is a miracle every time a human infant is born and begins to respond to his environment. There is more than a lack of parsimony in such an hypothesis. It has, rather, the appearance of giving up the problem altogether. This is clearly what J. J. C. Smart had in mind in likening a parallelism theory to the old theory about fossils, to the effect "that the universe just began in 4004 B.C. ... with sediment in the rivers, eroded cliffs, fossils in the rocks, and so on" (quoted by Brandt and Kim, p. 533).

Their reply that the identity theory requires the use of correlations anyway simply begs the question. It is still a queer kind of complexity in a scientific or philosophical theory to have to depend on so many massive occurrences *ex nihilo*. Smart is trying hard to eliminate that sort of anomaly. At the same time, it should be admitted that there is nothing logically impossible about the old theory of fossils or the widespread contemporary parallelism theories of mind. The objection to a parallelism theory is not only its lack of economy in comparison with an identity theory (which may or may not be true), but its lack of factual integration. What is fundamentally at issue is not the minor matter of economy of thought but the adequacy of a theory fully to handle the relevant evidence.

So now let us turn to the areas of evidence which an identity theory tries to organize.

One of the important evidential considerations underlying an identity theory is the mass of physiological data supporting what is usually called a causal or representative theory of perception. This is the view that the environmental object of perception is outside the organism and its response which gives the content of the perception. And in distal perception, such as the visual, there is a transmitting medium intervening between the object and the content of perception, so that the cognition of the object is representative and not direct. In fact, even in tactile perception on this view there are representative elements.

Recognition of the large amount of physical and physiological evidence for this representative theory is important for the identity theory, because it accounts for the obvious difference of qualitative content between the physiologist's observation of a person's brain activity and the introspective report correlated with it. The correlation so far as perceptual observation is concerned would be between the physiologist's qualitative visual content of an object of distal perception and the qualitative content of the subject's immediate introspective deliverance. The former would always be visual content; the latter could be any sort of qualitative content depending on the portions of the brain activated. As soon as this situation is fully realized, the nature of the correlation posited by any type of parallelism theory becomes enormously complicated, not to say implausible.

One of the commonest mistakes made by critics of the identity theory is to speak of the two modes of observation—the physiologist's visual perception of a brain and the subject's immediate introspection—as if they were on a par. In the crudest form, it is to assert that a physiologist should have a visual perception of green on the subject's brain if the subject reports a sensation of green. Brandt and Kim are alert to this sort of mistake. But I think they miss the intricacy and interrelatedness of the evidence adduced here—physical, physiological, and psychological—which renders any simple correlation theory extremely doubtful.

Another relevant evidential consideration is that of the large amount of conceptual interpretation that goes into the content of any perceptual response of a docile organism, particularly of a man, and most particularly of a trained scientist, observing objects of his specialty. He will project his extensive conceptualized experience—quite veridically as a rule—into the material he is perceptually observing. That is why a layman cannot "read" an X-ray plate. When a physiologist looks at a brain, his perception is expanded and saturated with the whole apperceptive mass of his neurological training. This empirical conceptualization is somehow connected with the subject's introspective report at the occurrence of a brain activation.

Another evidential consideration is that such a scientist's conceptual system is not a personal possession of the scientist. It is institutionalized in his science and consequently a public acquisition available to any man with the requisite training. Furthermore, a scientific system is not an institutionalized myth (at least, not in the generally accepted contemporary interpretation), but an institutionalized organization of evidence and of methods for verification and for the acquisition of more evidence.

Another relevant empirical consideration growing out of the preceding one is the ever-increasing explanatory, predictive, and (it would seem for these reasons) also descriptive powers of the natural sciences. An extrapolation of this trend leads to the empirical possibility that the concepts and methods of the natural sciences may be extended almost (or even quite) indefinitely. This last suggestion is speculative, but the trend is a genuine empirical consideration.

And, lastly, as a central empirical consideration, there are the introspective reports.

This is a rather massive sampling of empirical considerations. The two biggest problematic factors in trying to find a hypothesis adequate to bring these materials together are the highly integrated system of the natural sciences, on the one hand, and the apparently intractable introspective reports, on the other.

The parallelism theories in effect simply say: that is the way it is, and we are lucky to be able to set up some points of correlation. There is no use worrying further about it.

The identity theorists are not content to stop there. Lately there have been three main types of identity theory. They may be called the double language theory, the physical identity theory, and the qualitative identity theory. It is important to distinguish these types, particularly the last two. Critics tend to merge them, as if there were just one identity theory. Brandt and Kim may be doing this even though they make explicit references to all three.

The double language theory was held by Feigl in his early treatment of the subject. It consists in calling attention to the physical language of the natural scientists and the phenomenal language of introspection on the part of many psychologists and philosophers, and then suggests that the events designated by both languages in respect to what are physically described as neural events are identical. The trouble with this theory is that there is no specific characterization of the common object of designation. The difference between the physical and the mental is fully accounted for in the great difference between the two languages. But what are they about? That is not given by the theory. Then how can either linguistic account be verified? How can we know they have a strictly identical common object? For this reason, the view has been generally abandoned.

For an understanding approach to identity theories, however, it is still of more than purely historical importance. For in fact we do have the two linguistic reports with quite distinct vocabularies. No identity theory denies the existence of these two distinct linguistic reports. These have to be taken into account by any adequate identity theory. Both the physical and the qualitative identity theories attempt to do this. They differ from each other in terms of which pole of the "correlated" elements they take as basic. The one takes the neural descriptions as basic, the other the introspective.

Smart gives the most detailed exposition to date of a physical identity theory. He seeks to amalgamate all the qualitative elements of introspective reports into behavioristic and ultimately neural descriptions. The simplest expedient for doing this is in linguistic terms. The argument is that physical language is so much more comprehensive and precise than phenomenal language that we can safely dispense with the latter and identify what it is trying to describe with the former. It also appeals to the evidence for the comprehensive adequacy of physical language to embrace all evidence in the system of the natural sciences. Some identity theorists depend almost entirely on this argument, and Smart occasionally makes use of it. But in general he takes the introspective reports much more seriously and undertakes to show in detail how their qualitative vocabulary can be interpreted without loss into the terms of a physical language—indeed, not only without loss but with gain in both precision and discrimination. For instance, in *Philosophy and Scientific Realism*[2] he gives a detailed account of how blind men through testing the reports of seeing men on discriminations of differently dyed bits of wool can obtain a complete understanding of color "qualities" and their interrelations. He concludes "that experiences are brain processes, and that they have no qualia" (p. 82).

Smart's principal remaining difficulty is that introspective reports are less determinate than the descriptions of brain processes with which the experiences are identified. Most discussions of his theory in the journals center on this problem. He seeks to solve it in linguistic terms involving him in the logic of synonymity, definitions of identity, determinables, and so forth, with, I find, rather indifferent success. For the pith of the problem is not logical but factual. Are felt qualities immediately reported properly reducible without remainder to brain processes as described in physical terms? Qualia do not seem to be amenable to such a reduction by purely logical or linguistic manipulations. And this is the main point, I think, that Brandt and Kim are trying to insist upon in their article. How can you get rid of qualia when in every perception and aesthetic experience they so obviously stare you in the face?

The qualitative identity theory approaches the problem from the opposite direction. Feigl, for instance, in his more recent writings treats the brain process as a conceptual description of a physical event, and he identifies the event of the immediate experience had with the conceptual physical description of it.

"We may say," he writes, "what is *had-in-experience* and (in the case of human beings) *knowable by acquaintance* is identical with the object of *knowledge by description* provided first by molar behavior theory and this in turn identical with what the science of neurophysiology *describes* (or, rather, will describe when sufficient progress has been achieved) as processes in the central nervous system." [3] (Author's italics.)

The actual event is the felt qualitative one of immediate experience, and this is identical with the event which is cognitively referred to by the conceptual physical description as a brain process. The obvious difference between the phenomenal event and the physical description of it is explained. The one consists of the felt qualities experienced, the other of scientific concepts symbolizing the physical structure of the event. It is somewhat like the difference between a city map showing a certain street intersection and the full qualitative experience of a man standing at that intersection. The advantage of the map is that it shows the relation of the intersection to all the other streets in the city. But the map cannot give the actual full qualitative experience of the other locations. These have to be experienced at the locations. Nevertheless, the map is genuinely descriptive even in qualitative terms. For the experience had at the intersection does show the four corners as represented on the map and the angles of intersection and some other details.

In a way, what Feigl has done, starting with the double language theory, is to observe that the common object of the two languages is not unknowable. That object is immediately experienced as the object of the phenomenal report. The terms used in the phenomenal report are, of course, conceptual in their kind as truly as those of the physical language but quite differently derived. And as a linguistic report, it is by no means incorrigible. But the qualitative actual event it refers to is, of course, just what it is, and the introspectionist, through the medium of phenomenal language, tries to make his report as nearly true to the experience as he can.

But the qualitative identity theory is not a double language theory. Consequently, critics of the qualitative identity theory are on a wrong track if they try to equate the conceptual terms of the physical language literally in detail with the felt qualities of the experienced event actually had. It is as if a person holding a map on a street corner complained that the experienced streets are not black and white and bounded by thin lines, nor is there anything there corresponding to the texture of the paper. These are not the relevant characters of the map to be identified with the experience of the intersection. But so far as the map truly describes the intersection, the relevant characters of the map should correspond precisely with the features they refer to in the actual experience of the person reading the map at the intersection.

All this is understood by P. E. Meehl in his article "The Compleat Auto-cerebroscopist."[4] He finds the theory on the whole tenable but for one difficulty, a difficulty also previously noted by Wilfred Sellars as the difference of "grain" between the physical description in terms of brain process and the "raw feel" of experience with which it is identified. If I am not mistaken, this boils down to the fact that many more details ("properties," if you wish) are ascribed to the physical description of the events as "brain process" than to the event as a "raw feel." For instance, the "brain process" identified with a "raw feel" of "red quality" has a different "grain," many more details more atomized, than the simple continuous "red raw feel" introspectively reported. Moreover, Meehl does not find the "red raw feel" anywhere among the "functors" of the physical description.

Now, as I interpret the qualitative identity theory, if there is any such discrepancy of relevant details standing over in the last physical analysis, the difficulty should be ascribed to the physical analysis. Something still more is needed in the physical analysis in order to be taken as an adequate description of the actual qualitative event it refers to. I am afraid even Meehl does not fully appreciate this. For he allows himself to say in one place, "the reduction of raw feel statements to physical statements is obviously constitutive within identity theory" (p. 167). This would be true of the physical identity theory but not of Feigl's qualitative identity theory (at least in my interpretation of it). It would be, if anything, the other way around.

Let me interpolate a question which may be bothering some readers. What about the physiologist's visual perception of the multiple cell structure of the brain when quite surely a "red raw feel" as a *single* simple sensation must be identified with a *number* of activated interconnected brain cells, and moreover when every cell is itself an enormously complex structure of molecules, atoms, etc.? The answer here is that the physiologist, in terms of a representative theory of perception, is not having an immediate experience of the event which is the terminal object of his perception. Furthermore, as we also observed earlier, a trained physiologist has his visual perceptions loaded with all his conceptual knowledge of the neural structure of the brain. He perceives the brain as it would be physically described. He is a long way off (in his *distal* perception) from the actual event which he is distantly perceiving. So we are back where we began with a physical conceptual description of an event and an immediate experience of this event.

Now the objection about the difference of "grain" between the phenomenal and physical descriptions is that these are so different that they cannot be regarded as ascribed to strictly identical events. This difference, I suggest, can be partly accounted for on the analogy of the city map and the person experiencing a street corner. The map is much more detailed about all the streets of the city than the experience of the person at the corner can possibly be. For he can see only a little way up each of the streets. But the necessity for this discrepancy would come out clearly if we went into a detailed description of what is physically involved in the science of map making. The map is an assemblage of many surveyors' observations, each one as limited as that of the person at the corner.

Yet I admit that there is something more to the objection that needs to be answered. In terms of the physical description, the brain event actually is complex both in depth (as one might say) and in extensity, while the "raw red feel" (and note how cleverly the example is chosen) is a simple phenomenal element no further analyzable in depth (as distinguished from the phenomenal quality of a variegated textured background of an impressionistic picture or of a piece of woven goods with threads of different hues). This I admit is an objection that requires an answer if the qualitative identity theory is to hold up as an adequate hypothesis. My own suggestion is that the psychologically well-recognized empirical concept of "fusion" can do the job, with the addition that biologically, in the evolution of the human animal, the simple sensations mark the limit of man's capacity to analyze fusions, just as there is a limit to his capacities to respond visually to ultraviolet or infrared rays. And if there is as yet no suitable neural account of fusion, the defect is in the neural description.

Finally, I suggest that a qualitative identity theory is at least as tenable as any of the dualistic theories such as interactionism, epiphenomenalism, and the rest, and I repeat that the issue goes much deeper than a question of parsimony. The issue is over the relevant evidence and its coherent organization into an adequate hypothesis.

Moreover, I wonder if it would not remove a good deal of misunderstanding of the term "identity theory" were given up and the physical identity theory frankly called a "physical reduction theory," since what it seeks to do is definitely to reduce qualia[5] in terms of physical descriptions; and if the qualitative identity theory were renamed a "qualitative neural identification theory," since what it seeks to do is to identify within the physical scheme the actual qualitative events to which the descriptive conceptual constructs of the natural sciences refer as their ultimate objects.[6]

NOTES

1. Richard Brandt and Jaegwon Kim, "The Logic of the Identity Theory," *Journal of Philosophy* 66 (7 September 1967): 515–537.

2. J. J. C. Smart, *Philosophy and Scientific Realism* (London: Routledge & Kegan Paul, 1963), pp. 79 ff.

3. Herbert Feigl, "The 'Mental' and the 'Physical,'" in H. Feigl, M. Scriven, and G. Maxwell, eds., *Minnesota Studies in the Philosophy of Science*, vol. 2 (Minneapolis: University of Minnesota Press, 1958), p. 446.

4. In P. K. Feyeraband and G. Maxwell, eds., *Mind, Matter and Method: Essays in Philosophy and Science in Honor of Herbert Feigl* (Minneapolis: University of Minnesota Press, 1966), pp. 103 ff.

5. To remove another possible misunderstanding, let me say that "qualia," as used in this paper and in other writings by exponents of the qualitative theory, does not refer solely to ultimate elements of sensory discrimination such as "red," "sweet," and "pure tone" (of a tuning fork), etc., but to all felt qualitative experience, including color textures, savors, timbres, Gestalts, and any other qualitative complexities, such as an observed pictorial composition, a recognized face, a melody, a mood, an emotion, a situation of suspense—in short, all actual living immediate experience and its appreciated representation in drama, novels, and art generally.

6. For an extended analysis of this conception of the "ultimate objects" of scientific concepts as qualitative events, see the writer's *Concept and Quality* (La Salle, Ill.: Open Court Publishing Co., 1967), especially chapters 8 and 10.

3

Psychophysical and Theoretical Identifications

David Lewis

PSYCHOPHYSICAL IDENTITY theorists often say that the identifications they anticipate between mental and neural states are essentially like various uncontroversial theoretical identifications: the identification of water with H_2O, of light with electromagnetic radiation, and so on. Such theoretical identifications are usually described as pieces of voluntary theorizing, as follows. Theoretical advances make it possible to simplify total science by positing bridge laws identifying some of the entities discussed in one theory with entities discussed in another theory. In the name of parsimony, we posit those bridge laws forthwith. Identifications are made, not found.

In "An Argument for the Identity Theory,"[1] I claimed that this was a bad picture of psychophysical identification, since a suitable physiological theory could *imply* psychophysical identities—not merely make it reasonable to posit them for the sake of parsimony. The implication was as follows:

Mental state M = the occupant of causal role R (by definition of M).

Neural state N = the occupant of causal role R (by the physiological theory).

∴ Mental state M = neural state N (by transitivity of =).

If the meanings of the names of mental states were really such as to provide the first premise, and if the advance of physiology were such as to provide the second premise, then the conclusion would follow. Physiology and the meanings of words would leave us no choice but to make the psychophysical identification.

In this sequel, I shall uphold the view that psychophysical identifications thus described would be like theoretical identifications, though they would not fit the usual account thereof. For the usual account, I claim, is wrong; theoretical identifications *in general* are implied by the theories that make them possible, not posited independently. This follows from a general hypothesis about the meanings of theoretical terms: that they are definable functionally, by reference to causal roles.[2] Applied to commonsense psychology—folk science rather than professional science, but a theory nonetheless—we get the hypothesis of my previous paper[3] that a mental state M (say, an experience) is definable as the occupant of a certain causal role R—that is, as the state, of whatever sort, that is causally connected in specified ways to sensory stimuli, motor responses, and other mental states.

First, I consider an example of theoretical identification chosen to be remote from past philosophizing; then I give my general account of the meanings of theoretical terms and the nature of theoretical identifications; finally, I return to the case of psychophysical identity.

I

We are assembled in the drawing room of the country house; the detective reconstructs the crime. That is, he proposes a theory designed to be the best explanation of phenomena we have observed: the death of Mr. Body, the blood on the wallpaper, the silence of the dog in the night, the clock seventeen minutes fast, and so on. He launches into his story:

> *X*, *Y*, and *Z* conspired to murder Mr. Body. Seventeen years ago, in the gold fields of Uganda, *X* was Body's partner ... Last week, *Y* and *Z* conferred in a bar in Reading ... Tuesday night at 11:17, *Y* went to the attic and set a time bomb ... Seventeen minutes later, *X* met *Z* in the billiard room and gave him the lead pipe ... Just when the bomb went off in the attic, *X* fired three shots into the study through the French windows ...

And so it goes: a long story. Let us pretend that it is a single long conjunctive sentence.

The story contains the three names "*X*," "*Y*," and "*Z*." The detective uses these new terms without explanation, as though we knew what they meant. But we do not. We never used them before, at least not in the senses they bear in the present context. All we know about their meanings is what we gradually gather from the story itself. Call these *theoretical terms* (*T-terms* for short) because they are introduced by a theory. Call the rest of the terms in the story *O-terms*. These are all the *other* terms except the T-terms; they are all the *old, original* terms we understood before the theory was proposed. We could call them our "pre-theoretical" terms. But "O" does *not* stand for "observational." Not all the O-terms are observational terms, whatever those may be. They are just any old terms. If part of the story was mathematical—if it included a calculation of the trajectory that took the second bullet to the chandelier without breaking the vase—then some of the O-terms will be mathematical. If the story says that something happened because of something else, then the O-terms will include the intensional connective "because," or the operator "it is a law that," or something of the sort.

Nor do the theoretical terms name some sort of peculiar theoretical, unobservable, semi-fictitious entities. The story makes plain that they name *people.* Not theoretical people, different somehow from ordinary, observational people— just people!

On my account, the detective plunged right into his story, using "X," "Y," and "Z" as if they were names with understood denotation. It would have made little difference if he had started, instead, with initial existential quantifiers: "There exist X, Y, and Z such that. . ." and then told the story. In that case, the terms "X," "Y," and "Z" would have been bound variables rather than T-terms. But the story would have had the same explanatory power. The second version of the story, with the T-terms turned into variables bound by existential quantifiers, is the Ramsey sentence of the first. Bear in mind, as evidence for what is to come, how little difference the initial quantifiers seem to make to the detective's assertion.

Suppose that after we have heard the detective's story, we learn that it is true of a certain three people: Plum, Peacock, and Mustard. If we put the name "Plum" in place of "X," "Peacock" in place of "Y," and "Mustard" in place of "Z" throughout, we get a true story about the doings of those three people. We will say that Plum, Peacock, and Mustard together *realize* (or are a *realization* of) the detective's theory.

We may also find out that the story is not true of any other triple.[4] Put in any three names that do not name Plum, Peacock, and Mustard (in that order) and the story we get is false. We will say that Plum, Peacock, and Mustard *uniquely realize* (are the *unique realization* of) the theory.

We might learn both of these facts. (The detective might have known them all along, but held them back to spring his trap; or he, like us, might learn them only after his story had been told.) And if we did, we would surely conclude that X, Y, Z in the story were Plum, Peacock, and Mustard. I maintain that we would be compelled so to conclude, given the senses borne by the terms "X," "Y," and "Z" in virtue of the way the detective introduced them in his theorizing, and given our information about Plum, Peacock, and Mustard.

In telling his story, the detective set forth three roles and said that they were occupied by X, Y, and Z. He must have specified the meanings of the three T-terms "X," "Y," and "Z" thereby; for they had meanings afterwards, they had none before, and nothing else was done to give them meanings. They were introduced by an implicit functional definition, being reserved to name the occupants of the three roles. When we find out who are the occupants of the three roles, we find out who are X, Y, and Z. Here is our theoretical identification.

In saying that the roles were occupied by X, Y, and Z, the detective implied that they were occupied. That is, his theory implied its Ramsey sentence. That seems right; if we learned that no triple realized the story, or even came close, we would have to conclude that the story was false. We would also have to deny that the names "X," "Y," and "Z" named anything, for they were introduced as names for the occupants of roles that turned out to be unoccupied.

I also claim that the detective implied that the roles were uniquely occupied, when he reserved names for their occupants and proceeded as if those names had been given definite referents. Suppose we learned that two different triples realized the theory: Plum, Peacock, Mustard; and Green, White, Scarlet. (Or the two different triples might overlap: Plum, Peacock, Mustard; and Green, Peacock, Scarlet.) I think we would be most inclined to say that the story was false, and that the names "X," "Y," and "Z" did not name anything. They were introduced as names for the occupants of certain roles; but there is no such thing as *the* occupant of a doubly occupied role, so there is nothing suitable for them to name.

If, as I claim, the T-terms are definable as naming the first, second, and third components of the unique triple that realizes the story, then the T-terms can be treated like definite descriptions. If the story is uniquely realized, they name what they ought to name; if the story is unrealized or multiply realized, they are like improper descriptions. If too many triples realize the story, "X" is like "the moon of Mars"; if too few triples—none—realize the story, "X" is like "the moon of Venus." Improper descriptions are not meaningless. Hilary Putnam has objected that on this sort of account of theoretical terms, the theoretical terms of a falsified theory come out meaningless.[5] But they do not, if theoretical terms of unrealized theories are like improper descriptions. "The moon of Mars" and "the moon of Venus" do not (in any normal way) name anything here in our actual world; but they are not meaningless, because we know very well what they name in certain alternative possible worlds. Similarly, we know what "X" names in any world where the detective's theory is true, whether or not our actual world is such a world.

A complication: what if the theorizing detective has made one little mistake? He should have said that Y went to the attic at 11:37, not 11:17. The story as told is unrealized, true of no one. But another story is realized, indeed uniquely realized: the story we get by deleting or correcting the little mistake. We can say that the story as told is *nearly realized*, has a unique *near-realization*. (The notion of a near-realization is hard to analyze, but easy to understand.) In this case the T-terms ought to name the components of the near-realization. More generally: they should name the components of the nearest realization of the theory, provided there is a unique nearest realization and it is near enough. Only if the story comes nowhere near to being realized, or if there are two equally near nearest realizations, should we resort to treating the T-terms like improper descriptions. But let us set aside this complication for the sake of simplicity, though we know well that scientific theories are often nearly realized but rarely realized, and that theoretical reduction is usually blended with revision of the reduced theory.

This completes our example. It may seem atypical: the T-terms are names, not predicates or functors. But that is of no importance. It is a popular exercise to recast a language so that its nonlogical vocabulary consists entirely of predicates; but it is just as easy to recast a language so that its nonlogical vocabulary consists entirely of names (provided that the logical vocabulary includes a copula). These names, of course, may purport to name individuals, sets, attributes, species, states, functions, relations, magnitudes, phenomena, or what have you, but they are still names. Assume this done, so that we may replace all T-terms by variables of the same sort.

II

We now proceed to a general account of the functional definability of T-terms and the nature of theoretical identification. Suppose we have a new theory, T, introducing the new terms $t_1, \ldots, t_n$. These are our T-terms. (Let them be names.) Every other term in our vocabulary, therefore, is an O-term. The theory T is presented in a sentence called the *postulate* of T. Assume this is a single sentence, perhaps a long conjunction. It says of the entities—states, magnitudes, species, or whatever—named by the T-terms that they occupy certain *causal roles*; that they stand in specified causal (and other) relations to entities named by O-terms, and to one another. We write the postulate thus:[6]

$$\top [t].$$

Replacing the T-terms uniformly by free variables $x_1, \ldots, x_n$, we get a formula in which only O-terms appear:

$$\top [x].$$

Any n-tuple of entities which satisfies this formula is a realization of the theory T. Prefixing existential quantifiers, we get the *Ramsey sentence* of T, which says that T has at least one realization:

$$\exists x \top [x].$$

We can also write a *modified Ramsey sentence* which says that T has a unique realization:[7]

$$\exists_1 x \top [x].$$

The Ramsey sentence has exactly the same O-content as the postulate of T; any sentence free of T-terms follows logically from one if and only if it follows from the other.[8] The modified Ramsey sentence has slightly more O-content. I claim that this surplus O-content does belong to the theory T—there are more theorems of T than follow logically from the postulate alone. For in presenting the postulate as if the T-terms had been well defined thereby, the theorist has implicitly asserted that T is uniquely realized.

We can write the *Carnap sentence* of T: the conditional of the Ramsey sentence and the postulate, which says that if T is realized, then the T-terms name the components of some realization of T.

$$\exists x\,\mathsf{T}\,[x] \supset \mathsf{T}\,[t]$$

Carnap has suggested this sentence as a meaning postulate for T;[9] but if we want T-terms of unrealized or multiply realized theories to have the status of improper descriptions, our meaning postulates should instead be a *modified Carnap sentence*, this conditional with our modified Ramsey sentence as antecedent:

$$\exists_1 x\,\mathsf{T}\,[x] \supset \mathsf{T}\,[t],$$

together with another conditional to cover the remaining cases:[10]

$$\sim \exists_1 x\,\mathsf{T}\,[x] \supset t = *.$$

This pair of meaning postulates is logically equivalent[11] to a sentence which explicitly defines the T-terms by means of O-terms:

$$t = \imath x\,\mathsf{T}\,[x].$$

This is what I have called functional definition. The T-terms have been defined as the occupants of the causal roles specified by the theory T—as *the* entities, whatever those may be, that bear certain causal relations to one another and to the referents of the O-terms.

If I am right, T-terms are eliminable; we can always replace them by their definientia. This is not to say that theories are fictions, or that theories are uninterpreted formal abacuses, or that theoretical entities are unreal. Quite the opposite! Because we understand the O-terms, and we can define the T-terms from them, theories are fully meaningful; we have reason to think a good theory true; and if a theory is true, then whatever exists according to the theory really *does* exist.

I said that there are more theorems of T than follow logically from the postulate alone. More precisely: the theorems of T are just those sentences which follow from the postulate, together with the corresponding functional definition of the T-terms. For that definition, I claim, is given implicitly when the postulate is presented as bestowing meanings on the T-terms introduced in it.

It may happen, after the introduction of the T-terms, that we come to believe of a certain n-tuple of entities, specified otherwise than as the entities that realize T, that they do realize T. That is, we may come to accept a sentence

$$\mathsf{T}\,[r]$$

where $r_1, \ldots, r_n$ are either O-terms or theoretical terms of some other theory, introduced into our language independently of $t_1, \ldots, t_n$. This sentence, which we may call a *weak reduction premise* for *T*, is free of T-terms. Our acceptance of it might have nothing to do with our previous acceptance of *T*. We might accept it as part of some new theory, or we might believe it as part of our miscellaneous, unsystematized general knowledge. Yet having accepted it, for whatever reason, we are logically compelled to make theoretical identifications. The reduction premise, together with the functional definition of the T-terms and the postulate of *T*, logically implies the identity:

$$t = r.$$

In other words, the postulate and the weak reduction premise definitionally imply the identities $t_i = r_i$.

Or we might somehow come to believe of a certain *n*-tuple of entities that they *uniquely* realize *T*; that is, to accept a sentence

$$\forall x(\top [x] \equiv x = r)$$

where $r_1, \ldots, r_n$ are as above. We may call this a *strong reduction premise* for *T*, since it definitionally implies the theoretical identifications by itself, without the aid of the postulate of *T*. The strong reduction premise logically implies the identity

$$r = \cap x \top [x]$$

which, together with the functional definition of the T-terms, implies the identities $t_i = r_i$ by transitivity of identity.

These theoretical identifications are not voluntary posits, made in the name of parsimony; they are deductive inferences. According to their definitions, the T-terms name the occupants of the causal roles specified by the theory *T*. According to the weak reduction premise and *T*, or the strong reduction premise by itself, the occupants of those causal roles turn out to be the referents of $r_1, \ldots, r_n$. Therefore, those are the entities named by the T-terms. That is how we inferred that *X*, *Y*, and *Z* were Plum, Peacock, and Mustard; and that, I suggest, is how we make theoretical identifications in general.

III

And that is how, someday, we will infer that[12] the mental states M_1, $M_2, \ldots$ are the neural states $N_1, N_2, \ldots$.

Think of commonsense psychology as a term-introducing scientific theory, invented long before there was any such institution as professional science. Collect all the platitudes you can think of regarding the causal relations of mental states, sensory stimuli, and motor responses. Perhaps we can think of them as having the form:

> When someone is in so-and-so combination of mental states and receives
> sensory stimuli of so-and-so kind, he tends with so-and-so probability

to be caused thereby to go into so-and-so mental states and produce so-and-so motor responses.

Add all the platitudes to the effect that one mental state falls under another—"toothache is a kind of pain," and the like. Perhaps there are other forms of platitudes as well. Include only platitudes which are common knowledge among us; everyone knows them, everyone knows that everyone else knows them, and so on. For the meanings of our words are common knowledge, and I am going to claim that names of mental states derive their meaning from these platitudes.

Form the conjunction of these platitudes; or better, form a cluster of them— a disjunction of all conjunctions of most of them. (That way it will not matter if a few are wrong.) This is the postulate of our term-introducing theory. The names of mental states are the T-terms.[13] The O-terms used to introduce them must be sufficient for speaking of stimuli and responses, and for speaking of causal relations among these and states of unspecified nature.

From the postulate, form the definition of the T-terms; it defines the mental states by reference to their causal relations to stimuli, responses, and each other. When we learn what sort of states occupy those causal roles definitive of the mental states, we will learn what states the mental states are—exactly as we found out who X was when we found out that Plum was the man who occupied a certain role, and exactly as we found out what light was when we found that electromagnetic radiation was the phenomenon that occupied a certain role.

Imagine our ancestors first speaking only of external things, stimuli, and responses—and perhaps producing what we, but not they, may call *Äusserungen* of mental states—until some genius invented the theory of mental states, with its newly introduced T-terms, to explain the regularities among stimuli and responses. But that did not happen. Our commonsense psychology was never a newly invented term-introducing scientific theory—not even of prehistoric folk-science. The story that mental terms were introduced as theoretical terms is a myth.

It is, in fact, Sellars' myth of our Rylean ancestors.[14] And though it is a myth, it may be a good myth or a bad one. It is a good myth if our names of mental states do in fact mean just what they would mean if the myth were true.[15] I adopt the working hypothesis that it is a good myth. This hypothesis can be tested, in principle, in whatever way any hypothesis about the conventional meanings of our words can be tested. I have not tested it, but I offer one item of evidence. Many philosophers have found Rylean behaviorism at least plausible; more have found watered-down, "criteriological" behaviorism plausible. There is a strong odor of analyticity about the platitudes of commonsense psychology. The myth explains the odor of analyticity and the plausibility of behaviorism. If the names of mental states are like theoretical terms, they name nothing unless the theory (the cluster of platitudes) is more or less true. Hence it is analytic that *either* pain etc. do not exist or most of our platitudes about them are true. If this *seems* analytic to you, you should accept the myth and be prepared for psychophysical identifications.

The hypothesis that names of mental states are like functionally defined theoretical terms solves a familiar problem about mental explanations. How can my behavior be explained by an explanans consisting of nothing but particular-fact premises about my present state of mind? Where are the covering laws? The solution is that the requisite covering laws are implied by the particular-fact premises. Ascriptions to me of various particular beliefs and desires, say, cannot be true if there are no such states as belief and desire—cannot be true, that is, unless the causal roles definitive of belief and desire are occupied. But these roles can be occupied only by states causally related in the proper lawful way to behavior.

Formally, suppose we have a mental explanation of behavior as follows:

$$\frac{C_1[t], C_2[t], \ldots}{E}$$

Here E describes the behavior to be explained. $C_1[t], C_2[t], \ldots$ are particular-fact premises describing the agent's state of mind at the time. Various of the mental terms $t_1, \ldots, t_n$ appear in these premises, in such a way that the premises would be false if the terms named nothing. Now let $L_1[t], L_2[t], \ldots$ be the platitudinous purported causal laws whereby—according to the myth—the mental terms were introduced. Ignoring clustering for simplicity, we may take the term-introducing postulate to be the conjunction of these. Then our explanation may be rewritten:

$$\frac{\exists_1 x \left(\begin{array}{l} L_1[x] \& L_2[x] \& \ldots \& \\ C_1[x] \& C_2[x] \& \ldots \end{array} \right)}{E}$$

The new explanans is definitionally equivalent to the original one. In the expanded version, however, laws appear explicitly alongside the particular-fact premises. We have, so to speak, an existential generalization of an ordinary covering-law explanation[16]

The causal definability of mental terms has been thought to contradict the necessary infallibility of introspection.[17] Pain is one state; belief that one is in pain is another. (Confusingly, either of the two may be called "awareness of pain.") Why cannot I believe that I am in pain without being in pain—that is, without being in whatever state it is that occupies so-and-so causal role? Doubtless I am so built that this normally does not happen; but what makes it impossible?

I do not know whether introspection is (in some or all cases) infallible. But if it is, that is no difficulty for me. Here it is important that, on my version of causal definability, the mental terms stand or fall together. If commonsense psychology fails, all of them are alike denotationless.

Suppose that among the platitudes are some to the effect that introspection is reliable: "belief that one is in pain never occurs unless pain occurs," or the like. Suppose further that these platitudes enter the term-introducing postulate as conjuncts, not as cluster members; and suppose that they are so important that an *n*-tuple that fails to satisfy them perfectly is not even a near-realization of commonsense psychology. (I neither endorse nor repudiate these suppositions.) Then the necessary infallibility of introspection is assured. Two states cannot be pain and belief that one is in pain, respectively, in the case of a given individual or species, if the second *ever* occurs without the first. The state that *usually* occupies the role of belief that one is in pain may, of course, occur without the state that *usually* occupies the role of pain; but in that case (under the suppositions above) the former no longer is the state of belief that one is in pain, and the latter no longer is pain. Indeed, the victim no longer is in any mental state whatever, since his states no longer realize (or nearly realize) commonsense psychology. Therefore it is impossible to believe that one is in pain and not be in pain.

NOTES

1. *Journal of Philosophy* 63 (1966): 17–25.
2. David Lewis, "How to Define Theoretical Terms," *Journal of Philosophy* 67 (1970): 427–446.
3. Since advocated also by D. M. Armstrong in his *A Materialist Theory of the Mind* (New York: Humanities Press, 1968). He expresses it thus: "The concept of a mental state is primarily the concept of a state of the person apt for bringing about a certain sort of behaviour [and secondarily also, in some cases] apt for being brought about by a certain sort of stimulus" (p. 82).
4. The story itself might imply this. If, for instance, the story said, "*X* saw *Y* give *Z* the candlestick while the three of them were alone in the billiard room at 9:17," then the story could not possibly be true of more than one triple.
5. "What Theories are Not," in E. Nagel, P. Suppes, and A. Tarski, eds., *Logic, Methodology and Philosophy of Science: Proceedings, International Congress of Logic, 1960* (Palo Alto: Stanford University Press, 1962), p. 247.
6. Boldface names and variables denote *n*-tuples; the corresponding sub-scripted names and variables denote components of *n*-tuples. For instance, **t** is $\langle t_1, \ldots, t_n \rangle$. This notation is easily dispensable, and hence carries no ontic commitment to *n*-tuples.
7. That is, $\exists y \, \forall x (\top [x] \equiv y = x)$.
Note that $\exists_1 x_1 \ldots \exists_1 x_n \top [x]$ does not imply $\exists_1 x \top [x]$, and does not say that T is uniquely realized.
8. On the assumptions—reasonable for the postulate of a scientific theory—that the T-terms occur purely referentially in the postulate, and in such a way that the postulate is false if any of them are denotationless. We shall make these assumptions henceforth.
9. Most recently in Rudolf Carnap, *Philosophical Foundations of Physics* (New

York: Basic Books, 1966), pp. 265–274. Carnap, of course, has in mind the case in which the O-terms belong to an observation language.

10. $t = *$ means that each t_i is denotationless. Let $*$ be some chosen necessarily denotationless name; then $*$ is $\langle * \ldots * \rangle$ and $t = *$ is equivalent to the conjunction of all the identities $t_i = *$.

11. Given a theory of descriptions which makes an identity true whenever both its terms have the status of improper descriptions, false whenever one term has that status and the other does not. This might best be the theory of descriptions in Dana Scott, "Existence and Description in Formal Logic," in R. Schoenman, ed., *Bertrand Russell: Philosopher of the Century* (London: Allen & Unwin, 1967).

12. In general, or in the case of a given species, or in the case of a given person. It might turn out that the causal roles definitive of mental states are occupied by different neural (or other) states in different organisms. See my discussion of Hilary Putnam's "Psychological Predicates," in *Journal of Philosophy* 66 (1969): 23–25.

13. It may be objected that the number of mental states is infinite, or at least enormous; for instance, there are as many states of belief as there are propositions to be believed. But it would be better to say that there is one state of belief, and it is a relational state, relating people to propositions. (Similarly, centigrade temperature is a relational state, relating objects to numbers.) The platitudes involving belief would, of course, contain universally quantified proposition-variables. Likewise for other mental states with intentional objects.

14. W. Sellars, "Empiricism and the Philosophy of Mind," in H. Feigl and M. Scriven, eds., *Minnesota Studies in the Philosophy of Science*, vol. 1 (Minneapolis: University of Minnesota Press, 1956), pp. 309–320.

15. Two myths which cannot both be true together can nevertheless both be good together. Part of my myth says that names of color-sensations were T-terms, introduced using names of colors as O-terms. If this is a good myth, we should be able to define "sensation of red" roughly as "that state apt for being brought about by the presence of something red (before one's open eyes, in good light, etc.)." A second myth says that names of colors were T-terms introduced using names of color-sensations as O-terms. If this second myth is good, we should be able to define "red" roughly as "that property of things apt for bringing about the sensation of red." The two myths could not both be true, for which came first: names of color-sensations or of colors? But they could both be good. We could have a circle in which colors are correctly defined in terms of sensations and sensations are correctly defined in terms of colors. We could not discover the meanings both of names of colors and of names of color-sensations just by looking at the circle of correct definitions, but so what?

16. See Lewis, "How to Define Theoretical Terms," pp. 440–441.

17. By Armstrong, in his *A Materialist Theory of the Mind*, pp. 100–113. He finds independent grounds for denying the infallibility of introspection.

4

On Some Criticisms
of a Physicalist Theory
# of Colors

J. J. C. Smart

I WANT to discuss some criticisms made by M. C. Bradley[1] of the account of colors in my book *Philosophy and Scientific Realism*. I shall put forward a modified account of colors, which was first suggested to me by David K. Lewis, though a rather similar view has been put forward by D. M. Armstrong.[2] In fact there turn out to be certain differences between Lewis' present view of colors and that which he first suggested to me, and also between Armstrong's and Lewis', as also between Armstrong's and mine (or Lewis' original one). However, these differences seem to me to be of no ontological significance, but are rather differences as to which account of colors best fits our ordinary ways of talking. I suspect that our ordinary color discourse contains enough obscurity to make the choice between various philosophical analyses to some extent an arbitrary one.

In *Philosophy and Scientific Realism* I elucidate colors as dispositions of physical objects to evoke characteristic patterns of discriminatory color behavior by normal human percipients in normal circumstances. (Color discrimination, it will be remembered, can be elucidated antecedently to the notion of color, and so there is no circularity here.) Bradley brings up two imaginary cases to show the inadequacy of this view. One was originally C. B. Martin's, and is as follows. All colors can be represented on a color circle, where the various radii represent the various hues, and hues which are nearly indistinguishable from one another correspond to radii which are near to one another. The various amounts of saturation of a color are represented by distances along the radii. Thus, points near the center of the circle represent a high degree of additive mixing of white. (For simplicity of exposition I am here neglecting differences of brightness, and hence that between white, gray and black, but the full story can easily be adapted to the full color cone, which takes these differences into account. For "color circle" read "any cross section of the color cone.") Now let us envisage a miraculous transformation of things in the world so that the colors of things change into the diametrically opposite colors on the color circle. Thus if O is the center of the color circle and P and P′ are points on opposite radii such that O P = O P′, a thing whose color is represented by P will change to the color which is represented by P′, and vice versa. The only things that will not change will be those things (white ones) whose color is represented by the center O of the color circle.

In the envisaged case the physical constitutions of things will change and so will the wavelengths of the light radiated from them. That is, the change is a perfectly objective and scientifically detectable one. It might correctly be remarked that such a miraculous change would be physically inexplicable, and it would almost certainly lead to difficulties for even the existence of human life. Both food and human flesh would have to undergo changes in order for them to have the chemical constitutions required for the new colors. Moreover, we would have to make all sorts of assumptions about boundary conditions in order to keep our story compatible with the laws of physics. For example, we would have to suppose the nonexistence of rainbows. (For how could color interchange occur on a rainbow without there being a change in the laws of physics?) Such objections can probably be set aside as quibbles, because for the purposes of the objection we can even suppose the laws of physics to be different from what they are, so long as they remain the same throughout the story. After all, we are concerned with elucidating commonsense color concepts, which have mostly grown up before the rise of modern science.[3]

Now in the envisaged case, everybody will want to say (on the basis both of physics and of immediate experience) that there has been a systematic change of the colors of things in the world. Yet the patterns of discriminatory responses will *not* have changed. Normal human percipients will still find it hard to pick geranium petals from a pile of ripe tomatoes, but easy to pick them from a heap of unripe ones, and hard to pick out lettuce leaves from a distant part of the lawn, but easy to pick out delphinium petals which have fallen on to the lawn. Thus the systematic interchange in the constitutions of things will not lead to any change in discriminatory responses of normal human percipients. (This supposes, of course, that the nervous systems of normal human percipients will continue to function as before, even though the constitution of blood, nerve tissue, etc., may have changed. We have already agreed to neglect any objection of this sort as being something of a quibble.) On the basis of immediate experience, and also on the basis of physics, people will say that a systematic interchange of colors will have occurred. And yet there will be no change in the patterns of discriminatory responses which are evoked by things in the world. Consequently there must be something wrong with an account of colors in terms of powers to cause certain patterns of discriminatory behavior.

In my book I tried unavailingly to get out of this difficulty by bringing in color experiences; in the envisaged case we should notice that our color experiences had changed. I elucidated the experience of something looking red in terms of "something going on in me which is like what goes on in me when I am in normal health and in normal light and there is something in front of my eyes which *really is* red." That is, the experience of red is elucidated in terms of the redness of objects. (Not the other way round, as by John Locke, although my account is like the Lockean one, insofar as it elucidates colors as powers. But to elucidate redness as the power to cause red ideas or sense data, as in Locke, leads to obvious difficulties for a thoroughgoing physicalism.) Bradley shows convincingly that if I modify my account so that redness becomes not just the power to cause a certain pattern of discriminatory responses but the power to cause the experience of "seeing something red" as well, I am caught in a vicious circularity. Colors are elucidated in part in terms of color experiences, and these are elucidated in terms of colors, which are elucidated in part in terms of experiences, which are. . . .

I admit that this objection from color reversal is damaging to my original account of colors. I am therefore disposed to give up my original account in favor of a different one which is, however, equally compatible with physicalism. In correspondence, David Lewis asked me why I did not say that a color is a physical state of the surface of an object, that state which normally explains certain patterns of discriminatory reactions of normal human percipients. (Fairly obvious modifications would have to be made to deal with the colors of public yet illusory objects, such as the sky or a rainbow.) I replied at the time that I did not like this because the state would be a very disjunctive and idiosyncratic one. In effect, Lewis replied, "Very disjunctive and idiosyncratic—so what?" And I then thought to myself, "So what?" Let me explain this.

Consider the following absurd piece of fiction. A man (Smith, say) has a peculiar neurosis. If he sees a tomato, a rainbow, a bulldozer, or an archbishop, he goes red in the face and stands on his head. No other objects produce this odd behavior. Then doubtless the property corresponding to the open sentence "tomato *x* or rainbow *x* or bulldozer *x* or archbishop *x*" would be of some interest to this man and to his psychiatrist. It is a perfectly objective property, but because of its peculiar disjunctiveness (the oddity of the different components of the disjunction occurring within the same disjunction) it is both a disjunctive and an idiosyncratic property. Let us call this disjunctive and idiosyncratic property "snarkhood." Now, although snarkhood is a perfectly objective property, it is only Smith's neurosis which makes it of any interest to anyone. Were it not for Smith's neurosis, neither he nor his psychiatrist would have any reason to single it out from the infinity of other highly disjunctive and idiosyncratic properties. Similarly, the disjunction of physical properties which is the physical property of greenness seems to be a very disjunctive and idiosyncratic physical property. We single it out only because of certain highly complex facts about the human eye and nervous system. This is because infinitely many different mixtures of light of various wavelengths and intensities can produce the same discriminatory response. Just as the property of snarkhood is of no interest except to Smith or his psychiatrist, so we need not expect the physical property of greenness to be of any interest to extraterrestrial beings, who would have differently constituted eyes and nervous systems.

A simple formula F might be suggested which would describe all the mixtures of wavelengths which would give rise to the same color behavior (and color experience) in a normal percipient. For this reason Armstrong is tempted to say that if there is no such simple formula there are not really any colors, because it is an aspect of our color perception that all red things look to have some simple and nondisjunctive property in common. Compare the case in which a disease is described by some complex syndrome, and medical scientists come to divide it into two diseases characterized by different (although possibly overlapping) parts of the syndrome and ascertainably different etiologies. We would be inclined to say in such a case that the scientists had discovered the existence of two new diseases, and also the nonexistence of the original disease. There seems to be a choice here: we could redescribe the old disease as a disjunction of the two new diseases, or else say that the old disease is nonexistent. My own inclination in the case of colors would be to take the analogue of the former choice. That is, if no suitable F exists Armstrong would say that there are not really any colors. I do not think that any ontological issue depends on the difference, even if the simple formula F exists.

It may be worth recalling my reason for thinking that no simple formula exists. Consider an arrangement of three photoelectric cells in a circuit which approximately simulates the human visual system (as elucidated by the three-color theory of vision).[4] We should have to choose three cells with appropriately related characteristic curves (current plotted against wavelength of light) such that the shapes of the curves were such-and-such, and their maxima were such-and-such. These specifications would have a quite arbitrary look about them and would be dictated by the nature of the human visual system. In this way the properties of physical objects which explain human visual discriminations are idiosyncratic properties. Presumably they are disjunctive properties because quite different mixtures of light can lead to the same visual response. Moreover, a mixture of light for which the intensity-wavelength curve is single peaked, say at wavelength λ, can produce the same reactions as light with a many-peaked intensity-wavelength curve, and this last curve may even have a trough around λ. Nevertheless, there *may* be a nondisjunctive specification of the physical properties which are colors of objects although it is at least not obvious what this might be. I shall, however, mention an ingenious suggestion which David Lewis has communicated to me in correspondence. Consider a hyperspace of infinitely many dimensions, indeed as many dimensions as there are points in the real number continuum. A particular spectrum could be represented by a point in this hyperspace. Suppose that we give the space a metric, perhaps by taking the interval between two points in the hyperspace to be the mean square difference of intensities (for the two spectra) averaged over all wavelengths. Then, according to Lewis, it is possible that a color might correspond to (be the power to reflect light corresponding to) a simple shaped volume in this hyperspace. But at any rate it seems clear that if there is a simple formula of the sort for which Armstrong hankers, it cannot be anything very obvious, such as the capacity to reflect light of such-and-such a single wavelength. And if color should be such a simple property, so much the better. My defence of physicalism, however, will allow that it can be as idiosyncratic and disjunctive as you wish; like snarkhood it will nevertheless be a perfectly *objective* property.

Let me now revert to the earlier "So what?" A highly complex, disjunctive or idiosyncratic property would be objectionable at one end of a correlation law (nomological dangler). The assertion, however, that the color *is* the property, however disjunctive and idiosyncratic it may be, does not lead to this trouble. (If it should turn out to be less disjunctive or idiosyncratic than I fear, so much the better.) If the color *is* the physical property, then we have no nomological dangler depending from the property.

The property of snarkhood is disjunctive in that it might be defined by means of the disjunction:

Snarks $x =$ df tomato x or rainbow x or bulldozer x or archbishop x.

Nevertheless snarkhood could also be described nondisjunctively as the property which things have if and only if they cause the neurotic behavior in question. Snarkhood is the property which *causes* or which *explains* the peculiar behavior; it is the property such that it is a *lawlike* proposition that, if and only if Smith is presented with something possessing the property, then he stands on his head. Such a description of the property makes use of words like "causes," "explains," "is law-like." (Another possibility, related to the last one, is that we teach "snarks x" ostensively; snarkhood would then in a sense be indefinable, but we would be teaching someone to come out with the word "snarks" on any of a disjunctively describable set of occasions, whether or not he was aware of the disjunctiveness of the property of snarkhood.)

Notice that the identification of snarkhood with the property which causes the behavior in question is a contingent one. There is no difficulty about the contingent identification of properties, although it has for some reason been hard for many philosophers (including myself) to come to see this.[5] To use an example which I got from Lewis in correspondence, consider the statement that the property of conductivity is identical with the property measured by the piece of apparatus with such-and-such serial number. This statement is quite clearly a contingent and factual one. We must resist the temptation to suppose that all true statements of identity of properties would have to be necessary. It is clear, then, that although colors may be disjunctive and idiosyncratic physical properties, it need not be the case that those who use color words need know that this is so. For them, colors are described in a purely topic-neutral way (neutral between physicalist and nonphysicalist metaphysical theories). They are the properties, whatever they are, which could explain the characteristic patterns of discriminatory responses of normal human percipients. It would be perfectly possible for an Aristotelian type of person to agree with the analysis, but to suppose that the property which explains the pattern of responses is a nonphysicalist, emergent, and perhaps nondisjunctive one. We, with our scientific knowledge, will suspect that it is an idiosyncratic and possibly very disjunctive, purely physical property of the surfaces of objects. Not at first knowing or suspecting that the property is an idiosyncratic and possibly very disjunctive one, people might wrongly claim that they know that it is not an idiosyncratic and disjunctive one.

Armstrong suggests that mistakes of this sort can arise from a tendency of mind which gives rise to the headless woman illusion.[6] To cause this illusion, a dark cloth is put between the woman's head and the audience, and the background is similarly dark. Armstrong points out that the illusion arises from the tendency to suppose that because we do not perceive the woman to have a head we think that we perceive that she does not have a head, and he holds plausibly that a similar error causes people to think that they have an intuition that experiences are not brain processes. Such an error could occur in thinking about the possible identity of colors and physical states.

(I do not mean to say that Armstrong approves of this particular application of his idea about the headless woman illusion. He has told me that because all red things look to have something in common he does not think that the apparent simplicity of colors can be explained by a failure to perceive a real disjunctiveness.)

Notice now that though greenness is the very property which (in normal circumstances) explains a certain pattern of discriminatory reactions, a different color could explain the same pattern in the case of the miraculous color reversal. Two different things can explain the same thing. There is no reason why we should not therefore say that the colors had changed over. No doubt our inner experiences and memories would incline us to take this course because there will be a systematic change in our color experiences. (I go along with Martin and Bradley in supposing this; it seems to be probable. But since there would also have to be a complete change in our semantic habits we might simply feel dizzy or go mad.) Percipients will notice the change and will say (for example) that tomatoes are blue and that delphiniums are red. They will want to rewrite the *Concise Oxford English Dictionary* and interchange the entries "shades ... seen in blood" (see the definition of "red") and "colored like the sky" (see the definition of "blue"), though they might allow "red" and "blue" to be defined as "the shade *formerly* seen in blood" and "the color *formerly* of the sky." In short, then, the revised account of colors, which defines colors as the physical states of objects which (in our normal world) explain a pattern of discriminatory reactions, allows us consistently to describe the color reversal case: A and B can be different and yet each can explain the same phenomenon C. The trouble which arose for the account of colors as simply powers to cause patterns of discriminatory reactions does not arise. The colors are the physical states which explain these powers, but other states could explain the very same powers after the miraculous interchange.

I think that the revised account of colors also saves the physicalist from Bradley's objection that it is conceivable that everyone might have the appropriate discriminatory responses so that they would satisfy the behavioral tests for color vision, and yet everything would look gray to them. I am not completely sure that Bradley's case really is conceivable, because if someone has not at least a tendency not to discriminate (with respect to color) red things from gray things, can he really see red things as gray? Just as in Martin's example, however, the inability to think through the example in a scientific manner probably does not suffice to discredit the *philosophical* potency of the example, and so I shall waive this point. Now I think that we can accommodate this case to the revised account of colors as follows: Colors are the (perhaps highly disjunctive and idiosyncratic) properties of the surfaces of objects that explain the discriminations with respect to color of normal human percipients, and also the experiences of these percipients, the looking red, or looking blue, etc., of objects. They would also, however, help to explain the abnormal experiences of the people in Bradley's proposed case.

We might consider that there would be some abnormality in the brains of people who always had inner experiences of seeing gray even though their behavior showed a complete range of color discriminations. Then colors (properties of surfaces of objects) would help to explain the normal discriminatory behavior of these people and would also help to explain the abnormal color experiences of the people with the abnormal brains. It is interesting to speculate whether and in what sense these people would have a color language. They might learn color words purely by reference to discriminatory behavior and would have no words for color experiences. They would doubtless be able to describe illusory color perceptions, in the sense that someone might in slightly abnormal circumstances want to match A with B even though a normal human percipient (behavioristically speaking) would not want to do so. They would need at least a behavioristic analogue of "B looks the color of A."

Let us revert to Bradley's case. He strengthens it (so as to avoid the considerations of the last paragraph) by supposing that both the discriminatory color behavior and the looking gray of everything were *ex hypothesi* inexplicable. Then could I say, as I have done, that the colors of things are those objective physical properties (perhaps highly disjunctive and idiosyncratic) which explain the patterns of discriminatory behavior of human beings? If the answer is negative, I do not see how Bradley can suppose that there could be a color vocabulary at all. Surely a certain degree of explicability is presupposed by any color vocabulary? How would we teach or learn a purely private language of color discrimination or of color experiences? Both colors (which I am arguing to be objective properties of the surfaces of objects) and color experiences (which in my view are physical processes in human brains) are identified by their typical causes and effects (in the case of the colors themselves, mainly by effects, and in the case of color experiences, mainly by causes). This does not mean that for the purpose of giving sense to our color language we need strict causal laws, which would give strict necessary or sufficient conditions for color behavior or color experiences. The difficulties into which philosophical behaviorism has run provide sufficient evidence of the fruitlessness of a search for such strict conditions. Typical causes and effects in typical conditions are all that we need.[7]

I think that the revised account of colors will even enable us to follow Bradley in saying that color discriminations must be on "the different observed appearances of things."[8] For (a) we hypothesize colors as the (perhaps highly disjunctive and idiosyncratic) physical states of the surfaces of objects which in fact explain (from the side of the objects) typical color discriminations, and also (b) we hypothesize color experiences as those processes which (from the side of the person—in fact, the brain) explain this same discriminatory behavior. That the causal chain goes not direct from the surface of the object to behavior but goes via the person (his brain and hence his inner experiences) is perfectly consistent with the physicalist thesis.

A color sensation, in this view, is what is hypothesized as a typical cause of the typical response of normal color percipients in typical circumstances. ("Normal" can be defined without circularity.) Such a sensation will also partially serve to explain the nontypical false reports of percipients who suffer from illusion or from intention to deceive. (Illusion leads to false reports about external things, while intention to deceive can also lead to false sensation reports.) I therefore see no difficulty for the amended view in Bradley's remarks about false sensation reports which arise from intention to deceive.[9] Nor shall I touch on Bradley's argument[10] from the alleged incorrigibility of sensation reports, since he no longer subscribes to this argument.[11]

I have no doubt that I have been unable to do justice to all of Bradley's criticisms or even to the full subtlety of any of them, but I hope that I have been able to explain why I think that, although my earlier account of colors must be given up, there is nevertheless another physicalist account of colors which avoids these objections.

Ideally, for Quinean reasons, I should like to supplant my talk of colors as properties by a more extensional set theoretic account.[12] Ideally, too, the notion of "explains" or "causes" which comes into the account should rest on an extensional account in terms of the syntax (or possibly semantics) of the language of science.[13] It should be noticed, in any case, that this property talk, as well as the use of the concept of explanation ("colors are the physical states of objects which explain certain discriminatory behavior") is needed only to identify the colors of our ordinary commonsense talk with physicalist properties, that is, as a defense against someone who thinks that a physicalist world view leaves something out. Once this is conceded, we can drop the words "property" and "explain" within our statement of world view. But it would be good to do the job set-theoretically, rather than in terms of properties.[14]

NOTES

1. In his "Critical Notice of *Philosophy and Scientific Realism*," *Australasian Journal of Philosophy* 42 (1964): 262–283, and also in his "Sensations, Brain Processes and Colours," ibid. 41 (1963): 385–393.

2. D. M. Armstrong, *A Materialist Theory of Mind* (London: Routledge & Kegan Paul, 1968), pp. 256–260, 272–290.

3. It may be questioned whether the concept of the sort of color change which we are envisaging can be made structurally consistent. See Paul E. Meehl, "The Compleat Autocerebroscopist: A Thought-Experiment on Professor Feigl's Mind-Body Identity Thesis," in Paul K. Feyerabend and Grover Maxwell, eds., *Mind, Matter and Method: Essays in Philosophy and Science in Honor of Herbert Feigl* (Minneapolis: University of Minnesota Press, 1966), pp. 103–180, especially pp. 147–148. Also Bernard Harrison, "On Describing Colours," *Inquiry* 10 (1967): 38–52. I welcome such considerations if they can be made out, but even so I do not want my defence of physicalism to have to depend on them.

4. P. J. Bouma, *Physical Aspects of Colour* (Eindhoven, Netherlands: Philips Industries, 1949), pp. 154–156.

5. I myself learned this point from Lewis. N. L. Wilson argued, however, for the possibility of contingently identifying properties in his interesting paper, "The Trouble with Meanings," *Dialogue* 3 (1964): 52–64.

6. D. M. Armstrong, "The Headless Woman Illusion and the Defence of Materialism," *Analysis* 29 (1968): 48–49.

7. David K. Lewis, "An Argument for the Identity Theory," *Journal of Philosophy* 63 (1966): 17–25, especially 22.

8. Bradley, "Sensations, Brain Processes and Colours," p. 393.

9. Bradley, Critical Notice, p. 269.

10. Bradley, Critical Notice, pp. 272–278.

11. Bradley, "Two Arguments against the Identity Theory," in R. Brown and C. D. Rollins, eds., *Contemporary Philosophy in Australia* (London: Allen & Unwin, 1969).

12. See my paper, "Further Thoughts on the Identity Theory," *The Monist* 56 (1972).

13. To elucidate "explanation" we need to elucidate "law." A law is a universally quantified sentence which occurs either as an axiom or a theorem of an important and well-tested theory (or, in an informal theory, somehow "follows from" it) or is such that we guess that it will one day be incorporated in such a theory. Thus to elucidate "explanation" we seem to need value words (e.g.,

"important"). Value expressions enable us to avow preferences; there is nothing contrary to physicalist metaphysics about them.

14. I wish to thank Professor D. K. Lewis and Professor D. M. Armstrong for commenting on an earlier version of this paper.

5

Physicalism and the Contents of Sense Experience

Brian Ellis

I SUPPOSE that the main reason why physicalism is not generally accepted is that the physicalist's world picture seems essentially incomplete. It may be allowed that it is possible on a physicalist theory of the mind to account for what may be called the structure of sense experience, for example, to explain why one sense experience is like or unlike another. But it seems that no physicalist theory could possibly account for its content, for example, explain why our sense experience is as it is and not systematically otherwise. Here, I shall argue that, while there is a content of sense experience which no physicalist theory could possibly account for, it is not reasonable to require of any theory that it be able to account for it. We have to admit that the fact that our sense experience is as it is and not systematically otherwise is a brute and inexplicable fact, one that is perhaps on a par with the fact that the universe is predominantly a matter rather than an antimatter universe. It seems that we have to accept a doctrine of emergentism. Nevertheless, this doctrine of emergentism is not incompatible with physicalism as it is here understood, although it is incompatible with Feigl's physical$_2$-ism.

Physicalism

Physicalism is the theory that all events and processes are physical. If physicalism is true, those events or processes that we call reasoning, drawing inferences, having sense experience, forming beliefs, noticing similarities, focusing attention upon, and recognizing must be physical events or processes.

The distinction between the physical and the nonphysical has been drawn in various ways. Meehl and Sellars distinguish two concepts of the physical. A physical₁ event or entity is any that is located in the space-time network. A physical₂ event or entity is any that is "definable in terms of theoretical primitives adequate to describe completely the actual states though not necessarily the potentialities of the universe before the appearance of life."[1] The thesis that all events and processes are physical₁ is not very controversial, since, on at least some interpretations of "located in the space-time network," physical₁-ism is consistent with almost any kind of dualism. The more exciting thesis is that all events and processes are physical₂. This is the thesis defended by Feigl.[2]

Meehl and Sellars' definition of physical₂ events and entities is not at all clear. Are numbers or sets, for example, definable in terms of theoretical primitives adequate to describe the actual states, though not necessarily the potentialities of the universe before the appearance of life? The difficulty I find with this definition of physical₂ events and entities is that in actual cases I do not know how to apply it. Presumably the distinction between physical₂ and non-physical₂ is meant to be such that if any kind of ontological dualism or emergentism is true, then physical₂-ism is false. But that is about the only sense that I can make of it.

It seems to me that if a satisfactory distinction between the physical and the nonphysical is to be drawn, it must be made in the light of present-day physical theories. Accordingly I propose the following: a physical entity is anything that has energy; a physical event is any change of distribution of energy within the universe; a physical process is any causally connected sequence of physical events; a physical property is any property possession of which affects at least some physical processes; and a physical state is any that is characterized by physical properties. These definitions are proposed with a view to giving substance to the theory of physicalism.

I suppose that many defenders of physicalism would not wish to accept these particular definitions of the physical. There are at least two sorts of grounds on which they may object to them. The first is that they do not adequately capture the physical scientist's concept of the physical. For example, since forces do not have energy, the definitions require us to say that forces are not physical entities. This is a serious objection which I have discussed at some length elsewhere.[3] But for the purposes of this discussion it does not matter very much what conclusion we reach concerning the nature of forces. If anyone wishes to insist that they are physical entities, he is welcome to do so and modify my definition of a physical entity accordingly, that is, say that a physical entity is anything that is either a force or has energy.[4]

The second kind of ground on which objection may be made to these definitions is more fundamental. It is that physicalism is just not a doctrine related to present-day physical theory. If the concept of energy were to cease to have the central role that it has in present-day physics, these definitions of the physical might become clearly untenable. Future physicists might come to accept that there are all sorts of entities and events existing or occurring in inorganic nature that neither have energy nor involve any transfers of energy—and are not forces either. My only reply is to admit that the objection is a sound one, but plead that there is nothing that I or anyone else can do about it. I can discuss whether physicalism is now a tenable doctrine, but there is no way of discussing whether for any future acceptable definition of the physical all events are physical.

A Physicalist Theory of the Mind

I assume that the beliefs that we acquire as a result of sensory stimulation are, as a matter of fact, neurophysiological states that are probably encodings of information about the events which stimulated our sense organs and the sensations that we have experienced. I also assume that we are caused by events going on in our surroundings and in our heads to acquire a number of different kinds of beliefs about a variety of different kinds of things and to hold them with various and varying degrees of confidence. I suppose that the degree of confidence with which a belief is held is a direct function of its degree of resistance to erasure or modification; that is, our belief states have a kind of inertia. A belief acquired by inference is presumably a belief state that has been acquired as an effect of the acquisition of some other belief, or as a result of such physical processes as those we call thinking about, concentrating upon, and so on. It is reasonable to suppose that our brains have encoded within them enormously complex systems of beliefs to which new elements are frequently being added (by perception) and others dropped out, modified, reinforced, or undermined by processes of reasoning, forgetting, and so forth.

There must be a kind of dynamics of belief: those beliefs that are more firmly entrenched, that is, more stubbornly held, tend to remain, and those that are less firmly held are more subject to erasure, weakening, or modification. A system of deductive logic should be regarded as a *partial* dynamics of belief. For it circumscribes the kinds of systems of beliefs that could be held by an *ideally rational man*. It does not tell us what beliefs an ideally rational man would hold any more than Newtonian dynamics tells us what the actual motions of Newtonian point-masses in an inertial system would be. But it does enable us to say that if a belief-set is such and such, then it is not the belief-set of an ideally rational man. Similarly, Newtonian dynamics enables us to say that if the motions of actual bodies are such and such, then the system in which they occur is not inertial, or its elements are not Newtonian point-masses.

The ideal of a rational man is not easy to explain, although it is clear that we all have some such ideal. It is apparent that our systems of beliefs can be modified in several ways. We can acquire new beliefs by perception, and we can lose beliefs by forgetting. But our beliefs states can also interact or be caused to interact with each other by processes we call reasoning, drawing inferences, and so on. A completely nonrational being would be one in which such processes never occurred. A completely rational being is presumably one in which all such processes of rational interaction which could occur do so, and whose system of beliefs while stable under all such rational interactions is nevertheless flexible enough to admit new perceptually acquired beliefs and to accommodate them within a modified system of beliefs which again is stable under all processes of rational interaction.

It is a problem for the physicalist to say what makes a belief true, or what it is for one belief to be contrary to or to contradict another. If a belief is a neurophysiological state of some kind which is caused to come into being by events occurring in our heads or elsewhere, then it must correspond to the reality that caused it in the sort of way that *any* effect corresponds to its cause. Hence, to say that a belief is true if and only if it corresponds to reality is to make all beliefs true unless some distinction can be drawn between proper and improper encodings. But if such a distinction can be made, I have no idea how to make it.

The idea of a conflict of beliefs is easier to understand. For just as it is physically impossible for an object to be hot and cold simultaneously it may be physically impossible for two particular belief-states to coexist. Such would be the case for those belief-states that are the immediate contradictories of each other. Let us agree to say that a belief is acquired inferentially if and only if it is acquired as an effect of the acquisition of some other belief, or as an effect of those physical processes we call thinking about, considering, or attending to the consequences of other beliefs. Let us say that any belief that is not acquired inferentially is acquired immediately. Then it is particularly easy to see how a conflict can occur between immediately and inferentially acquired beliefs. For there is nothing very mysterious about countervailing causal tendencies. What happens in such cases, typically, is that a dynamic equilibrium is established, but often only after an initial period of oscillation and instability. Much the same seems to happen to a system of beliefs when a conflict arises. The processes of adjustment and accommodation which may occur as a result of such a conflict would be far too complex to be described here, even if I could do so. But, typically, both of the conflicting beliefs are weakened in the ensuing readjustment.

I do not know what to say about the *objective truth* of a belief. I can understand a *subjective* concept of truth. For we may say that a belief B is true for a person x if and only if x has been caused to hold B firmly, and nothing has occurred to cause x to weaken or to change B. But I cannot understand what it is for a certain kind of neurophysiological state to be true in any objective sense. Of course, I can understand it in an abstract way. For we may suppose that there exists a certain function ϕ appropriate to an ideally rational human being which maps events occurring in our environments onto brain states, and that a belief B about an event e is true if and only if $B = \phi(e)$. But since we know nothing whatever about this supposed function ϕ, we are incapable of applying this objective concept of truth.

Most philosophers who are physicalists seem nevertheless to use an objective concept of truth as though it were unproblematic. Maxwell, for example, says that most of our beliefs about the outside world (although, strangely, not those about our own sense experiences) are probably false.[5] For me this is the claim that most of our beliefs are not "proper" encodings of the events occurring in our surroundings, although some of our beliefs are proper encodings of events occurring in our heads. But since we have no idea what an encoding proper for an ideally rational human being might be, it seems to me that this is a claim we cannot say anything at all about. If you ask me whether it is probable that most of my beliefs are false, I can only reply, given my subjective concept of truth, that I have the beliefs that I have, and that I cannot without (pragmatic) contradiction assert that most of my beliefs are probably false. To make sense of the claim one would need an objective concept of truth which at present we do not have.

The physicalist theory of mind that I wish to defend is epistemologically as well as ontologically monistic.[6] It is epistemologically monistic in the sense that it denies the existence of any distinction between immediate and inferred, or direct and indirect, knowledge other than the introspectively based distinction between those beliefs that are acquired without *conscious* inference and those that are acquired as result of attending to or thinking about or trying to explain other beliefs. On my view, what is immediate is simply a function of what neural hookups have been established, and this is presumably a function of the observer's past history of sensory stimulation. For my part, the beliefs that I can acquire immediately include beliefs about things external to my head (that there is a cup in front of me), about causal relationships (that I am holding a pen), about future outcomes (that the telephone on my desk is an enduring physical object and not a transient chimera), about your sense experiences (that you are in agony), about my own sense experience (that my feet feel cold), about causal relationships between external events and the experiences they produce (that the metal feels cold), and about my own intentions, desires, wishes, beliefs, and so on.

I do not deny that my capacity to acquire such beliefs immediately, without conscious inference, is an acquired capacity. But that goes for all beliefs. I see no reason to suppose that there is any simple intensionally definable class of belief-acquiring capacities which is epistemologically primitive, and such that all other beliefs are acquired by processes of conscious or *unconscious* inference from them. Yet philosophers, even those who claim to be physicalists, commonly do make such an assumption, and in doing so they incur all of the epistemological problems of classical dualism. On my account, there is no one kind of belief acquired by sensory stimulation from which all others are inferred. A landscape is shaped by wind, rain, running water, vegetation, volcanic upheavals, and so on. A particular stretch of land, for example, a field, is thus formed and shaped by its environment. The same with us. Our beliefs are formed, shaped, weakened, strengthened, and undermined by events occurring in our environments and in our heads. To think of a system of beliefs as a construction out of a primitive set of beliefs is to think of the system not as a landscape but as a building. But since the existence of a building implies the existence of a builder, to think of ourselves in this way is to think dualistically. And this is so, even if we think that the foundations of our buildings are insecure, as most neo-empiricists do.

Physicalism and Sense Experience

Perhaps the most serious objection to this physicalist theory of the mind is that such a theory cannot adequately account for the content of sense experience. It might be possible, on such a theory, to account for the fact that our *beliefs* about our sense experience are as they are. But even if we could do so, it might be argued, it would still be a fact, unexplained on our theory, that our sense experience is as it is and not systematically otherwise.

Let us suppose that we have a highly developed psychophysiological theory of taste experience that is capable of predicting every fact about my taste experience that I am capable of describing. Let the theory be physicalist in the sense that every event of having a taste experience is identified as a neurophysiological event. Let A and B be two new substances, and suppose that my physicalist theory predicts that when the substances are tasted the following neurophysiological events will occur:

(a) I will judge that the taste of A is pleasant, but utterly unlike anything else that I have ever tasted before.

(b) I will judge that the taste of B is pleasant, but utterly unlike anything else that I have ever tasted before.

(c) I will judge that the taste of A is quite different from the taste of B.

Let us suppose that after tasting the substances A and B, the predictions (a), (b), and (c) were all verified. And, further, let us suppose that when questioned I was quite unable to add to my descriptions.

Now the point about this imagined case is that the best descriptions that I was able to offer of my taste experiences were identical; *both taste experiences fitted the one best description.* But since my physicalist theory was capable of yielding only that best description, it follows that it could not explain why one taste experience was had rather than the other.

Let the experiences had when the substances A and B are tasted be e_A and e_B respectively. Let D be the common best introspective description of e_A and e_B. Then we have

(i) $\forall \phi \, (\phi e_A \equiv \phi e_B)$, where ϕ ranges over introspective psychological predicates

(ii) $e_A \neq e_B$

(iii) $De_A \wedge De_B$

Then because of the symmetry of (i), (ii), and (iii) with respect to e_A and e_B, it is evident that the predictions of the physicalist theory would have been as well confirmed if e_B had occurred when the substance A was tasted and e_A had occurred when the substance B was tasted.

Let N_A be the predicate "is a neurophysiological response of the kind K_A," O the predicate "occurs at," and T the predicate "is tasted at." Then my neurophysiological theory should enable me to predict that

(iv) $T(A, t) \supset \exists x (N_A x \wedge O(x, t) \wedge Dx)$.

Similarly, it should also enable me to predict that

(v) $T(B, t) \supset \exists x (N_B x \wedge O(x, t) \wedge Dx)$.

But without postulates to the effect that

(vi) $\forall x (N_A x \equiv x = e_A)$

and $\forall x (N_B x \equiv x = e_B)$

it would appear that

(vii) $T(A, t) \supset O(e_A, t)$

and $T(B, t) \supset O(e_B, t)$

could not possibly be predicted. That is, without postulates like (vi) the theory would be incapable of predicting the occurrence of e_A rather than e_B when the substance A is tasted.

The equivalence relations (vi), which are contigent identity statements, would have to appear as *fundamental* postulates of the theory because (a) they are not analytic, (b) they cannot be derived from more basic postulates, and (c) they are required for the explanation of (vii)—which is what is observed. But if the relations (vi) appear as fundamental postulates in such a theory, then for these reasons they are emergent and inexplicable facts. For we are assuming that the theory is as good as any physicalist theory could be. Therefore, as physicalists, we must suppose that no more fundamental theory could be constructed.

However good my physicalist theory may be, therefore, without ψ-ϕ (psychophysical) correlation laws it is incapable of explaining why the taste experience e_A is had when the substance A is tasted rather than some other introspectively distinct experience such as e_B. If, when I tasted the substances A and B, I did not know beforehand which substance was which, I still would not know after the test was completed. There must therefore be some kind of ineffable quality of e_A which no physicalist theory is capable of accounting for. For if there were no such quality, how could e_A be known introspectively to be different from e_B, even though e_A and e_B are introspectively descriptively identical? This, in a greatly simplified form, is the inverted spectrum argument for the existence of ineffable qualia or contents of sense experience and for the necessity of ψ-ϕ (psychophysical) correlation laws (nomological danglers) in any theory adequate to account for them.

There are several objections to this argument. First, it may be said that we *can* discriminate descriptively between e_A and e_B. For we can say that e_A is the taste of the substance A while e_B is the taste of the substance B. This, however, is not to describe the tastes e_A and e_B. It is simply to say what the words "e_A" and "e_B" refer to. We need neither theory nor experience to say that e_A is the taste of A and e_B the taste of B. It cannot, therefore, be any part of the description of e_A that it is the taste of A or that it tastes A-ishly. For whatever else description is, it always involves relating what is described to something else. If I say that something is blue, then I classify that thing in a certain way, and hence relate it to other things that are similarly classified by a relationship of similarity.

A second kind of solution is to deny that such a situation as that described in the example could ever in fact arise, that it is contrary to some physical law that it should do so. The law would have to be something like the following:

> We cannot discriminate between experiences which we cannot describe differently.

Such a law, however, is highly implausible. A blind man whose sight is restored can certainly say whether or not his visual experiences are changing, even though he may be quite incapable of describing them. It is true that we can learn to discriminate, and that once we have learned it seems inconceivable that we could ever have failed to discriminate. Hence it may well be true that out ability to discriminate between experiences is a function of our history of sensory stimulation. But there is no evidence to suggest that a law anything like as strong as the above holds. A blind man's first visual experiences may not be such a blooming confusion as we are apt to imagine, but there is no good evidence to suggest that they are uniform and unchanging, either.

A third kind of solution is to deny the premise that a physicalist theory could never do more than yield the best description of an experience that I am now capable of giving of it. A really good physicalist theory might be capable of predicting that there exists a substance C which has never yet been synthesized that will taste more like A than B. If this is so, then the physicalist theory might yield a description of e_A that is distinct from the description of e_B. So it may be argued that we do not lack an adequate theory here, but only adequate means of testing it.

But I do not find this solution wholly satisfactory. For surely, however elaborate the descriptions of e_A and e_B and the relationships of similarity and difference between e_A, e_B, e_C, ... where e_C ... are the taste experiences produced by as yet unsynthesized substances, it is always logically possible that these relationships could be satisfied by any of a range of sets of possible experiences. No matter how elaborate a consistent axiom system may be, it is always possible that more than one physical model can be found for it. Similarly, it would not appear to matter how well the experiences e_A and e_B were triangulated, it would always seem to be possible that these same relationships could hold between a different set of experiences. That being so, the physicalist theory would seem to be logically incapable of explaining why one particular set of experiences which satisfy all of these relationships is had rather than some other.

If none of these solutions is acceptable, however, then we must accept nomological danglers into our psychophysics. For now we shall need a law which says that *this* experience (e.g., e_A) is the neurophysiological response K_A rather than some other e that fits the description D that is derivable from a knowledge of K_A and the physicalist theory. Calling it a contingent identity does not destroy its nomological character. If it is a contingent fact that K_A is the experience e_A rather than, say, e_B which it could also be according to the theory, then, relative to the theory, this contingent fact is emergent.

It can now be seen how this inverted spectrum argument applies generally to the whole of our sense experience. Imagine a Martian neurophysiologist describing our sense experience. Let us suppose that the description he offers is introspectively (to us) complete and accurate in every detail. Let us assume, furthermore, that he is able to predict accurately and fully our future sense experiences. Then clearly his neurophysiological theory of sense experience which enabled him to make these predictions would be as good as any such theory could be. And yet we may want to say that he may not really understand what it is to have sense experience. We may grant that he knows all that there is to know about the structure of sense experience, but if somehow he could take on human form and actually *have* human sense experiences he might nevertheless be surprised to discover that they are as they are. Therefore, the fact that human sense experiences are as they are and not systematically otherwise is necessarily inexplicable, and no theory of sense experience that is not anchored by at least one ψ-ϕ correlation law could possibly explain why we have the sense experiences that we do.

My response to this argument is to admit its soundness, but to deny the implication that physicalism is thereby shown to be inadequate. For a precisely analogous argument demonstrates that if nomological danglers are required for psychology they are also required for physics.

Incompleteness and Emergence

Consider the following description: "This particular object is a spiral. It has a radius of three inches and an interval of one inch. It is made of copper wire $\frac{1}{16}$ inch in diameter. It is seven inches long." Obviously, this particular description could be satisfied in more than one way; that is, there is a multi-membered set of possible objects satisfying the description. Is the wire tarnished or untarnished? Are there markings on it? Is it pure copper? Is it a right-handed or a left-handed spiral? We can add details to the description. But however much we do so there is always a range of possible objects which would satisfy the description. We therefore postulate:

1. THE PRINCIPLE OF INCOMPLETENESS OF DESCRIPTIONS: *Any true description of a physical object or event, however elaborate, can be satisfied in more than one way.*

But any explanation of an object or event, however elaborate, can never do more than yield a true description of that object or event. We therefore obtain:

2. THE PRINCIPLE OF INCOMPLETENESS OF EXPLANATIONS: *No explanation of a physical object or event, however elaborate, can explain why that object or event is precisely as it is, or occurred precisely as it did.*

Assuming for the purposes of this argument Hempel's explanation-prediction symmetry thesis, it follows that any prediction of the occurrence of an event yielded by a physical theory could always be borne out in more than one way.

These conclusions are not startling and I state them only to avoid a possible misunderstanding. The argument of the previous section is not based upon the principle of incompleteness of explanations, but on a much stronger principle which I shall soon elaborate. If the argument were based upon this weaker principle it would not be a sound one. For there is nothing in it to suggest that there is anything *essentially* inexplicable about any object or event. The fact that an explanation that explains the occurrence of an event e_1 would equally well have explained an event e_2, had it occurred instead, does not entail that the occurrence of e_1 rather than e_2 is inexplicable—only that it has not yet been explained.

Let us suppose that I am in radio contact with someone on Mars. He seems to be speaking English. He describes his world to me and I describe my world to him. Gradually, I build up a picture of his world, its plants, animals, processes, machines, customs, geography, and so on. The picture he describes is coherent and intelligible in terms of all of the physics that I understand. But we have to suppose that throughout the whole process of communication there is never any one thing to which we can both refer. Apart from the verbal communication between us, each is isolated in his own world, neither able to perceive anything that the other can also perceive.

Eventually I get an opportunity to pay him a visit. I find that his world is not as I expected it to be. His manuscripts are all in mirror writing, his typewriters all chug off to the right, his magnetic north is at my magnetic south pole, and so on. In short, his world is a kind of mirror image of the one that I thought he had described.

The point about this example is that, assuming that the principle of parity holds, our systematic misunderstandings of each other could not have been cleared up by further communications of the kind outlined. And since it is at least logically possible that the principle of parity holds, it is logically possible that systematic misunderstandings of this kind should exist between us which cannot be resolved without some common ostensive reference. When I can show the Martian a right-hand screw and say that *that* is what I mean by a "right-hand screw," it may be possible to remove this systematic misunderstanding (although, as Quine has pointed out, because of the essential ambiguity of referential gestures, even then the logical possibility of continued misunderstanding remains).

Let us say that two languages, L_1 and L_2, are syntactically similar if and only if they have the same vocabulary, grammar, and syntax. That is, every well-constructed sentence of L_1 is a well-constructed sentence of L_2, and conversely; and every analytic sentence of L_1 is an analytic sentence of L_2, and conversely. Let us change the example by assuming that the Martian's description of his own world exactly fits ours. He describes accurately our trees, rivers, people, and cities, and calls them all by their proper names. We think, naturally, that he is describing our world in English although, in fact, he is describing a different world in a language syntactically similar to English. Now think of the Martian world not as a distant actual world to which we have no direct access, but as just another possible world. Let W_1 be the actual world and W_2 this other possible world. Let L_1 be the English language of the actual world and L_2 the syntactically similar language spoken by the inhabitants of W_2. Then every sentence of L_1 that is true of W_1 is a sentence of L_2 that is true of W_2. Moreover, as the example has been described, the L_1 description of the possible world W_2 would be identical to the L_2 description of the actual world W_1. Let us agree to say that the worlds W_1 and W_2 are *structurally similar* relative to the languages L_1 and L_2. In general, we may define structural similarity thus:

Two worlds W_1 and W_2 are structurally similar relative to a language L_1 if

(a) every sentence of L_1 that is true of W_1 is a sentence of a syntactically similar language L_2 that is true of W_2, and

(b) every sentence of L_1 that is true of W_2 is a sentence of L_2 that is true of W_1.

We may now formulate:

3. THE PRINCIPLE OF STRUCTURAL INDETERMINACY: *For any given world W_1 and language L_1 it is possible that there exists a structurally similar world W_2.*

This principle is much stronger than the principle of incompleteness of descriptions. For it does imply that, whatever language we use to describe the actual world, there are facts about that world that cannot be explained.

Consider the sentence of L_1 that the actual world is W_1 rather than W_2, where W_2 is a possible world structurally similar to W_1. This is surely true. But the fact that it is true cannot be explained in L_1. For if it were possible to explain it, precisely the same explanation of why the world is W_2 rather than W_1 would be acceptable to an inhabitant of W_2 speaking the syntactically similar language L_2. Thus we obtain:

4. THE PRINCIPLE OF EMERGENCE: *For any given world W_1 and language L_1 it is impossible to explain why the set of all true L_1 descriptions of W_1 is instantiated in the way that it is.*

It follows from the principle of emergence that if the world that is the mirror image of the actual world is structurally similar to the actual world relative to the English language, then no explanation of why the world is as it is, and not its mirror image, is possible in English. Similarly, if there is a possible world composed primarily of antimatter that is structurally similar, relative to a given language, to the actual world composed primarily of matter, then no explanation of why the world is predominantly a matter rather than an antimatter world is possible in the language. Therefore, to explain why the world is as it is, and not systematically otherwise, we require nomological danglers of precisely the kind required for psychology. Therefore, it cannot be any kind of failing of a physicalist theory of the mind that it is incapable of accounting for the content of sense experience. For, if this is a ground for claiming that no physicalist theory of the mind can be adequate, there is an analogous ground for claiming that no physicalist cosmology can be adequate. Nomological danglers are not peculiar to psychology.

Emergent Physicalism

The argument of the previous section invites the following comment: It is easy to believe that one or more content-fixing anchors (nomological danglers) are required to explain why the physical world is as it is and not systematically otherwise, but if the events which comprise our having sense experience are physical events, why should *additional* content-fixing anchors be required? Doesn't the fact that they are required demonstrate that these events cannot be fully explained in terms of a physics that is adequate for the explanation of the world before the appearance of organic life, and hence that physical$_2$-ism is false? The answer to the second question depends on what is considered a reasonable requirement on an explanation. A physicalist theory of sense experience is in principle capable of explaining why our sense experience is as we describe it to be, completely and in every detail. What it is incapable of explaining is why this description is fulfilled in the way that it is, and not systematically otherwise. But to demand an explanation of the latter is to require an explanation where no explanation could possibly be given. On any theory of sense experience, whether physicalist or not, we have to suppose that the fact that it is as it is and not systematically otherwise is emergent. Hence we may wish to say that the events which comprise sense experience can in principle be fully

explained in terms of a physics that is adequate for the explanation of the world
before the appearance of organic life. Since those who have argued in favor of
physical$_2$-ism have generally thought it necessary to argue against emergentism,
however, it is probably fairer to allow that physical$_2$-ism, as it is generally
understood, is false.

But if physical$_2$-ism is false, what should one say of the doctrine of physicalism as it is here understood? Certainly, there is no good reason to deny that all
events and processes are physical in the sense explained earlier. The event of my
having a sense experience is still a physical event, whether or not there exists a
structurally similar world in which an introspectively qualitatively different
event would have occurred. We do have to allow, however, that the necessity for
additional content-fixing anchors for the explanation of why our sense experience
is as it is and not systematically otherwise provides a good case for accepting a
form of emergentism.

NOTES

1. P. E. Meehl and W. Sellars, "The Concept of Emergence," in H. Feigl and
M. Scriven, eds., *Minnesota Studies in the Philosophy of Science*, vol. 1 (Minneapolis: University of Minnesota Press, 1956), p. 252.

2. H. Feigl, *The "Mental" and the "Physical." The Essay and a Postscript*
(Minneapolis: University of Minnesota Press, 1967).

3. In an unpublished paper, "The Existence of Forces," I argue that forces
are not physical entities and that we have no good reason to believe that they exist.

4. Nevertheless, the point should be made that if one is prepared to admit such
nonenergetic causes and effects as forces into one's scientific ontology, then one is
already a kind of dualist. And since forces are supposed somehow to mediate
between energetic causes and effects in the sort of way that mental events are
often thought to do, we should not be too disparaging of the idea that certain
physical (energetic) brain states or events produce certain nonphysical (nonenergetic) effects (feelings, thoughts, sensations, etc.) which in turn act to produce
certain other physical effects (movements, speech acts, etc.). Feelings, thoughts,
and sensations might even *be* forces if there were any such things.

5. Maxwell says this in a number of places. His view is that any statement that
involves reference to a publicly observable physical object (such as a table) and
which ascribes observable (first-order) properties to that object is, strictly
speaking, almost certainly false. See his "Structural Realism and the Meaning
of Theoretical Terms," in S. Winokur and M. Radner, eds., *Minnesota Studies
in the Philosophy of Science*, vol. 4 (Minneapolis: University of Minnesota Press,
1970), pp. 181–192. It seems to me, however, that we have more reason to be sure
of statements concerning publicly observable objects than we have to be sure of
statements concerning our own sense experiences. This is so because our ability
to make judgments concerning our own sense experiences has been less well
tested. Before the advent of psychoanalytic theory, no one doubted that he knew
his own intentions, wishes, and motives. Now we don't think ourselves to be quite
such good judges. Today we have a high degree of cocksureness about our

judgments concerning our own sense experiences, thoughts, and beliefs, Maybe one day we'll have this knocked out of us, too.

6. For a more complete account of epistemological monism, see my "Physical Monism," *Synthese* 17 (1967): 141–161.

6

Mind and Body:
Aspects of Identity

Chung-ying Cheng

THE PURPOSE of this article is to clarify a number of issues and observations found in recent writings on the identity theory of mind and body. The identity theory as first proposed by H. Feigl[1] serves two purposes: First, it will resolve certain puzzles about the relations between mind and body, among which the causal one is most likely to be conjured. Second, it purports to represent a scientific hypothesis which will ideally characterize the true nature of mind in terms of physicalistic concepts and which is in principle capable of being scientifically confirmed and disconfirmed, when suitably elaborated.[2]

Given this understanding of the identity theory, we confront two problems. On the one hand, there is the question of how to distinguish the monistically interpreted identity theory from carefully formulated parallelism, epiphenomenalism, and the like, in the light of theoretical and empirical considerations. This is the question of empirical justification. On the other hand, there are various possible semantic interpretations of the identity relation in the identity theory. In the first place, there is Feigl's interpretation of the identity thesis as a double-knowledge theory, according to which, even though the mental and the physical are one, our distinction between them represents two different ways of knowing the same reality. In the second place, there is the replacement interpretation: the identity between the mental and the physical is derived from the fact that the meaning of mental terms in our language can be ultimately explicated, and therefore redefined, in terms of a neurophysiological or physicalistic language, and this means that the mental terms can be supplanted by physicalistic or neurophysiological terms.

In his "Postscript" written ten years later, in 1967, Feigl rejects his earlier double-knowledge interpretation of the identity theory in favor of a replacement interpretation. Yet at the same time Feigl, following Sellars, contrasts the manifest image (suffused with phenomenal concepts) with the scientific image of the world and seems to consider their relation as devoid of any empirical scientific connections. In fact, Feigl is even willing to admit that there are a great many perspectives, or frames, with the purely egocentric perspective at one end ("lower limit") and the completely physical account at the other. He considers that this difference of perspectives is to be explicated by the logic of categories, but not to be formulated as a feature of the world.[3] It is not clear in what sense the mental terms in our language can be ultimately supplanted by physical terms. The existence of possible manifest constructions at a stage of intended complete physicalistic understanding of the world presents new problems of explanation, and their relationships need clarification. One can be further puzzled by the simultaneous banishment of parallelism of one form and introduction of parallelism of another.[4]

In the light of these ambivalences of the notion of identity between mind and body, it will be fruitful to ask what aspects of identity are involved, how they are related in the actual theories proposed by recent philosophers, and how they should be related in a final account of the relation between mind and body. In this paper I will specifically discuss these questions in regard to a distinction of three aspects of identity in the identity theory—the logical, the empirical, and the philosophical or metaphysical.

Identification as an Axiomatic Decision

Philosophers have variously spoken of the mental or phenomenal states, events, or properties (such as in the case of a green after-image or a toothache) which represent how things look, sound, smell, taste, and feel. These have been contrasted with physical states, events, or properties. To these philosophers, the mental states, events, or properties such as consciousness, thoughts, sensations, and feelings are intrinsically different from physical properties, states, and events. The latter are intersubjectively ascertainable and spatially localizable, and can be probablistically recognized. The former are privately accessible, not necessarily spatially localizable, and supposedly can be expressed with certainty. In these terms the identity theory would therefore mean identity of states, events, or properties. But if the identity theory is formulated in this way, some difficulties present themselves.

In the first place, the expressions for mental properties, states, and events are assumed to refer to different objects. The question, therefore, is how the referents of expressions for mental states, events, or properties can be said to be identical with those for physical events, and so forth. The answer is that they cannot, for once it is assumed that their referents are distinct and different extensional entities, the expressions for them will not refer to same entities.

The moral from this discussion is that the identity theorist cannot permit the talk of mental states, events, or properties as clearheaded, for this talk will inevitably introduce puzzles over the identity in question and pave the way for semantical objections, which the identity theorist can only reject by noting that the introduction of the conception of mental states, events, or properties is gratuitous. The rejection consists in pointing out that since the mental has been assumed to be incapable of being characterized in accordance with scientific method, the talk of mental states, events, or properties cannot be scientifically justified. The point, of course, is not to regard the talk of mental states, events, or properties as simply meaningless. It is to urge that we make clear what the expressions for the mental states, events, or properties could mean and in what way they function to mean. Before suggesting an answer to this question, one can call attention to the fact that there are no logical or empirical reasons (in the strict sense) to believe that mental states, mental events, or mental properties are well-defined entities because we can use the terms "mental states," "mental events," or "mental properties" in a seemingly referring way. For example, there is no empirical nor logical reason for us to believe that there are green after-images, or toothaches, simply because we can say, "I see a green after-image" or "I have a toothache."

For a positive account of the meanings of mental terms, we might suggest that in so far as they can be used either as logical subjects or as logical predicates in statements, they must perform the double functions of referring and characterizing. Their meanings must be therefore explained in terms of these two functions in the discourse. As logical subjects they are intended to refer to entities of which we can make some characterization (in terms of logical predicates or relations). As logical predicates, they are intended to characterize entities referred to by the logical subjects in the sentences in which they appear. Thus, in statements like (1) "My sensation of red is dazzling" or "I had a dazzling red sensation," the expression "My sensation of red" refers to some entity characterized by "dazzling"; whereas in (2) "I am sensuously conscious of a red triangle," the expression "am sensuously conscious of a red triangle" is intended to characterize the entity which the egocentric expression "I" is intended to refer to. Now it should be noted that as a referring expression a mental term is always related to some egocentric expression such as "my" or "this," and can be always transformed into a characterizing expression in relation to the egocentric particulars "I," "he," etc. Thus (1) can be transformed into (3) "I have a dazzling sensation of red." Keeping this possibility of transformation in mind, we may also note that the referring forces of mental terms are in fact derived from the referring forces of singular egocentric expressions. On the basis of this observation we suggest that part of the meanings of mental terms is derived from the referring force of the singular egocentric expressions and part from their purported characterizations of the egocentric particulars which the singular egocentric expressions stand for.

In our earlier criticism of the unexamined use of terms like "mental events" and "mental properties," we noted that they are not well defined and need not be assumed to be definite or determinate in meaning. The egocentric particulars which they intend to characterize are not well defined and need not be assumed to be definite and determinate entities of which we have clear understanding. On this analysis, we conclude that mental terms can be said to refer if their referents are to be identified with egocentric particulars, and can be said to characterize or describe if their meanings are left open to be specified or explained in the light of empirical theories. What we wish to stress is that mental terms can be considered performing a purely referential function in language and the question as to how to characterize objects to which they refer can be left open.

Once we have distinguished the referential function of mental terms from their descriptive function, we see no logical objection to identifying the referents of mental terms (or more precisely the referents of the egocentric expressions to which mental terms are necessarily related) with the referents of nonmental terms. There is no logical or empirical reason for assuming that the referents of the mental terms cannot be scientifically explained and therefore explained in terms of physical-chemical laws and theories.

Within the broad category of the nonmental terms, we can distinguish between the *molar behavior terms* on the one hand and *physical object terms* on the other. The molar behavior terms characterize molar behaviors of men and animals. They are exemplified by such words as "walk," "drink," "write," and "dance." Apparently the molar behavior terms are similar to the mental terms in that they can be normally predicated of the egocentric particulars in such statements as "I write" and "He walked home." But the difference is that whereas the mental terms when predicated of the first person egocentric particulars appear to describe, and when predicated of egocentric particulars of the third person appear to ascribe, the behavior terms in both these types of predication appear to describe. I will not carry further this analysis of various uses of these terms. It suffices here to point out that the meanings of these two types of terms are explicitly independent: they do not explicitly entail each other in all constructions. Yet one might argue that they are implicitly related. Logical behaviorists like Ryle and others have tried to show by analyzing the use of our ordinary language that the meanings of the mental words are implicitly defined in molar behavior terms including those for behavioral dispositions. On the other hand, the scientific behaviorists like Skinner have a theory of explaining the mental variables in terms of variables of behaviors and external environments. In both cases, the semantic relations between the mental and the molar behavior terms are to be discovered or constructed (by analysis or by experimental observation). Since normally we can predicate behavior terms as well as mental terms of egocentric particulars, there is at least prima facie reason for assuming that they are intended to characterize, and therefore implicitly refer to, the same type of entity.

In the case of physical object terms, we can distinguish between the nonbehavioral neurophysiological terms and physical-chemical terms. Both kinds of terms are normally implicitly defined in scientific theories and in such theories they do not implicitly refer to egocentric particulars.[5] The physicalists believe that all neurophysiological terms can be ultimately explained in physical-chemical terms, which means that the neurophysiological theories can be reduced to fundamental microphysical theories. The possibility of this reduction is clearly indicated in that both types of terms implicitly refer to nonegocentric objects in a broad sense. What these objects are is for each individual theory to explain and characterize. Yet there is no reason why in both neurophysiological and microphysical schemes the ultimate objects of investigation should be identical. The difference between the two types of theory consists ultimately in the scope and powerfulness of explanation achieved by the individual theories.

Returning to the question of identification of implicit referents of mental terms with those of nonmental terms, the question is not essentially different from identifying referents of molar behavior terms with those of neurophysiological terms, or that of identifying referents of neurophysiological terms with those of microphysical terms. There are no logical inconsistencies in making the identification. It is an axiomatic decision, based on the consideration that (1) it is conceivable that a single type of entity may have widely divergent properties, and that (2) no set of predicates with descriptive meanings uniquely characterizes. For the function of referring of a used term is different and distinct from the function of characterizing (or intended characterizing) of the same term. To identify or refer is one thing, to describe or characterize is another. In the light of the fact that the egocentric expressions share the same referring force as the expressions for objects such as "this" and "that," the identification is a decision not totally without theoretical basis, apart from considerations of apparent simplicity.

In identifying the implicit referent of a mental term with that of a nonmental term, we naturally face the question of how adequately to characterize the common referent. Indeed, there are various ways of characterization which perhaps can be in general ordered according to degrees of explanatory power, or size of the scope of explanation. This means that these characterizations must be formulated in theories of various complexities and in view of various pragmatic purposes. At one end of the characterizations we have the intended characterization in mental terms. This characterization is poor in content, for there is no scientific theory relating these terms on their own basis. They are perhaps used as demonstratives are used.[6] In this sense we might ignore their minimum meaning content and seek explanation of their referents in objectively constructed theories. Along this line of thought, one might explain the meanings of mental terms in a neurophysiological theory of brain states, or finally one might explain their meanings in a microphysical theory of elementary particles.

The above three characterizations represent three semantically independent and distinct levels of characterizations. By semantically independent and distinct levels of characterization, I mean that each such level constitutes a semantic field of meaning which is not logically reducible to the other. The meaning of a term on each level is determined by its relationship to other terms on the same level.

Identification as an axiomatic decision does not imply that the mental and nonmental predicates must be intensionally isomorphic or even that there must be lawlike connections between the mental and the nonmental. *They need not be known to be related in any definite ways.* In fact, without a perfect theory on each level of characterization, we cannot even assign definite (or determinate) meanings to these terms. Because of this possibility, mental terms as purely referential are like labels or proper names which, when used, have existential import, but which need not have descriptive meanings in their being used. Their implicit referents can be regarded as events, or states whose occurrences are occasions for theoretical interpretations.

For our purpose, we emphasize that identification as an axiomatic decision is logically, ontologically, as well as epistemologically, justifiable. In order to devise a theory which will interpret the identical reality in an intended completeness, and therefore will explain various other possible interpretations, we need always inquire into the empirical evidences revealed and implicitly used on each level of characterization.

Briefly, we might construct three distinct theories of referents or intended meanings of the mental terms. Let the list of ostensible mental predicates be $M_1, M_2, \ldots, M_n$ in ordinary language. Let the structure underlying our ordinary mental language be called T_0. Then T_0 consists in $M_1 \cdot M_2 \cdot \ldots \cdot M_n$ $(x_1, x_2, \ldots, x_n)$, where $x_1, x_2, \ldots, x_n$ are purely referential terms for egocentric particulars of the first person or third person. For theoretical reinterpretations and explanations of $x_1, x_2, \ldots, x_n$, let T_1 be a theory of molar behavior of egocentric particulars of the first or third person, which contains molar behavioral predicates $B_1 \cdot B_2, \ldots, B_n$. The theory T_1 can be represented by $B_1 \cdot B_2 \cdot \ldots \cdot B_n$ $(x_1, x_2, \ldots, x_n)$. Similarly we may construct two more theoretical characterizations of $x_1, x_2, \ldots, x_n$ in terms of a neurophysiological theory T_2 and a microphysical theory T_3, etc. Then T_2 can be represented by $N_1 \cdot N_2 \cdot \ldots \cdot N_n (x_1, x_2, \ldots, x_n)$ and T_3 by $P_1 \cdot P_2 \cdot \ldots P_n (x_1, x_2, \ldots, x_n)$ where $N_1 \cdot N_2, \ldots, N_n$ and $P_1 \cdot P_2, \ldots, P_n$ are respectively theoretical predicates in T_2 and T_3. Now we can see that it is only by an axiomatic decision that we regard all the theories T_1, T_2, T_3 as sharing the same primitive individuals to which the manifest structure purports to refer.

In practice each theory will have its own distinctive primitive individuals just as it will have its own distinctive theoretical predicates. Thus we may assume a *theory of psychology* T_m to be represented by $M_1 \cdot M_2 \cdot \ldots \cdot M_n (x_1, x_2, \ldots, x_n)$ and a *theory of microphysics* T_p to be represented by $P_1 \cdot P_2 \cdot \ldots \cdot P_n$ $(y_1, y_2, \ldots, y_n)$. Our axiomatic decision to identify referents of T_m and T_p means positing a new set of entities represented by $(z_1, z_2, \ldots, z_n)$ such that $(x_1, x_2, \ldots, x_n)$ and $(y_1, y_2, \ldots, y_n)$ should be reinterpreted in terms of some new predicates to be introduced in the new theory T_q which contains $(z_1, z_2, \ldots, z_n)$ as primitive individuals. Let these new predicates be M' and P', respectively. Then we may redefine T_m and T_p as follows:

$$(M_1 \cdot M_2 \cdot \ldots \cdot M_n) x_i \equiv (Ez_i)(M'z_i \cdot (M_1 \cdot M_2 \cdot \ldots \cdot M_n) z_i)$$
$$(P_1 \cdot P_2 \cdot \ldots \cdot P_n) y_i \equiv (Ez_i)(P'z_i \cdot (P_1 \cdot P_2 \cdot \ldots \cdot P_n) z_i)$$

In this way the different and distinctive universes of T_m and T_p can be fused or unified in a larger universe defined by the new theory T_q. This axiomatic decision is guaranteed by the logical possibility of reducing a many-sorted theory to a one-sorted theory. Of course, in actual construction of a one-sorted theory we should proceed in terms of some completely new predicates such as $Q_1 \cdot Q_2 \cdot \ldots \cdot Q_n$ so that T_q can be represented by $Q_1 \cdot Q_2 \cdot \ldots \cdot Q_n (z_1, z_2, \ldots, z_n)$. The reduction of the original theories T_m and T_p means that (1) the sets $(x_1, x_2, \ldots, x_n)$ and $(y_1, y_2, \ldots, y_n)$ are to be reconstrued in terms of $(z_1, z_2, \ldots, z_n)$ by suitable definition in T_q and the predicates $(M_1 \cdot M_2 \cdot \ldots \cdot M_n)$ and $(P_1 \cdot P_2 \cdot \ldots \cdot P_n)$ are to be effectively redefined in the new predicates $(Q_1 \cdot Q_2 \cdot \ldots \cdot Q_n)$ in T_q.

Compare the standard reduction procedure of T_m and T_p to T_q with the unification of universe without a reduction of predicates in the case of T_0, T_1, T_2, T_3.[7] In the overall theory T_q we can explain T_m and T_p by deducing T_m and T_p from T_q under suitable conditions, whereas we can not use the overall theory $T_4 \equiv M_1 \cdot M_2 \cdot \ldots \cdot M_n. B_1 \cdot B_2 \cdot \ldots \cdot B_n. N_1 \cdot N_2 \cdot \ldots \cdot N_n. P_1 \cdot P_2 \cdot \ldots \cdot P_n (x_1, x_2, \ldots, x_n)$ to deduce T_1, T_2, T_3 in a nontrivial sense of scientific derivation. The reason is that in T_4 the interanimation and conceptual fusion of the predicates in T_0, T_1, T_2, T_3 are not yet effected. Not even empirical correlation of predicates is assumed. Yet we must see that the axiomatic decision to have a unified discourse (universe) is a step forward to examine how logically and empirically different theories can be integrated together.

As we can adopt scientific explanatoriness and predictiveness as the fundamental principles for evaluating a theory, we can make T_3 the basic theory in terms of which T_0, T_1, T_2 can be defined in the light of empirical discoveries. The ultimate and ideal fusion of T_0, T_1, T_2 into T_3 is the achievement of an ideal microphysical theory in terms of which not only will we predict and explain every bit of human behavior and mental process, but we will exhibit clearly in a lawful fashion the mutual relations of $T_0, T_1,$ and T_2 to one another, analogous to the explanation of mutual relation between T_m and T_p in T_q. In conceiving such a powerful theory we also need to raise the question whether, therefore, T_0, T_1, T_2 can be said to disappear or be replaced completely, and in what sense of disappearance or replacement. We will deal with this question in relation to the completeness and self-referential explanatoriness of this powerful scientific theory after we have considered the question of the empirical import of the identification of referents of mental terms and nonmental terms as an axiomatic decision.

Empirical Import and Basis of Identity Theory and Its Superiority to Parallelism

We have argued that the identification of referents of mental and nonmental terms can be made independently of empirical considerations and that it is a matter of imputing referential identity to two sets of concepts which are yet to be specified in empirical theories. This logical move is, as we have seen, not without logical and ontological significance. It presents a simple universe of one sort. It leads us to inquire into the mutual semantical relations of the mental and nonmental terms and urges us to formulate a satisfactory theory in terms of which mental terms can be given adequate meanings.

Apart from its logical and epistemological basis, the logical move of identification independent of empirical considerations is not without empirical import either. As any imputation of identity leads to the positing of a set of new entities other than those assumed in prior universes, we can always regard the imputation of referential identity to mental and nonmental terms as posing an empirical hypothesis to be explored and confirmed according to scientific principles. This point does not seem to be sufficiently recognized. A recognition of the empirical import of the identity theory, together with an appropriate appreciation of its empirical basis, will dispel any doubt about the logical as well as the empirical superiority of the identity theory to parallelism.

According to this formulation, one need not in fact impute identity to referents of the physical and the mental. Parallelism will do as well as the identity theory. Therefore, one asks, why an identity theory?

This criticism of the identity theory is understandable. The nomic correlation need not be a good reason, nor direct evidence for the underlying referential identity. It is true that referents of P and M are not like referents of the expressions "morning star" and "evening star," which can be identified by simple observation in a continuing spatio-temporal process. It is further unlike the case of identifying the same type of theoretical entities in physics through identifying typical and yet peculiar observable similar tokens of the same type. Nor is it like the case where electrical conductivity is identified with thermal conductivity on the basis of more fundamental laws. Certainly we cannot hope to establish a situation which approximates to simple observation of identity by perceptual similarity or by spatio-temporal contiguity. The autocerebroscopic experiment only reveals correlation of tokens of different types through different media.[8] The properties of a tokening event corresponding to a brain state to be observed on the autocerebroscope certainly ostensibly differ from the raw-feel directly experienced by the subject of the experiment. For there are no clear spatio-temporal contiguities or recognizable perceptual patterns of similarity.[9] It has also been pointed out by both Meehl and Sellars that the ostensible manifest phenomenal objects have surface homogeneity which is not found in the theoretical entities of microphysics or neurophysiological theory. In view of this, there is no clear simple empirical basis for the identification of the physical and the mental.[10]

The lack of direct evidence for the identity theory, discussed above, does not constitute a positive argument against the supposition of the identity theory any more than it is a positive argument for the supposition of parallelism. On the contrary, the argument against the identity theory on the basis of lack of empirical evidence is itself unsound in the light of our analysis of the possible meanings of the mental terms. Use of the term "phenomenal property" by Brandt and Kim prejudices the issue whether phenomenal terms do clearly indicate a class of simple properties, as well as the issue whether the presupposition that the meanings (in terms of sense and reference) of phenomenal terms such as "directly aware" are clear and determinate is a correct one.[11] As we are not able to identify phenomenal properties in a way ostensibly similar to that by which we can identify spatio-temporal objects, we can raise doubt concerning whether the meanings of phenomenal terms are determinate and definite. Apparently one need not interpret the meaning of a phenomenal term as consisting in the existence of a simple irreducible quality. Instead, one should attempt to analyze phenomenal properties and explain the meanings of phenomenal terms in accordance with scientific methodology of explanation and confirmation. Until we have a clear scientific theory of phenomenal properties, we will not know what criteria will really enable us to identify them and what will not.[12]

As there is no adequate pre-existent explicit theory of phenomenal properties (mind), there is no a priori reason to suppose that a *tertium quid* object may not be independently determined by a simple observation to satisfy the neurophysiological description and at the same time satisfy the phenomenal description fully developed in a theory.[13] The identity thesis, when adequately presented, therefore carries with it the requirement that a scientific theory of ostensible phenomenal properties is to be fully developed and formulated. It provides an empirical basis for any clear and precise empirical understanding of the ostensibly phenomenal properties and some specification of the meanings of the phenomenal terms. This point can be regarded as a first reply to the criticism of Brandt and Kim.

The second reply is related to the first. As we have seen, imputation of identity is a device for determining or positing an entity as the object of reference of two sets of applicable concepts. The positing of an entity is an invitation to characterize the entity in a scientific theoretical investigation. Without positing such an object of investigation, we will never advance to high-level theories. Suitably formulated parallelism will be sufficient to account for the ostensible empirical correlations between the physical and the mental, but as such it lacks explanatory power; the correlation law is merely an inductive statistical generalization which attains only crude probabilistic validity. In the light of lessons of the history of science, there is no reason why we should not inquire into a powerful explanatory account of the correlation between the physical and the mental in terms of microcosmic processes. It is in this direction that the hypothetic referential identification of the mental and the physical terms should be understood. No present neurophysiological theory is capable of actually explaining everything about ostensible phenomenal properties. Certainly one reason for this is that our understanding of the brain processes is still far from being adequate. Another reason is that we do not really understand what we call phenomenal experience, and will not until we can explain this in terms of a scientific theory. Thus it is unfair for Brandt and Kim to criticize the identity theory as not genuinely explanatory and predictive, for it is only in terms of the identity theory that a theory of mind or phenomenal experience can become genuinely explanatory and predictive. Herein lies the superiority of the identity theory over parallelism.

It is one thing to maintain that the identity theory is a methodological doctrine which opens the way for future theory construction; it is another to see how this theory construction is to be anchored. If the theory in question is to be a scientific theory, it must be empirically formulated. Therefore, one must undertake the construction of such a theory in the light of our understanding of what constitutes the empirical basis for corroborating or refuting a scientific theory. If such a basis consists (as it must) of only intersubjectively observable data, then only such observable data will be taken into account. In this sense, the ostensible data of our "primary" and "private" introspection and direct awareness will not even be part of the empirical basis. One may indeed raise the question: Are these data after all intersubjectively observable? If they are, of course, they are part of the empirical basis, and therefore should not be called private and merely subjective. Holding this position is not necessarily incompatible with holding that the introspective data and data of "direct awareness" are indeed primary and private in a different sense. *The primariness, the immediacy and the privacy are to be regarded as demonstrative forces of pure referentiality.* They indicate, express, and exhibit the occurrences of events, or occasionings of states to be described or characterized, which they do not intend to describe or characterize. The feelings of primariness, immediacy, and privacy are factually related to outward events as one physical event is related to another in a physical system.[14]

In the light of this view, we can recognize that it is in terms of our individual "private" or "primary" reports that we conduct verification of scientific theories, and at the same time answer the question: How do the "subjective," "private" data provide an empirical basis for an intersubjectively verifiable theory? The answer, to risk redundancy, is that the *subjective phenomena are occasions for intersubjective verification of a scientific theory.* The reports of subjective phenomena merely refer to, without describing, something that can be in principle intersubjectively observed. Without the referring reports of private data, and without the factual occurences to which these reports are directed, we will have no occasion to conduct verification and hence no occasion to construct scientific theories.

On the basis of the above discussion of the interplay of the phenomenal and the theoretical, we conclude that if theory construction is empirically justifiable, the identity theory as a hypothesis is also empirically justificable. We should note that this argument does not depend upon the downfall of parallelism as a suitable competing hypothesis. It depends only on a correct and adequate understanding of the role of phenomenal terms and the role of theory construction in our understanding of the world.

As an empirical hypothesis, parallelism cannot be a competing thesis. Three considerations count against parallelism which do not count against the identity theory. First, parallelism like dualism has to assume the existence of a mental substance corresponding to the existence of a material substance. This assumption is itself based on an imputation of identity: the imputation of referential identity to all phenomenally unrelated and disconnected ostensible phenomenal terms. This has been made clear by Hume. Our rejoinder to the parallelist is, therefore: What is the genuine empirical basis for the imputation of identity to mind, as contrasted with the lack of empirical evidence for the imputation of identity to both mind and neural processes? Second, in pragmatic contexts we do regard the correlation between the physical and the phenomenal as characterizing individual persons. There must be an explanation why individual persons exhibit two different yet correlated processes. The explanation must be basically monistic if it must explain the singleness of persons or egocentric particulars of the first or second person. Finally, as pointed out by Sellars,[15] the phenomenal experiences are *ex hypothesi* needed to explain how we come to recognize appearances in the manifest world. In the rigorous sense of scientific explanation there is no reason why the explanation in question cannot be made by a monistic neurophysiological theory. Thus the possibility of achieving a theory of stronger explanatory power should be a reason for identifying the referents of the phenomenal terms with those of the neurophysiological terms which are defined in a theory intended for stronger explanatory power.

Completeness and Self-Referential Explanatoriness of a Universal Scientific Theory

We have shown that the identity theory is logically warranted, methodologically sound, and empirically significant. It is not a full-fledged scientific theory, but one which such a theory would necessarily presuppose. Now I will deal with how an ideal universal scientific theory, which will genuinely explain the relation between the physical and the mental, should be characterized. Such an ideal universal theory should provide a final solution to whatever puzzles the problem of mind and body may pose. We will show in what philosophical sense the solution is achieved and in what other senses the solution may appear illusory. We will also examine whether such a solution can be said to be replacement of some inadequate theories or views and whether such inadequate theories will naturally disappear.

In the first place, if one does not wish to adopt the Rylean conceptual analytic approach to the identity of the mental and the nonmental, one will have to recognize the necessity of explaining the cross-categorial identity of the mental experiences expressed by the structure T_m and the physical events described in the physical theory T_p. Is this explanation to be made in terms of some *tertium quid* object which can be characterized in some set of new predicates? Assume such an explanation to have been developed and assume the theory which incorporates this explanation to be T_q (which we discussed above). The explanation of T_m and T_p in T_q then means that there exist correspondence rules or bridge laws among T_q, T_m and T_p so that (1) T_m and T_p can be suitably deduced from the postulates of T_q in a network of nomic connections, and (2) the relation between T_m and T_p will be made clear in this deduction.

At this point we are interested in answering two questions. The first is whether T_q as a universal theory is physicalistically defined or is completely neutral in a certain sense. The second question is in what exact sense is T_q (the scientific image in Sellar's sense) a complete image of the world, explaining, but not explaining away, the structure T_m which represents our mental and phenomenal experiences.

An answer to the first question will reveal the basic nature of our ideal universal scientific theory. An answer to the second question will reveal the nature of our conception of an ideal scientific theory. In earlier accounts of the identity theory, these two questions are not distinguished. The failure to make this distinction accounts for an insufficient appreciation of the metaphysical, not just the scientific, significance of the identity theory.

Now our answer to the first question depends upon how one takes the categorial difference between mental and nonmental terms. If there is a genuine difference between the two, T_q should be a neutral theory, neither properly mentalistic nor properly physicalistic, yet one from which the structure of the mental (T_m) and the theory of the physical (T_p) can be derived. However, to make this suggestion is in a certain sense misleading. For the suggestion presupposes that we can come to know T_q independently of T_m and T_p. As we have pointed out, a universal scientific theory will develop in accordance with scientific principles of explanation and confirmation, and therefore must be in an important sense a continuation of the theory of the nonmental. It should be basically a microphysical theory of what it is intended to be based on intersubjective confirmation. For this reason T_q will be more a materialistic theory than a nonmaterialistic one. But in saying this, as we shall see, I am not sure what more we can signify than merely that T_q is basically a development of our known scientific theories about neurophysiology and microphysics.

We come to the second question regarding the intended completeness of the universal scientific theory T_q. If T_q is complete in the sense that it will explain everything and give us total knowledge, then it should be capable of explaining the mental and the phenomenal. But what does this mean? To explain the mental and the phenomenal could mean at least two things; that is, we could distinguish two senses of explanation of the mental and the phenomenal within T_q: the weak and the strong sense. In the weak sense of explanation, T_q explains T_m if the universal scientist is able to derive and predict T_m from T_q without knowing that T_m is explained by T_q, that is, without knowing that what are intended by the mental predicates and phenomenal concepts are nomically correlated with the physicalistic predicates and concepts in T_q, even though the mental and phenomenal are represented or redefined in terms of the microphysical properties within T_q. In this weak sense of explanation we may also say that the universal scientist does not have to know that there exists such a structure as T_m in whatever sense of existence.[16]

On the other hand, in the strong sense of explanation, T_q explains T_m if the universal scientist is able to derive and predict T_m from T_q as well as claim to know that T_m is explained by T_q, namely, that T_m is correlated with part of T_q in a certain way and that the derivation of T_m from T_q is a result of such correlation expressed in T_q. Since the set of the correlation laws between T_m and the universal scientific theory T_q can be expressed by the following two formulas:

$$(1) \quad T_m \equiv (Ez)(Tz \cdot Qz)$$
$$(2) \quad (z)(Tz \equiv Q_1 \cdot Q_2 \cdot \ldots \cdot Q_n z)$$

where z is the type of entity postulated in T_q, and Q_1, Q_2, ..., Q_n are basic predicates in the vocabulary of T_q, when the universal scientist claims to know that T_q explains T_m, he in fact claims to know that T_m is reduced to T_q by the reduction (1) of entities and the reduction (2) of predicates.[17]

Now we face the question of how the universal scientist can be said to know this. Is what he knows about the reduction of T_m to T_q precisely the same thing as his actual ability to draw T_m from T_q? Can we make a distinction between knowing how to perform one act and knowing that some act is performed at all? If some such distinction can be made, then the universal scientist in a strong explanation case has to be assumed to know the phenomenal and the mental independently of the universal scientific theory T_q. This will immediately destroy the intended completeness of T_q. In view of this difficulty, one might suggest that in knowing how to derive and predict T_m from T_q the universal scientist will naturally come to know what the phenomenal and the mental mean as well as come to know that the phenomenal and the mental in whatever sense they are understood are derived from T_q. The reason why he can come naturally to know this is that the fact of understanding T_m as such and knowing T_m as being reducible to T_q are derived and predicted in T_q. Whatever T_m stands for and whatever knowing T_m as such stands for can be perhaps treated as some emergent qualities defined in T_q.[18] On this suggestion one can say that in the strong sense of explanation of T_m within T_q the universal scientist not only actually derives T_m as a part of T_q but perceives (or recognizes) part of T_q as T_m, because he can perceive (or recognize) part of T_q as representing an emergent quality defined in T_q which he can designate as T_m. For example, the universal scientist will not only predict and derive the neural states of his brain corresponding to his feelings of pain, he will actually experience the pain as pain and know that what he experiences as pain is in fact a neural state of his brain.

In order to make our strong sense of explanation logically clear, we might conceive the universal scientific theory T_q as a universal translating procedure for translating the mental talk in our language into the uniquely correct microphysical talk. In order to do correct translation, the procedure will enable us not only to translate a given sentence involving mental terms into some corresponding sentence of the microphysical theory, but to translate a given microphysicalistic sentence into a corresponding phenomenolistic sentence if it has such a corresponding sentence. The process of translating back is important because it will enable us to check errors and eliminate mistakes. Since there is good sense in speaking of checking errors and eliminating mistakes, we can imagine that our universal scientific theory will enable us to discover errors and eliminate mistakes by enabling us to compare the original structure T_m with the corresponding representation of T_m in T_q. This presupposes then that the original T_m will be preserved in T_q and can be identified as such.

With this illumination of the strong sense of explanation, we come to clarify and evaluate the intended completeness claims of T_q. As a microphysical theory, it should contain a full microphysical description of life, consciousness, and sensations without use of any mental or phenomenal terms. Granted this, it is clear that this characterization of T_q does not preclude it from being characterized in reference to the phenomenal on two counts. First, the universal scientific theory must be established as a true and sound theory on the basis of perceptual data. In other words, to understand T_q one cannot ignore the basis of confirmation rooted in the experience of the phenomenal. This basis can be construed as an occasion referred to by egocentric expressions and the phenomenal terms, an occasion which invites scientific theoretical interpretation. Second, when a universal scientist entertains the universal theory, he does so in the form of *knowing* the theory. Until we have explained satisfactorily *knowing* in terms of the universal theory, the theory itself will remain to be the *propositional content* of the knowledge of the universal scientist. The point of this is that if *ex hypothesi* the phenomenal and the mental have no place in the universal theory, one must (apparently) deny the existence of the universal theory. As a result, the universal theory cannot be said to be known if it exists. If it can be said to be known, it cannot be complete in the sense that it will not be able to account for its being known as a theory.[19]

The above argument of *reductio ad absurdum* is not intended to reject the completeness claims of the universal scientific theory. It is used to reveal difficulties to be surmounted in our attempt to conceive a complete universal scientific theory. Perhaps following our distinction between the weak sense of explanation and the strong sense of explanation of T_m in T_q, we may suggest a similar distinction between T_q as a weakly complete theory and T_q as a strongly complete theory. T_q is weakly complete if it explains the phenomenal in the weak sense of explanation; T_q is strongly complete if it explains the phenomenal (which includes the egocentric experiences of feelings and sensations as well as the mental entertainment or contemplation of a proposition) in the strong sense of explanation. It is apparent that T_q can be weakly complete without being strongly complete.

Given our analysis of the completeness claims of T_q, we can see that T_q is intended to be strongly complete. We can also see that for the sake of the consistency of T_q its being strongly complete should not contradict its being weakly complete. In fact, we must now show that the consistency of T_q as a universal theory demands that its being weakly complete should *naturally* coincide with or lead to (not just be logically equivalent to) its being strongly complete. In other words, T_q should weakly explain its strong completeness, whereas its strong completeness should enable T_q to strongly explain its weak completeness. I will argue that the necessity of this aspect of identity involved in coherently thinking of a universal microphysics which explains everything is essential for clarifying the nature of our universal theory.[20] The lesson from this is that we should not conceive the success of the identity theory as consisting in replacing our mental talk by purely physicalist talk, nor as consisting in simply advancing a double- or multiple-knowledge theory according to which the implicit referents of the mental expressions in our language can be at the same time described in a microphysical theory.

A further step to clarify our notion of the strong completeness of the universal theory T_q consists in requiring T_q to explain two things: (1) how various possible interpretations and reinterpretations (such as represented by our earlier theories T_0, T_1, T_2) of implicit referents of egocentric expressions in pragmatic contexts are possible (not just in the sense of microphysically possible, but in an independent sense); and (2) how its own existence as a universal theory is possible. To require this is to require that T_q be not merely self-explanatory but *self-referentially* explanatory.

The first requirement can be regarded as a reformulation of the case of explaining the existence of mental terms which are meaningful in pragmatic contexts. In order to fulfill this requirement, the theory must recognize a place for the phenomenal within the theory in order to justify its substitution in pragmatic theories and to justify the compatibility or complementariness of the pragmatic theories with itself. This leads us to the difficulty of reconciling the monistic basis of the theory with the pragmatic or semantic dualism or pluralism within the theory.

As to the requirement of self-referential explanatoriness,[21] the theory has to explain and predict its own occurrence in terms of microphysical terms, say, as a brain state of the universal scientist. As such it is merely manifested as a microphysical event. But as the theory is strongly complete, it should predict and explain its being held as a theory. This indeed involves an infinite regress, but there is no harm in this. For the theory will identify itself as a neural process and at the same time as a theory entertained by the universal scientist. In other words, the universal scientist should, as demanded by the universal theory, conceive or entertain the universal theory as a neural process as well as a theory. This parallelistic thinking implied by the strong completeness of the universal theory constitutes another difficulty for our notion of the nature of a complete universal theory T_q.

Now the difficulty related to self-referential explanatoriness and the earlier difficulty related to the problem of strong explanation of the mental are serious difficulties. For they threaten to avenge parallelism and anticipate its ghostly rise from the grave. In the face of this challenge, I suggest that we recognize a fundamental postulate of identification, namely: For all theoretical as well as pragmatical purposes the identity thesis and parallelism are the same. This sameness or identity is to be recognized as a perceptual fact, a fact which can therefore be explained or represented in the universal theory T_q. In terms of this identification, which is an assertion of the equivalence of the weak completeness and strong completeness of the universal theory in a metalanguage, we can say that we *recognize* or *know* the universal theory both as a neural process and as a theory in whatever sense it is intended. In this sense, it is meaningful as well as consistent to say that the mental is not only identical with the physical, but is *recognized* or *experienced* as being identical with the physical. Consequently we may say of the theory T_q that it is not only identical with a brain state, but that it is experienced or recognized as being identical with a brain state and vice versa. In the sense of this fundamental identity, we may regard the identification of the mental with the physical as a *simple* observation which is describable in T_q in microphysical terms, but which has nevertheless an experiential status like any phenomenal experience. Indeed, it is in the light of a correct understanding of the complete universal theory that one perceives this fundamental unity and identity of mind and body.

I do not know to what extent I have made my notion of a fundamental identity in the universal theory clear. It should be clear, however, that this identity goes beyond the referential identity axiomatically determined, as well as the hypothetic identity based on scientific and methodological considerations. It is furthermore not strictly intensional identity, although the mental and the physical terms will receive the same base meanings in the universal theory. For it represents an understanding of interchange of meanings of the mental and physical terms not in an explicit analytic sense, but in regard to or in reference to all theoretical as well as pragmatical contexts which may not yet have been specified in the formulation of the universal theory. This decision is therefore not only a logical and methodological one, but a pragmatic one.

The significance of the above philosophical identity perhaps can be made a little more clear in the light of Sellers' and Feigl's contrast between the "manifest image" of the world and the "scientific image" of the world.[22] Sellars introduces the image term "manifest" to denote our understanding in terms of commonsensical notions of mind and body, and the image term "scientific" to denote our understanding of the world in terms of imperceptible objects as postulated by science. Sellars, like Smart and Feyerabend, contends that the present scientific image could develop into a complete image, and as a consequence should replace the manifest image. But the question is how the replacement will take place. This is the question which Feigl has entitled "great transformation." Sellars considers that this great transformation should take place, yet he is not clear as to how the scientific image will replace or supplant the manifest image.

The fundamental identity which we postulate for the universal theory can now be formulated as the principle that the universal scientist will perceive the manifest image as a scientific image as well as perceive the scientific image as a manifest image where the process of perceiving is a neural state in the brain of the universal scientist, and therefore describable in terms of the microphysical. It also amounts to perceiving an identity between an egocentric account of the world and an account of the world without egocentric terms. Examples of this perception in the universal theory are the following: Perceptual water is perceived to be H_2O. Clouds are perceived to be droplets of water. Tables are perceived as clouds of electrons. The sensation of pain is perceived as a stirred brain state. This "perception" is to be regarded as a primitive term (or relation) posited in the universal theory as a result of collating multiple pragmatic contexts of understanding which, however, are fully explainable in the universal theory.

If our observations above make sense, the fundamental principle of identity implied by the consistency of the universal theory as a theory enables us to realize that a replacement interpretation of the identity theory will not do justice to the complete scientific image of the world. For in the complete scientific theory, as we have seen, the scientific image does not replace or supplant the manifest image (for it cannot), but will *embrace* or *comprehend* the manifest image. By virtue of the intended *perceptual* identification of the scientific with the perceptual, the *embracing* and *comprehending* of the manifest image in the scientific image means a genuine fusion of the concepts of theories or structures on various pragmatic levels. This fusion is indexed by our pragmatic decision on viewing these various types of concepts as cohering in a theory which as a whole can be scientifically explained.

This view of the relation of the manifest image to the scientific image which underlies that of the mental to the physical is not a revival of the double- or multiple-knowledge interpretation of the identity theory. For the double- or multiple-knowledge interpretation of the identity theory as represented by Feigl's original 1958 essay does not postulate, and indeed does not see the necessity of postulating, the identity (in a certain sense) of the multiple knowledge involved. It postulates only the referential and structural identity of mind and body. Our present view has given a new dimension to the identity of mind and body. It is the *epistemic* identity necessitated by a clarification of the notion of a complete universal scientific theory. We shall call our present view a *comprehen-*

sion interpretation of the identity theory. As such, it differs from the double- or multiple-knowledge interpretation of the identity theory, on the one hand, and from the replacement interpretation of the identity theory, on the other. In the light of this view, we need not take seriously the suggestion that, although we may not replace the manifest image by a complete scientific image in a swoop, we might, however, as a result of linguistic evolution, learn to forget the meaning of terms in the manifest image.[23]

In his postscript, Feigl agrees with the assertion that the scientific image and the manifest image do not represent two different sorts of reality, but "are two ways of providing a conceptual frame description." In fact, Feigl suggests that there could be a great many "perspectives" to describe or label the referents of the manifest image. This suggestion makes it difficult to interpret Feigl's present view, that is, difficult to determine whether it is a replacement interpretation of the identity theory or a double- or multiple-knowledge interpretation. But perhaps Feigl's position in his patient discussion is not far from the above comprehension interpretation of the identity theory.

Summary and Conclusion

I have argued that the identity of mind and body can be regarded as resulting from an axiomatic decision on identification which is logically warranted. Then I attempted to show that the identity theory is both logically and methodologically superior to parallelism. It has been argued that a negative logical criticism of parallelism is as essential to clarifying the position of monistic microphysicalism as a positive empirical confirmation of the latter.

In the last part of the article, where my main contribution lies, I have attempted to clarify the notion of a universal scientific theory. Such a theory will have to explain its own existence as a theory as well as the existence of the individuating or referential forces of the phenomenal or mental terms used in pragmatically significant contexts of life. Such a theory, it has been argued, must involve a fundamental philosophical, or, for that matter, a fundamental metaphysical, postulate of identity between mind and body, if the theory is not just a tautology (in the sense that the theory explains everything which the theory is capable of explaining) or a nontheory (in the sense that, even though the theory is complete, we are not in a position to maintain or ascertain that it is one, or in fact not even in a position to know the theory was a theory, but merely to experience it as a brain state or a neural process).

The fundamental philosophical or metaphysical identity in question can be described as the identity between the knowledge of the mental and the knowledge of the physical in the overall complete scientific theory. It is a form of *epistemic* identity realized in such cases as knowing x *as* y or recognizing x *as* y or perceiving x *as* y.

In the light of this aspect of identity in the complete scientific theory, neither the double- or multiple-knowledge interpretation of the identity thesis, nor the replacement interpretation of the identity thesis, is an adequate characterization of the complete scientific image implied by the identity thesis. We propose to call our view, which is based on our clarification of the notion of the complete scientific image and the identity postulate necessitated by such a notion, a *comprehension interpretation* of the identity thesis. This view is intended to provide a basis for further analysis of the complete scientific image, as well as a ground for criticizing existing opinions regarding the validity of the identity theory, on the ond hand, and the interpretation of the identity theory, on the other.

NOTES

1. Herbert Feigl, "The 'Mental' and the 'Physical,' " in H. Feigl, G. Maxwell, and M. Scriven, eds., *Minnesota Studies in the Philosophy of Science*, vol. 2 (Minneapolis: University of Minnesota Press, 1958), reprinted with a postscript as *The "Mental" and the "Physical." The Essay and a Postscript* (Minneapolis: University of Minnesota Press, 1967).

2. Feigl argued for the scientific value of the identity theory ("The 'mental' and the Physical,' " p. 105). In his postscript, however, he maintains that philosophical analysis is continuous with scientific research, and he allows possible refutation of his identity theory in future scientific research (*The "Mental" and the "Physical," Essay and Postocript*, p. 160).

3. He adds that "the mutual exclusiveness of the phenomenal and physical conceptual frames is to be explicated by the logic (semiotic) of the respective categories and not as a formulation of a feature of the world. Correspondence rules connecting physical with phenomenal terms, however, are 'cross-categorical.' They should be formulated in a semiotic (semantic-pragmatic) language" ("The 'Mental' and the 'Physical,'" p. 157).

4. Clearly, in a complete physicalistic description of the world, parallelism finds no place. But the semantic-pragmatic contrast between the "manifest image" and the "scientific image" certainly is a new form of parallelism which needs to be not merely logically analyzed, but scientifically explained.

5. Here, one might note that to say that "John is in brain state E," without a proper construal of what the statement is intended to mean, is a case of category mistake.

6. Feigl frequently refers to them as mere labels but does not sufficiently bring out their demonstrative forces.

7. This can also be achieved in another form by constructing Ramsey sentences of T_0, T_1, T_2, T_3 over the same set of variables, this being again an axiomatic decision.

8. Paul E. Meehl, "The Compleat Autocerebroscopist: A Thought Experiment on Professor Feigl's Mind and Body Identity Thesis," in Paul K. Feyerabend and Grover Maxwell, eds., *Mind, Matter and Method*, (Minneapolis: University of Minnesota Press, 1966), pp. 103–180.

9. Meehl has cited a case whereby the identity thesis can be refuted easily if

the experienced properties of a raw feel are taken to be the raw feel, instead of properties of it. The refutation, based on Wilfred Sellars, consists in the following: Suppose I am experiencing a circular red raw feel, large, clear, saturated, and focusing my attention upon its center. Our introspection will not be able to refute the statement: "There is a finite subregion $\triangle R$ of the raw feel red patch ϕr, and a finite time interval $\triangle t$, such that during $\triangle t$ no property of $\triangle R$ changes." Now the autocerebroscopic tokening of this raw-feel state will consist in the production of the corresponding physicalist statement: "There is a finite region $\triangle R'$ of the brain state ϕr and a finite time interval $\triangle t$, such that during $\triangle t$ no property of $\triangle R'$ changes." But this statement is neurophysiologically false. This refutation of the identity theory only pertains to the identity between the raw feel and the cerebroscopically tokened brain state, but not to the identity between a *tertium quid* referent of the phenomenal term and the referent of the physicalist term. For one still can maintain, as Feigl apparently does, that the raw feel designates the red patch, but denotes something else to be identified with the brain-state-tokening term. See Meehl, "Compleat Autocerebroscopist," pp. 167–168. See also W. Sellars, *Science, Perception and Reality* (London: Routledge & Kegan Paul, 1963), p. 37.

10. Feigl himself admits that the step from parallelism to the identity view is essentially a matter of philosophical interpretation. He seems to regard the principle of parsimony as a major reason for preferring the identity theory to parallelism. Another reason for Feigl seems to be that there is no logical reason why the identity is not possible in analogy to the case where one can know a friend in person and another knows him only by description. But this example is misleading for, in the case of knowing a person, we can trace by descriptions in terms of time and space to someone who knows the friend by acquaintance. There are ways of establishing identity in the elementary sense of perceptive similiarity and identity in spatio-temporal whole. Thus, Feigl in his 1957 writings fails to establish the identity claim except on parsimony basis. Moreover, Feigl's suggestion to construe the difference as a matter of logical analysis is unsatisfactory. For the logical distinction which one can draw between the identity theory and parallelism is analogous to that between the meanings of mental terms and physical terms. If there is any reason to recognize that there is no distinction between the identity theory and parallelism, it is that this can be shown empirically in a complete theory of the identity between the mental and the physical. This also means the fusion of the meanings of mental terms with those of physical terms.

11. Richard Rorty, "Mind–Body Identity, Privacy and Categories," in Stuart Hampshire, ed., *Philosophy of Mind*, (New York: Harper and Row, 1966), p. 57.

12. It is along this line of thought that the logical behaviorists reach the position that the phenomenal terms in fact refer to intersubjectively observable patterns of overt molar behaviors of persons, which should be explained by neurophysiological laws. In this sense, the introspective reports of pains, etc., can be treated as evidence for the attribution of the theoretical brain states to persons as well as basis of the explanation of the overt pain behavior.

13. This is essentially David Lewis' argument in Chapter 3 of this volume.

14. This distinction between private data and the privacy of the private data should enable us to see why one can hold private data to be intersubjectively

observable without contradicting himself: or the private data are merely occurrences, reports of which carry no descriptive meanings but merely a referential force to invite characterization and understanding in an intersubjective sense. To call private data merely "ineffable," as many philosophers do, does not clarify the nature of private data, although it is correct to observe that, as such, reports of private data cannot constitute knowledge claims and therefore can be ignored from an outsider's point of view. But it is precisely in this sense that they need not be ignored by an outside observer if he is in a suitable position to observe.

15. Sellars, Science, Perception and Reality, p. 36.

16. In terms of Feigl's example of the Martian superscientist in his postscript, the Martian superscientist will not know what our raw feels feel, yet he would be able to explain and predict "all of human behavior on the basis of his micro-theories." But this explanation and prediction are to be understood totally in a weak sense, i.e., that they are explanation and prediction of microphysics, not of human behavior or raw feels.

17. In this strong sense, part of T_q is known to be identical with T_m. Perhaps it is in this strong sense of identity that Brandt and Kim raise the issue as to whether a full materialistic description of the world is possible, i.e., whether the term "materialistic" retains its meaning, for, as they point out, the identity in question is a symmetrical relation: the mental being identical with the physical means that the world is both mentalistic and physicalistic.

18. That is, if emergence is regarded as a perceptual fact just to be accepted but not questioned, then the intended identity will be preserved.

19. One may simply ask: If we are correct in identifying the mental with the physical, how do we know that we are correct? To suppose that we do know as a matter of fact is to suppose a metaphysical postulate of identity of some sort.

20. A difference in our notion of the nature of a theory will make a difference in our notion of the theory.

21. In general, Feigl has recognized the difficulty of self-referential explana-toriness. For example, he notes that the ultimate physical processes would be "opaque" to one who did not know how to classify them. Feigl also notes that one would not know that a physical notation is also music notation if one is not familiar with rules of musical notation. See The "Mental" and the "Physical." Essay and Postscript, p. 151.

22. Sellars, Science, Perception and Reality, pp. 6–40; Feigl, The "Mental" and the "Physical." Essay and Postscript, p. 142.

23. This view is presented and considered an alternative to the replacement view in Rorty, "Mind–Body Identity, Privacy and Categories," cited in note 11 above.

7

Asymmetries and Mind-Body Perplexities

Keith Gunderson

"O wad some Pow'r the giftie gie us
To see oursels as others see us!"

from *"To a Louse" by* Robert Burns

I

Any satisfactory solution to the mind-body problem must include an account of why the so-called "I," "subjective self," or "self as subject of experiences" seems so adept at slipping through the meshes of every nomological net of physical explanations which philosophers have been able to imagine science someday bestowing upon them.[1] Until this agility on the part of the self is either curtailed or shown to be ontologically benign, not forcing us to attribute inexplicable properties to our self-consciousness or consciousness of self, the mind-body problem is not going to go away. Unless the self itself, however characterized, can be shown to be comfortably at home within the domain of the physical, many of its putative attributes—thoughts, feelings, and sensations—will not seem to be at rest there either.

Nor will it do to attempt to preempt the playing out of these perplexities by launching a frontal attack à la Hume or Ryle on allegedly quixotic views about the nature of the self. The problem I am alluding to does not arise because of quixotic views of the self. It is just the reverse: Philosophers find themselves forced to endorse quixotic views of the self primarily because they systematically

Reprinted, with minor editorial changes, from *Minnesota Studies in the Philosophy of Science*, Vol. 4, ed. M. Radner and S. Winokur (Minneapolis: University of Minnesota Press, 1970).

fail to show how a human being might conceive of himself as being completely in the world.

Some kind of thoroughgoing physicalism seems intuitively plausible mainly because of a dramatic absence of reasons for supposing that were we to dissect, dismantle, and exhaustively inspect any other person we would discover anything more than a complicated organization of physical things, properties, processes, and events. Furthermore, as has been emphasized recently, we have a strong sense of many of our mental features as being embodied.[2] On the other hand there's a final persuasiveness physicalism lacks which can be traced to the conceptual hardship each person faces when trying to imagine himself being completely accounted for by any such dissection, dismantling, or inspection. It is not so much that one boggles at conceiving of any aspect of his self, person, or consciousness being described in physicalistic terms; it is rather that one boggles at conceiving of every aspect being simultaneously so describable. For convenience of exposition I shall sometimes use the word "self" to refer to whatever there is (or isn't!) which seems to resist such description. Such reference to a self or aspect thereof will not commit me to any positive characterization of it. Neither will it commit me to the view that one's self remains unchanged from moment to moment or to the view that it doesn't or to the view that it is a thing, process, or bundle of events.

What I am committed to is phrasing and unpicking the following problem: If a thoroughgoing physicalism (or any kind of monism) is true, why should it even *seem* so difficult for me to view my mind or self as an item wholly in the world? And this independently of how I may construe that mind or self: whether as a substance or as a cluster of properties, processes, or events. The paradox becomes this: A physicalistic (or otherwise monistic) account of the mind at the outset seems quite convincing so long as I consider anyone except myself. If, however, physicalism provides an adequate account of the minds or selves of others, why should it not, then, provide an adequate account of the nature of my mind or self so long as I lack any reason to suppose that I am utterly unique?[3] But if I am unable to see how physicalism could account for the nature of my mind or self, why then should it not seem equally implausible as a theory about the mind or self of anyone else, again assuming that I lack reasons for supposing that I am unique? In this way we teeter-totter between the problem of viewing our self as wholly in the world, or physical, and the problem of viewing other people who seem wholly in the world as being somewhat mental. But if the mental is after all physical, why should this be so? Although I may not initially believe that in my or anyone else's investigation of the world I or they will find need to riddle our explanations with references to immaterial selves or spirits, it still remains easy to believe that I will never turn up the whole of my self as something cohabiting with items in the natural world. Hence the presumptuousness of assuming I really do find other selves in the world.

II

Descartes claimed that it made sense to suppose the set of limbs called his body and whatever physical thing—gas, air, fire, or vapor (animal spirits)— might infuse it were nonentities, but that he would still be left with the need to assert that "nevertheless *I* am something."[4] And by doing so he called attention in a roundabout way to the seeming difference between whatever is associated with the expression "I" when I use it and whatever else there is which is characterized by my use of (generally physicalistic) descriptions.

In a different metaphysical setting Bishop Berkeley was to write: "But besides all that endless variety of ideas or objects of knowledge, there is likewise something which knows or perceives them; and exercises divers operations, as willing, imagining, remembering, about them. This perceiving active being is what I call MIND, SPIRIT, SOUL, or MYSELF. By which words I do not denote any one of my ideas, but a thing entirely distinct from them, wherein they exist. . . ."[5] This is tantamount to Berkeley's having asserted that he does not come upon his mind, spirit, soul, or self as an item of the world in the way in which he is able to come upon cogs or pulleys, dendrites or axons. His claim that we only have notions of the mind, spirit, soul, or self and not ideas (perceptions) of it is another way of expressing his belief that there is a basic difference between how it is we can have knowledge of our own mind(s) and how it is we can have knowledge of nature.

And Kant, in spite of his general disaffection with Descartes and Berkeley, echoes to some extent their sentiments concerning the mind when he claims that he "cannot have any representation whatsoever of a thinking being, through any outer experiences, but only through self-consciousness."[6]

Furthermore, I believe it can be shown in writings from Fichte to Sartre that a well-advertised view of the self as a free or autonomous subject occurs as a simple corollary to the just discussed claim that whatever its nature the self will not be found to reside as do objects at any spatiotemporal address. As occupant of a more ethereal dwelling, the self can hardly be expected to feel constrained by the zoning laws of determinism. (Compare the quotation from Schopenhauer in section VI.)

In a contemporary vein, Herbert Feigl's view[7] that even with the weapons of a "Utopian neurophysiology" at our disposal the (admittedly suspect) argument from analogy for the existence of "raw feels" in others would not be obsolete but, indeed, necessary is still another way of claiming that the "subjective" selves of others are beyond the pale of physical descriptions. This conclusion need not, yet may, be arrived at by way of the belief that it is difficult to make sense out of one's own raw feels being located in the net of physical descriptions ("physical$_2$ descriptions" in the terminology of Sellars and Meehl.[8] This is not the same as, but is a companion to, the view that one's self seems to slip through the net.

Strictly speaking, Professor Feigl's identity thesis commits him to the claim that mental states are wholly characterizable in terms of features within the nomological net (of physical$_2$ descriptions). This should cast the admittedly controversial "argument from analogy" into disuse. But I believe that his desire to retain that argument in his repertoire of inferences can be appreciated not as a blatant inconsistency (which it seems to be) within his physicalistic theory, but as an honest ackowledgment that to date there remains something fishy about viewing one's own self and hence other selves, or other selves and hence one's own self as items within the net. This in spite of the fact that physicalism may seem in most other respects impeccable. In short, Feigl's espousal of the argument from analogy is a way of admitting that something very like the paradox stated at the outset of this essay exists.

Thomas Nagel in his recent article "Physicalism" writes: "The feeling that physicalism leaves out of account the essential subjectivity of psychological states is the feeling that nowhere in the description of the state of a human body could there be room for a physical equivalent of the fact that I (or any self), and not just that body, am the subject of those states."[9] No doubt (as Nagel himself intimates) such puzzlements are to some extent reflected in (perhaps in some sense caused by?) the peculiar linguistic role played by expressions such as "I" ("now," "this," and so on) or what have been called egocentric particulars (by Russell),[10] token reflexives (by Reichenbach),[11] indicators (by Goodman),[12] and indexicals (by Bar-Hillel).[13] Even so, what then needs to be shown is that the pragmatic conditions underlying the difference in use between the indexical "I" and nonindexicals do not add up to a metaphysical difference between whatever the indexical "I" denotes when it is used and the sorts of things which the nonindexicals might refer to or characterize. Only after this is done will it be easy to concur with Russell's claim concerning egocentric particulars "that they are not needed in any part of the description of the world, whether physical or psychological."[14]

In brief, I believe that a major temptation to reject a physicalistic theory of mentality, or *any monistic doctrine*, and by default flirt with some variety of Cartesianism or epiphenomenalism derives from the as-yet inadequately assessed asymmetry between (a) how I am able to view myself as a potential object of investigation (within a spatiotemporal setting) and (b) how at first sight it seems one would be able to investigate virtually anything else including (supposedly) other people within such a setting. Given this asymmetry it is cold comfort to be told that my sensations and feelings may be identical with certain brain processes in the way that a lightning flash is identical with an electrical discharge or a cloud is identical with a mass of tiny particles in suspension.[15] Such comparisons may serve to assuage whatever logical qualms had been felt concerning the compatibility of an identity statement ("Sensations are identical with brain processes") with the supposedly synthetic empirical character of the mind-body identity thesis. (For we have learned that although a lightning flash is identical with an electrical discharge, we had to make empirical discoveries to disclose it.) But as long as we seem systematically unable to view our own mind or self as something which can be wholly investigated in the way in which lightning flashes or electrical discharges or, as it seems, other people can be wholly investigated, illustrations involving lightning flashes, electrical discharges, and the like will seem less than illustrative. It is for this reason that the seeming duality of the phenomenal and the physical does not constitute an analogue to the "complementarity" involved in the Copenhagen interpretation of quantum mechanics. For both particles and waves are, *in some sense*, equally at home *in* or "out of" the world.

The invisible bull in the china shop of the physicalist's analogies is the ominous absence of whatever those arguments might be which would show one that his own self is as wholly amenable to physical investigation as are *either* clouds *or* molecules *or* lightning flashes *or* electrical discharges. The identity analogies usually engaged in the service of physicalism involve only identities between entities rather obviously susceptible to eventual specification and characterization by expressions which conveniently locate them within a spatio-temporal framework and describe them in physicalistic ways. The question of whether my mind or self is wholly amenable to even roughly this sort of description is one of the major points at issue. It is not sufficient to argue that if other minds seem to consist of nothing other than that which can be physically located and characterized then my mind must be too, unless I suppose it is unique; for the failure to suppose it's unique can be utilized to show that other minds cannot be accounted for in a purely physicalistic way.

If the diagnosis above is correct, any solution to the mind-body problem must proceed through (at least) two stages: At the first stage what must be overcome is a natural resistance to viewing one's own mind or self as something which can be wholly investigated in a way in which other people and things can be imagined as being wholly investigated by one's own mind or self. I shall refer to the difficulties encountered at this first stage as the *Investigational Asymmetries Problem*. Once such difficulties have been dissolved one may go on to attempt to answer the question of whether one's mind (and hence other minds) which is amenable to such investigation can best be characterized after such an investigation as "a certain kind of information processing system," as "a coalition of computerlike routines and subroutines," or instead as "a certain type of entelechy" or as "a certain sort of vital force" and so on. I shall refer to the difficulties encountered at this second stage as the *Characterization Problem*.

I mention entelechies and vital forces in passing because I wish to emphasize that a solution to the Investigational Asymmetries Problem does not settle in favor of physicalism the question of whether physicalism is true. The extent to which this latter question remains unanswered is the extent to which a theory such as vitalism could blossom from our investigation of nature in general. For example, it might seem reasonable to conclude on the basis of current physical theory that there are entities (say entelechies) inexplicable within the framework of that theory. (Compare Hans Driesch's vitalistic conclusions insofar as they were based on his investigation of the development of sea urchins and not based on his investigation of Hans Driesch.[16])

Also, as I have already intimated, the problem of the first stage is not just a problem for a physicalist view of the mind.[17] (I shall, however, generally treat this problem as a problem for physicalism since I currently view this as the most persuasive monism abroad in the land. But see my final spooky footnote.) Suppose we wish to ask, sensibly, whether my mind, self, or consciousness is identical with some entelechy or vital force. Then, too, we must first establish that my mind, self, or consciousness is the sort of thing which is amenable to the investigations we use for finding out about entelechies or vital forces. It is obvious, for example, that even if Descartes had been willing to contend that he could imagine entelechies or vital forces as being nonentities he would *still* have thought himself left with the need to assert that "nevertheless *I* am something." The "residue" of self or the I which remains once one has doubted away the existence of all physical and/or vital things or features is precisely that which seems intuitively so implausible to identify with any physical and/or vital thing or feature. So, too, the dualism of the "knowing subject" and the "objects of knowledge" so prominent in a variety of idealist writings can be argued for quite independently of how nature in general is conceived—whether, say, in panpsychic or materialist terms.

An unsettling feature of most altercations concerning the mind-body relationship during recent years is that the disputants have often (a) ignored the necessity for passing through what I have called the first stage or (b) prematurely argued about the details of the second stage possibly in the hope that once these were worked out this might settle the perplexities encountered at the only dimly defined first stage, or (c) restricted their attention to asymmetries closely akin to, yet not fully reflecting the Investigational Asymmetries Problem. These asymmetries are closely associated with the "other minds" problems, but they are not identical with it. In what follows I shall concentrate on the first stage, and propose a solution to the Investigational Asymmetries Problem. I shall set aside for the most part the issue of Characterization. This issue at the moment, I believe, can be best dealt with by developing and assessing analogies between minds and machines. But first some remarks on (c).

III

In the context of current controversies concerning the problem of "other minds" much attention has been given to the asymmetries[18] expressed by the claims (A) that first-person psychological statements when honestly proffered are incorrigible and that third-person psychological statements are generally corrigible, and (B) that in order to know about my own thoughts, feelings, sensations, and so on, I need know nothing about my own neurophysiology, whereas if physicalism were true you could be certain of my thoughts, feelings, and sensations only by knowing something about my neurophysiology. The overlap between the problem of other minds and the problem of the mind-body relationship is that where there seem to be radically different ways of knowing about my own as opposed to your thoughts, feelings, and sensations, there is some reason to suppose that the sort of things I know about on the one basis, my own thoughts, feelings, and sensations, cannot be identical with any things of the sort I know or find out about on the basis of the other. The semantically unpalatable view that when I say "I am in pain" and when I say "you are in pain" I mean two different things by "pain" retains an edge of reasonableness only because it's not wholly unreasonable to deny that my sensation, say, could be identical with any brain process. For it seems I need know nothing about my brain processes in order to know that I am in pain, whereas all that I can ever know in order to know (if I can know) that you are in pain is something like a brain process (together with behavior). This line of reasoning, of course, often leads to the claim that I don't really know anything about your mind at all. So, too, if first-person psychological statements when honestly proffered really are incorrigible, then how could the items which they are statements about (thoughts, feelings, sensations) be identical with the items which statements about neurophysiological events processes are about? For these latter statements are generally thought to be not incorrigible. In brief, as long as these asymmetries persist, there may be ways of arguing that physicalism is not home safe.

Claims (A) and (B) are at best crude paraphrases of richly textured positions which are celebrated enough to need no detailed recounting here. In some important respects progress has been made in clarifying the exact nature of these asymmetries and the extent to which they jeopardize a physicalistic interpretation of mentality. Two of these respects should be briefly discussed:

I think recent writers have convincingly argued that whatever the nature of the asymmetry with respect to me vis-à-vis my own mind and vis-à-vis someone else's mind, it does not consist simply in the capacity to frame incorrigible psychological statements pertaining to my own case, as distinct at best corrigible statements with respect to other people. For it seems conceivable, though perhaps surprising, that I might, with good reason, be persuaded to doubt and relinquish honestly proffered first-person reports of my own thoughts, feelings, and sensations. One of the most recent proponents of this claim, Paul Meehl, has sketched a persuasive case[19] of a person becoming convinced that he is not experiencing a "visual raw feel of red" although it seems to him that he is. The person is brought to the point of believing that his own honestly offered report on his current experience may be inappropriate due to his overwhelming conviction that the neurological theory which tells him he should be experiencing something other than what he has said he is, is true. It's not simply a case where a person comes to *feel* that his first-person psychological statements are in error.

He may, in fact, persist in *feeling* they are correct. It's rather a case where the person has sound theoretical backing for believing himself mistaken. (Compare some of the claims set forth in Richard Rorty's imaginative article "Mind-Body Identity, Privacy, and Categories"; see section 5.[20]) Consequently if the asymmetry between what and how I can know about my psychological self and what and how I can know about the psychology of others which poses a problem for physicalism had consisted simply in the asymmetry between first-person psychological statements which were seemingly incorrigible and third-person psychological statements which were seemingly corrigible, then the problems encountered at what I have called stage one of any solution to the mind-body problem would have been solved.

I also think that J. J. C. Smart and others[21] have undermined the assumption that physicalism can be refuted simply by proving that I may know that I am in a certain mental state without knowing anything at all about my neurophysiology. They argue as follows: Just as I may know something about Cicero without knowing that what I know is also true of Tully without thereby threatening the identification of the person Cicero with the person Tully, so too I may know something about my own psychological states or processes without knowing that what I in effect have knowledge of is the same thing you have knowledge of through knowing about my neurophysiological states or processes. Thus if the asymmetry between how and what I can know about my own psychological states and what and how I can know about the psychological states of others which poses a problem for physicalism had turned out to be simply the asymmetry between needing no neurophysiological knowledge in my own case and much neurophysiological knowledge in the case of others (or this asymmetry plus the first-mentioned one), then again there would be reason to suppose that the problems encountered at stage one of any solution to the mind-body problem would have been dissipated by recent writings.

Along these lines Professor Feigl reports[22] that Bruce Aune had suggested (in conversation) that because of the "referential opacity" we do not at first realize that in talking about raw feels you are "really" (also) talking about certain (configurational) aspects of the cerebral states or processes. Feigl thinks that Aune's suggestion implies that by introspection we can do a crude sort of neurophysiology! He goes on to say "perhaps, if you try hard 'three times before breakfast' (*Alice in Wonderland*) you'll manage to believe this." But apart from reservations one might have concerning this approach, I think that Smart's remarks and Aune's suggestion at least point out that it's not a conclusive objection to the identity thesis of mind and body simply to show that I can know about my own psychological states without apparently knowing neurophysiology, whereas you can know about my psychological states only by knowing about my neurophysiology. Furthermore, it is not at all clear to me that Aune's suggestion implies that introspection is a *crude* sort of neurophysiology. However it is we obtain information about Tully, there is no reason to suppose that this amounts to a *crude* version of however it is we obtain information about Cicero.

But I am not summarizing these views with which I am in general sympathy in order to defend or develop them. Instead what I wish to argue is that even if the incorrigibility claims made on behalf of first-person psychological reports could be undermined, and even if it could be established that "talking about raw feels" might really amount to "talking about certain (configurational) aspects of the cerebral states or processes," physicalism is not free from trouble. A reasoned resistance to it would remain. For the feeling would linger that wherever and however I might investigate the physical universe I could never come across the whole of the self which I am. In particular, I would never come across the self or aspect of it which was doing the investigation. Hence discussions of the asymmetries mentioned above do not really tune in on a basic mind-body perplexity. They do not, in short, exhaust the Investigational Asymmetry Problem as I have stated it.

It is, of course, helpful to be shown that first-person psychological statements are not incorrigible simpliciter. And it is clarifying to see that even if my mental state is identical with a certain physical state it does not follow by Leibniz's law that if I know I am in that mental state then I know I am in that physical state (since the context is intensional). But we are not thereby informed how it is that we could ever view ourself as a purely physical being. For in order to do this it certainly seems that I must be able, at least in principle, to see myself simply and wholly as one among many physical things in a physical universe. But this is precisely what remains so very difficult to do. And given that this is difficult to do, one is disinclined to accept the claim that descriptions of brain states are *in fact* descriptions of mental states. One might even suggest that the difficulty is of such magnitude that it is more appropriate to claim that it hardly makes sense to propose that talk about mental states might really be talk about neurophysiological states in the way that talk about Cicero is really (often) talk about Tully. (Compare "talk about $\sqrt{-1}$ might really be talk about the wind in the way that talk about Cicero is really talk about Tully." But why should anyone ever believe this?) *So the problem I wish to focus on is not simply that my self seems so private to me and hence could not be a physical object of scientific investigations carried out by others, but rather that it seems in some part so unpublic to me, and hence cannot be viewed by me at any given time as an item wholly susceptible even in principle to scientific investigations by me.* (We might call this the problem of empirically "underprivileged access" to ourselves.) But if my self could never be wholly public to me in the way that cogs or pulleys, dendrites or axons seem to be, it is easy to be persuaded that it is not really wholly public to anyone else either. Hence a thesis such as physicalism, which certainly ought to be committed to the view that my mental states are public in virtue of their being physical states or processes which are incontestably public, still seems implausible.

So what I now hope to show is that the asymmetry between how I am able to investigate myself (and thereby the subject of my thoughts, feelings, and sensations) and how it is I can investigate what I regard as other selves and other things within some spatiotemporal scheme is structurally similar to other ontologically benign asymmetries. By seeing why it is that these analogous asymmetries fail to thrust upon us any dualistic ontology of things, processes, or features, I think it will be shown that there is no need to suppose that the Investigational Asymmetries underlying the mind-body problem force upon us a dualistic ontology of things, processes, or features. If this is correct we shall pass through what I called the necessary first stage of any solution (and hence any physicalistic solution) to the mind-body problem. What will remain of the mind-body problem will be the Problem of Characterization, or the problem of providing an adequate inventory and anatomy of those features which we, in fact, find other persons to possess. Given the notable absence of any (current) arguments on behalf of vitalism or kindred antiphysicalist doctrines, the inventory and anatomy of other persons at present is heavily weighted in favor of physicalism.

IV

Although I regard each of the following cases to involve asymmetries analogous to the Investigational Asymmetry, the first will seem somewhat removed from it and as it stands is more problematic and perhaps less ontologically benign than the other cases. I include it in spite of some unsettled opinions about it mainly because it provides some indication of the variety of ways in which an Investigational Asymmetry Problem may be stated. If I am correct, it can be used to illustrate the manner in which problems concerning the mind-body relationship have a bearing on certain problems in linguistic theory: namely, the problem of disambiguation and the formulation of an adequate speaker-hearer model. But this I shall only hint at and not develop.[23] The second case bears more directly on the issues at hand, and has in slightly different forms appeared in the writings of others (for example Wittgenstein[24] and Ruyer[25]). As I shall try to show, the wrong conclusions are generally drawn from this sort of case. The third case and a curious corollary to it are, I trust, wholly on target.

Case I: The My Meanings Problem

Speaker-hearer asymmetries. When I say "I'm going to the bank," you (the hearer) may have to "disambiguate" my utterance. You may need to interpret whether I'm going to the river bank or to a bank where one deposits money. But I do not, in the normal case, need to disambiguate for myself my own utterance. And not only do I not need to do so, in the usual case I could not do so. We can, of course, imagine a speaker going through the motions of doing this. For example, we can imagine Professor Chomsky asserting that "flying planes can be dangerous" and then asking himself whether he meant "flying" to be construed as a verb or as an adjective. But here we have only imagined someone going through the motions of disambiguating an utterance. Given that the speaker is actually making an assertion, it is absurd to suppose he should have to figure out for himself what he has asserted at the time of asserting it. (That someone may later have to disambiguate his own utterance for himself—coming across it in a diary or because he has a strange memory such that he can hardly remember the last two words he has spoken—is a logically possible case which need not be discussed once it is acknowledged.) Hence in the usual case we find that there is an asymmetry between the speaker vis-à-vis his utterance and the hearer vis-à-vis the speaker's utterance. One could say, following Ziff,[26] there is an asymmetry between the encoding process involved in producing an utterance and the decoding process involved in interpreting that same utterance. This fact I shall redescribe for the purpose at hand by saying that for the usual case we as speakers are unable to make our utterances items for public interpretation by ourself after the manner in which we find, as hearers, the utterances of others to be public items for interpretation by ourself (or anyone else excluding the speaker). Why, in general terms—not in terms of any specific information processing system—is this so?

Let us try to imagine its being otherwise. In what sense could my utterances be *my* utterances if I had to interpret them in a speaker-hearer context in the way a hearer does, if the problem of disambiguating my own utterance arose as naturally for me vis-à-vis my utterance as it does for a hearer vis-à-vis my utterance? There would, of course, still be an output (syntactic, lexicographic) which was mine, in a sense, but in what sense or to what extent would it be my assertion? To put it in a slightly different way, in what sense could my linguistic output be treated as a specific locutionary act with a specific illocutionary force (following Austin[27])? For example, in what sense could I in saying "I am going to the bank," where I too need to disambiguate what I have said, be making a statement? If I was meaning to say something, if I know what I was saying when I was saying it, and so on, the question of disambiguation for me would not arise. For to say that I would need to know what I was meaning to say in order to perform a certain illocutionary act is the same thing as saying I would not need to disambiguate my own utterance in the way that someone else would. For a condition for saying something and meaning it is simply that one is choosing to utter those phrases which will get his meaning across, and to say that one is doing this is to say that one does not need to disambiguate what he means, for what he is saying is being determined by what he means.

Suppose we tried to break down the asymmetry between a speaker's stance toward his utterance and the hearer's stance toward that some utterance. What would this involve? It would involve attempting to treat the locutionary meaning and illocutionary force as a hearer's input. But how could this be done if what the speaker is saying is being determined by what he means? How can he reasonably be put in the position of having to ask "What does what I am saying (which is being determined by what I mean to say) mean?"

So suppose I utter "I am going to the bank" and someone else one minute later utters "I am going to the bank." The two utterance tokens are tokens of the same utterance type, but the problem of disambiguating for me arises only in the case of the utterance token which was not mine. In other words, I am unable to view my utterance as an item for my own interpretation in the way I must treat the other speaker's utterance as an item demanding interpretation by me. There is, it seems, a systematic difference between any of my ambiguous utterances and any of anyone else's ambiguous utterances uttered as potential items in interpretation by me. But could such differences provide a basis for some kind of dualism with respect to the nature of my utterances as distinct from the utterances of others? Would, for example, such differences justify the claim that the nature of my utterance is utterly unlike the nature of utterances which I hear, since the latter can need interpretation by me, but my own do not need interpretation by me? (Consider: "*My* utterances could never be identified with the sorts of things which utterances needing interpretation consist in.") Of course not. So long as what I am saying is determined by what I mean, and what someone else is saying is being determined by what that someone else means, there is bound to be an asymmetry. In the usual case, I can never be a full-blown hearer, as it were, of my own utterance at the time of the production of that utterance, and so, if you produce the same utterance that I do at roughly the same time, I will stand toward your utterance in a way I do not stand toward mine. But that does not mean that there is anything peculiar about my utterance as distinct from any other utterance I may hear which stands in need of interpretation. To think so would be to overlook the fact that my output is for everybody else except myself like everybody else's verbal output vis-à-vis me. (*As I will claim later, my self also is to everyone else except myself like everybody else's self vis-à-vis me.*) The temptation to imbibe a dualistic ontology with respect to the nature of utterances can be seen to derive wholly from the harmless though ultimately exciting fact that I cannot be the receiver and sender of a particular message simultaneously. Consequently whenever I am sending a message, there will be at least one particular utterance in the world, the meaning of which I seem to have a privileged access to, namely, the utterance I am uttering. To wish to be either in as unprivileged a position with respect to the meaning of the utterance I am uttering, or in as privileged a position with respect to the utterances of others, is to wish that there was no such thing as the difference between a speaker and a hearer, or an encoder and a decoder of utterances.

But the bearing which an asymmetry of the speaker-hearer sort has on the problem of the self, as well as the metaphysical harmlessness of its character, can be made clearer and more convincing by considering another case.

Case II: The My Eyes Problem

How can I tell what both my eyes look like (at one time)? Not in the same way I can tell what some else's eyes look like, not simply by observing them. Only by looking in mirrors, or at photographs, or at movies of me, or by asking others to tell me what my eyes look like.

There are two ways of finding out what a person's two eyes look like at one time: (1) a way of finding out about the eyes of others, and (2) a way of finding out about my own. A familiar division. Here we have a kind of other-minds problem in reverse. I can know by directly looking at them what other people's eyes look like, but I can never know what my own eyes look like by looking at them—except with the aid of mirrors, photographs, and so on. (I shall hereafter rule out the latter.)

I can imagine what it would be like to be in a position to see what anybody else's eyes look like, but I cannot imagine what it would be like to be in a position to see with my present eyes what my present eyes look like. At least I cannot imagine being in a position to see what my eyes look like, without, say, imagining something like the case where I have my current eyes removed and replaced by a different pair of eyes. But this changes the case. By "my eyes," I mean to mean "the eyes which I now possess in my body and which I now see through."

But is there any reason to suppose that the general characteristics which my eyes have differ in kind from the sorts of features which other people's eyes have and which I can see that they have by looking at them? That is to say, are we in the least bit tempted here to propagate a double ontology concerning eyes: (1) the sorts of features my eyes have and which from my point of view seem nonvisible, and (2) the sorts of features (or looks) everybody else's eyes have and which I am aware of whenever I look at them? Are we to imagine that there is more (or, better still, less) to other people's eyes than meets my eye since I have no reason to suppose I am unique, and, seemingly, every reason to suppose there is something in eyes which cannot be investigated since I cannot investigate my own?

Consider the complications which would arise if we tried to refute the testimony of mirrors, photographs, and other people as wholly adequate for our own case. We would have to assume that though we know what everyone else's eyes looked like, and know that they looked just as they looked in the mirror, ours do not look as they look in the mirror to everyone else. Ours, we might insist, have nonvisible features. If we were to do this we would also have to assume that the looks of our eyes differ from any other part of the body with respect to their reflections in a mirror. We know our hands look as our hands look in the mirror; we know our stomachs look as our stomachs look in the mirror; and so on. But eyes, well, no, or maybe, or we can't tell whether they do look as they look in the mirror or that they are even the sorts of things of which it makes sense to say "they look a certain way," and so on. We would have to believe that everybody else lies with respect to our eyes, and that mirrors "lie" with respect to our eyes, though they "tell the truth" with respect to every other reflectable feature of us.

I do not conclude that my eyes look as they look in the mirror because I adopt a simple "reverse" argument from analogy: "Since other people's eyes look like what they look like in the mirror, therefore my eyes must look like what they look like in the mirror." Rather, it is because it would take an immensely complicated and implausible theory to try to explain my eyes not looking as they look in the mirror, given that my hands do, given that my feet do, given that other people's eyes do, given that I have no reason for thinking other people are lying when they tell me what my eyes look like, and so on. Lacking a special theory for my own case, I not only accept what other people say about the looks of my eyes, and what is shown in the mirror, I have excellent reasons for accepting this. And certainly I do not conclude that my eyes are, say, "featureless." This latter absurdity, however, is one we would be bossed into accepting were we to decide to "start from our own case" and reason by analogy to the nature of the eyes of others. We would be forced to submit to the conclusion, even in the face of other faces, that the eyes of others have no visible features, for our own eyes seem to us to have none. But we never seemed pressed to such calamitous conclusions, and this is because we have a perfectly good explanation of why we could never be in a position to see the features of our own eyes in the way we are in a good position (potentially) for seeing the features of anyone else's eyes. And the explanation is that in order for me to see my eyes with my eyes, my own eyes would have to be in two (actually four) places at once: in front of themselves to be looked at as well as at the point from which they are are being looked at. Note too the conceptual absurdity involved in supposing we know how eyes (in general) look by "starting from our own case" and then reasoning by analogy that other eyes are as ours seem to us, i.e., featureless. What possible sense could be given to the claim that our eyes seem to us to have or lack features of any sort whatsoever if we suppose there are no mirrors about, etc.?

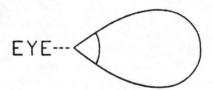

Wittgenstein remarked in the *Tractatus*: "For the form of the visual field is surely not like this,"[28] that is, like the diagram, which connects up with his earlier remarks at 5.631: "There is no such thing as the subject that thinks or entertains ideas." "If I wrote a book called *The World as I Found It*, I should have to include a report on my body, and should have to say which parts were subordinate to my will, and which were not, etc., this being a method of isolating the subject, or rather, of showing that in an important sense there is no subject, for it alone could not be mentioned in that book."[29]

Surely Wittgenstein here has his eye on what I have called the Investigational Asymmetries Problem. In other words, just as the eye does not, cannot, see itself in its own visual field, so too, the self will never, in its inventory-taking of the world, find itself in the world in the manner in which it finds other people and things. But Wittgenstein wrongly concludes from this that the self ("the subject") in "an important sense" does not exist. What I am arguing is that there's no more reason to suppose the self does not exist because it is unable to observe itself than there is reason to suppose eyes have no visible features since they are unable to observe them for their own case. Compare: The speaker's meaning does not exist for utterance tokens because only items which require some degree of interpretation or disambiguation can have meaning, and a speaker doesn't interpret or disambiguate his own remarks! Note that Wittgenstein anticipates this move but seems willing to accept the consequences: "You will say this is exactly like the case of the eye and the visual field. But really you do *not* see the eye."[30]

Of course. But we really *do* see eyes, and (1) have an explanation of why it is we cannot observe our own, and (2) have no reason to assume our case is unlike the case of other eyes which we do observe. But if our having eyes does not guarantee that we ourselves will be able to inspect their looks, their visible natures, why should we suppose that our being or having selves should guarantee that we will be in a position fully to inspect their natures, and so on? The way back into the world for the self which seems to itself not to be there is simply its coming to realize that it is to other people what other people are to it.

The case of "my eyes," though it is a kind of other-minds problem in reverse, about which I'll have something to say later, is exactly parallel to that problem of the self which has concerned me here. For the problem of convincing myself that the looks of my eyes are (more or less) exactly like the looks of other eyes is parallel to the problem of becoming convinced that the nature of my self is (more or less) exactly like the selves of others which, it seems, can be exhaustively described by reference to their behavior and physiology.

But one last case will help us to consolidate and further clarify the conceptual theses advanced in the first two cases. It might be noted that nowhere in our third case is any mention of a living organism involved. This should serve to erase any suggestion that the form which the Investigational Asymmetry Problem takes is peculiar to sentient agents.

Case III: The Self-Scanning Scanner Problem

Suppose we have a nonconscious scanning mechanism, call it SM_1, which is able to scan what we shall call its communication cell, CC_1, somewhat after the manner in which current computing machines are able to scan symbols in their communication cells. We shall imagine CC_1 to be a cell of rather flexible size. It will be able to expand and contract. We shall suppose that SM_1 could scan CC_1 for the appearance of symbols or the presence of objects, say a bug or a watch or a feather. Let us also imagine that SM_1 could scan other scanners, SM_2, SM_3, . . . , SM_n, all of which would differ from SM_1 only in that they'd be smaller than SM_1 during the time at which they were being scanned. Whenever a scanner such as SM_1 scans another scanner, the scanner being scanned will have to shrink suitably in order for it to appear in CC_1. (Later we shall relax the restriction that any object being scanned by SM_1 must appear in SM_1's CC_1. This will lead us to temper some of the following claims.) Suppose that SM_1 could scan other scanners while they were in the state of scanning things. Scanners SM_1, SM_2, . . . , SM_n will be similar in all interesting respects: in design and structure, and in the sorts of inputs, outputs, and so on which are possible for them. So now let us suppose that SM_1 is able to perform what we shall call a "complete scan" of the workings of SM_2, while SM_2 is scanning its communication cell CC_2 in which there appears some symbol or thing. Thus the nature of SM_2, its program, its actual operation while scanning CC_2, will be made available to SM_1 in the form of descriptions. Each scanner we shall suppose to be endowed with certain pattern recognition or generalization capacities. For example, each scanner will be able to recognize various instances of triangles as triangles, apples of different sizes and color, all as being apples, and so on. Thus a scanner will be equipped to answer simple questions about how a certain item is classified. Let us imagine that such information could be stored as an entry to a list contained in some storage system which is an appendage of SM_1. Let us call this list SM_1's "World List." And let us call the list of all possible World Lists (of scanners SM_1, SM_2, . . . , SM_n) "The World List." So now let us imagine that SM_1 goes on to scan SM_3, SM_4, . . . , SM_n while each is in a state of scanning a symbol or a bug or a watch or a feather. Thus a description of each scanner scanning would be potentially available to SM_1 and could be stored in SM_1's storage system on its World List. And if we imagine the universe in which SM_1 exists as being a universe in which there are only other scanners SM_2, SM_3, . . . , SM_n and a few objects and events—feathers, bugs, watches, scanners scanning—then we can imagine SM_1 being able to describe virtually everything in its universe. That is, it could in principle scan almost everything in its universe and store a description of each item on its World List. But obviously there is going to be one description which SM_1 will never be able to insert on its own World List: namely, any complete description of SM_1 while it is in a state of scanning. SM_1 is, of course, not able to obtain information about itself while scanning in the same way that it is able to gain information about SM_2, SM_3, . . . , SM_n. In order for SM_1 to obtain information about itself scanning an X, say, in the way that it obtains information about SM_2 scanning an X, SM_1 would have to be in two places at once: where it is, and inside its own communication cell.

Nevertheless, a description of SM_1 in a state of scanning will be available to the World List of some other scanner—say SM_{27}. Hence, such a description could appear on *The* World List. All descriptions of scanners in a state of scanning could appear on *The* World List. So if we think of scanners SM_1, SM_2, ..., SM_n as all being of a comparable nature, and the descriptions of them in a state of scanning as depicting that nature, then we can see that SM_1 in a state of scanning is the same in nature as the other scanning scanners it scans, though it will never be able to locate a description which depicts its nature of other scanners scanning which are descriptions on its (SM_1's) World List. In other words it would be utterly wrong to conclude from SM_1's failure to find a description of its own state of scanning on its World List (or for SM_1 somehow to report on the basis of this) that SM_1 possessed features different in nature from the features which other scanners scanning had and which could be revealed to SM_1. For this would be to suggest that a comparison between SM_1's features and the features of other scanners made available to SM_1 while scanning had been made and that radical differences had been found. Although scanner SM_1 is in principle unable to construe itself on the model of other scanners in a state of scanning in the restricted sense that it cannot construct a list of information about itself comparable to the lists of information it can compile about other scanners, there is no reason for it to report or for us to suppose that some kind of scanning dualism is in order. In other words, there is no reason to assert that SM_1 while in the state of scanning differs in nature from the sorts of features it finds other scanners to possess while in a state of scanning X. Hence, there is also no reason to suppose that there is more to other scanners in a state of scanning than that which could be revealed to SM_1.

An alternative and somewhat more formal way of stating some of the points above together with further ones suggested by them is to construct a "grammar" with which we can generate all possible semantically well-formed descriptions of any scanning mechanism, SM_i, which is in a state of scanning. Our grammar will be a "device" for parsing or analyzing any SM_i in a state of scanning into its constituent parts. Following, metaphorically and incompletely, Chomsky's account (in *Syntactic Structures*[31]) of phrase structure grammars, we can conceive of a thing-structure "grammar" for describing nonabstract objects, SM_i's, in a state of scanning as being "a finite set F of instruction formulas" of the form $X \rightarrow Y$ interpreted: "rewrite X as Y." Thus given our grammar (Σ, F) we can "define a *derivation* as a finite sequence of strings, beginning with an initial string of Σ, and with each string in the sequence being derived from the preceding string by application of one of the instruction formulas of F." Those derivations which cannot be rewritten by any further application of the rules F will be called terminated derivations.

So now let $SM_i s$ be the symbol for a given scanning mechanism in a state of scanning. Given our previous account of the nature of SM_i's, their flexible communication cells, the variety of objects they might scan, etc., we can ask: What according to our grammar should be the permissible combinations of constituents for $SM_i s$'s? And the answer seems to be that our grammar should consist of, and certainly not violate, the following rules:

(1)   (i) $SM_i s \rightarrow S_i + CC_i$

        (ii) $CC_i \rightarrow ($ $)_i +$ _____, $SM_i s$, Object$_i$, etc.

where each rule $X \rightarrow Y$ of (1) involves a left-to-right rewrite, and where a given $SM_i s$ is the symbol for a scanning mechanism in a state of scanning; S_i is the symbol for a scanner; CC_i is the symbol for $Sm_i s$'s communication cell; ($\quad$)$_i$ is the symbol for the space in that communication cell; _____$_i$ is the symbol for the absence of any object in CC_{ii}; and for any object in SM_i's communication cell other than an SM_i we shall use italicized terms such as *bug, feather, watch.* (Restrictions on $SM_i s$ in (ii) will be discussed in due course.)

    Now consider:

(2) $SM_1 s$

        $S_1 + CC_1$ (i)

        ($\quad$)$_1 +$ _____$_1$ (ii)

where the second line of (2) is derived from the first by rewriting $SM_1 s$ in accordance with rule (i) of (1), and the third line is obtained by rewriting $S_1 + CC_1$ as ($\quad$)$_1 +$ _____$_1$ in accordance with rule (ii) of (1). We can also represent (2) by means of a tree diagram:

(3)

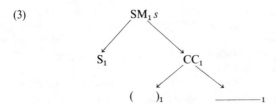

$S_1 + ($ $)_1 +$ _____$_1$ may be thought of as a *terminated* derivation in our grammar since, given our restricted vocabulary, we have no way of rewriting either S_1, ($\quad$)$_1$, or _____$_1$. This terminal line we may interpret as describing a possible $SM_i s$ with the nature of its constituents fully analyzed by the tree with which the terminal string is associated. If we were to substitute *feather* for _____$_1$, however, we would get a terminal line showing $SM_1 s$ as a scanning mechanism scanning its communication cell in which there was a feather, etc.

    Interesting problems arise, however, when we ask what, if any, constraints should be placed on the occurrence of other $SM_i s$'s in SM_1's communication cell. Certainly for any $SM_i s \neq SM_1 s$ it is permissible to substitute $SM_i s$ (say $SM_2 s$) for _____$_1$ in tree diagram (3). Thus we could have:

(4)

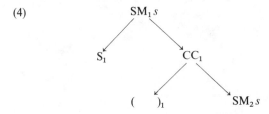

where S_1 + ( )$_1$ + $SM_2 s$ would not be a *terminated* derivation since $SM_2 s$ could itself be parsed. Hence the complete tree, call it (4′), might be:

(4′)

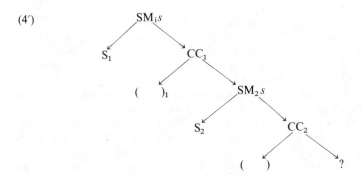

where if? is replaced by_____$_2$ or *feather* we would have a terminated derivation; whereas if another $SM_i s$, say $SM_3 s$, where substituted for? we would have an *unterminated* derivation, etc.

But now we must ask: Can we allow an $SM_i s = SM_1 s$ to recur as the label of some right-most node in a tree which finds $SM_1 s$ as the label of the top-most node? Certainly one conclusion of our less-formed previous discussion would seem to preclude this. For it was explicitly stated that SM_1 could not occur in its own communication cell. And since "contained in" denotes a transitive relation $SM_1 s$ could not occur in any communication cell, say $SM_2 s$'s, if the scanning mechanism to which that communication cell belonged occurred in SM_1's communication cell, etc.

There is, so far as I can tell and as I shall subsequently show, no way of relaxing this restriction without falling into contradiction. And given our thing-structure "grammar" we are now in a position to say, in a rather novel and I think interesting way, exactly why this is so. We can do this by comparing the role of the $SM_i s$ in our grammar to the role of S = *sentence* in an actual phrase-structure grammar. Suppose we have:

(5)

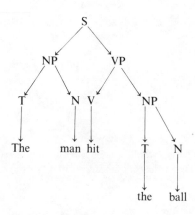

where S = sentence, NP = noun part, VP = verb part, etc., and The + man + hit + the + ball is a *terminated* derivation. (For rules parallel to our (1) above and further details of phrase-structure grammars see Chomsky, *Syntactic Structures*.) What is of primary interest to us in (5) is whatever restrictions are to be placed on the recurrence of S. S is a category symbol for sentences in the same way SM_is is a category symbol for scanning mechanisms in a state of scanning. Clearly there is no reason why S should be prohibited simpliciter from recurring at nodes of either right- or left-branching paths descending from S. For such a recurrence would be a convenient way of indicating a sentence which had as one of its constituents an embedded sentence.[32] Note, however, in *Syntactic Structures* reference to two distinct sentences, S_1 and S_2, does not occur in (Σ, F) type grammars. (The nature of this constraint need not trouble us here.) On the other hand it is obvious that some restrictions must be placed on the embedding of sentences within sentences. And clearly one restriction, the restriction that is of most interest here, must be that a sentence cannot embed itself. For what would this involve? It would involve the recurrence of S, call it S′, such that S′ = S. But this would be tantamount to allowing S with itself embedded as one of its constituents to be equivalent to S, which is a contradiction. (Compare: The man hit the ball ≠ The man hit The man hit the ball the ball. And a still different yet analogous example suggests itself: the difficulty of a painting of a painting where the first painting = the second painting. I might paint a painting of "Guernica" and preserve all the dimensions of "Guernica" in doing so. So might Picasso; but not while painting "Guernica.") Hence S can recur in a tree only if it is understood that the initial string S ≠ the recurrent string S. Part of a sentence, or another sentence, can, of course, occur in a sentence as one of its constituent parts, e.g., the main clause of a sentence can occur in the subordinate clause of the same sentence as in "The man who told me that the man hit the ball," etc. (Compare: Any SM_is might scan part of itself.)

So now let us suppose, as seems reasonable, that total consciousness of one's self would be analogous to a scanner completely scanning itself. Further let us suppose that $SM_i s$'s are describable in terms of a thing-structure grammar which has a formal equivalent in a phrase-structure grammar (of the sort mentioned above). Then the following conclusion emerges: *Total consciousness of one's self is formally equivalent to a self-embedded sentence; any self-embedded sentence involves a contradiction, for no whole sentence can be one of its own constituents; hence any example of total consciousness of one's self involves a contradiction.* And the corollary of this which interests us is: *For one's self to observe one's self as a wholly physical object would be an example of one being totally conscious of one's self, which is a contradiction.*[33]

We have reached this conclusion by a most curious route; namely by extending our (allegedly) ontologically benign asymmetries so that they now include the asymmetry between any whole sentence S vis-à-vis its constituents and certain sentences $S \neq S_i$ vis-à-vis S_i's constituents.

It might seem, however, that some of our conclusions above would be left begging for premises were we to relax our restriction that for SM_1 to scan an object, that object must appear in SM_1's communication cell. Instead we might allow SM_1 to scan any objects which, while remaining wholly external to SM_1, come within what we may call the "scope" of SM_1's scan. Further suppose that any scanner scanning an object internalizes some sort of image of that object which it uses as the basis for its derivation of a description of the object being scanned. Now let us imagine the case where $SM_1 s$ is being scanned by $SM_2 s$ and where $SM_1 s$ is able to scan the image of itself appearing in $SM_2 s$. It might then be argued, would not this be a way of $SM_1 s$ wholly inspecting itself? In a sense, of course. But not in a sense which abrogates the sort of asymmetry which has been troubling us. For $SM_1 s$ can only store a description of itself by way of an examination of the image it obtains from the image of itself which appears in $SM_2 s$. Thus $SM_1 s$ can confront the whole of itself only in the sense that I can, through my current eyes, see those eyes, namely by looking in a mirror. But there is no way that $SM_1 s$ can confront the whole of itself which does away with the asymmetry between its confrontation with the whole of itself and its confrontation with the whole of some other $SM_i s$.

So too we can easily imagine $SM_1 s$ at time t_i scanning, together with a feather, say, a description of itself at t_i. Thus:

(6)

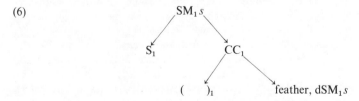

where $dSM_1 s$ = a token of the tree diagram (6).

But if we suppose that in order to be informed that a description actually describes a given object the description must in some sense be seen to apply to or be true of that object, then we cannot imagine $SM_1 s$ being able (1) to scan a description of itself scanning, and (2) recognize the applicability of the description to itself, if recognizing the applicability of the description involves making $SM_1 s$ wholly available to $SM_1 s$. But of course, $SM_1 s$ could do this in the case of $SM_2 s$. Hence the troublesome asymmetry persists.

The case of the scanning mechanism is very much like a case of a periscope which is able to sight other ships, even parts of the ship to which it belongs, but which is unable to place itself in its own crosshairs (compare R. Ruyer's *Neo-Finalisme*[34]).

The import of such examples for the mind-body problem should by now be transparent: The difficulty in construing our self at any given moment as an item wholly susceptible to third-person physicalistic and behavioristic descriptions is comparable to the difficulty a periscope would face in attempting to place itself between its own crosshairs.

V

On the basis of the foregoing cases, I think it is correct to conclude that the following statements are true: (1) My (potentially ambiguous) utterance tokens are identical in kind with members of the class of utterance tokens requiring disambiguation even though I am, as encoder of my utterances, never in a position of needing to disambiguate them. (2) Even though I can never be in a position to look at them, the visual appearances which my eyes possess are identical in kind with members of the class of visual features to which the visual features of the eyes of others belong, which features are revealed to me simply by looking at other eyes (sans mirrors, photographs, etc.). (3) Whenever scanner SM_1 is in a state of scanning its communication cell, it is in a state identical in kind with the sorts of states other scanners in a state of scanning are in, and which are revealed to SM_1 whenever other scanners scanning are placed in SM_1's communication cell. (A periscope$_1$ is identical in kind with members of the class of periscopes$_2 \ldots_n$ any one of which periscope$_1$ can place between its crosshairs.)

The three statements above might all be called metaphysically neutral. For even though it can be shown that X, say, is identical in kind with Y's, it leaves open the question what kind of things Y's are. Yet such a metaphysically neutral identity statement is, I believe, exactly what must first be shown to be true if a theory such as physicalism is to seem justified. The statement which the analogies above are designed to support is this: "I am identical in kind with what I find other people to be" where by "what I find other people to be" is meant as they are (or might be) revealed to be on the basis of empirical investigation, etc. (which could in principle be found out by me). This latter qualification must be made in order to distinguish our case from the case where someone accepts the claim that he is identical in kind with other people but asserts that other people all have private selves not amenable to empirical investigation where this is derived from his belief that he is a self not amenable to such investigation. That is, I am assuming that what we find other people to be will no longer be colored by the assumption that since I cannot wholly investigate myself, then since there is no reason to assume I am unique, there is something for all people which does not yield to empirical investigation either. In other words, "what I find other people to be" will be construed as "what I find them to be sans use of the just mentioned assumption." This again, as argued earlier, does not load the dice in favor of physicalism. It simply seems that way, since it is obvious at the moment that unless we resort to such an assumption there is no reason to suppose other people are not wholly physical beings.

It is easy to saddle oneself unwittingly with the view that if I am an object wholly amenable to scientific investigation, I had better be able to imagine myself as being an object which I myself could wholly investigate. This, I have argued, is an absurd demand. And for the same reason that it's absurd to demand that I be able to see my own eyes if I am to credit them with the same sorts of features I ascribe to the eyes of others. Yet the self-centered insistence that if I am an item susceptible to empirical investigation I ought to be able, at least in principle, to carry out the complete investigation is quite understandable. For what this really adds up to is the insistence that anyone, myself or others, be able to demonstrate *to my satisfaction* that I am such an item. And the insistence that it be possible to demonstrate to my satisfaction that I am such an item slips into seeming comparable to the demand that I be in a position to appreciate the demonstrations. (Compare: I must be the sort of creature which can never die, since I cannot imagine being in a position to observe my own death. And since I'm not unique, perhaps we are all immortal.)

But given that what I have called the "metaphysically neutral identity statement" is true, the main obstacle is removed from the path leading to the conclusion that I am exactly like the sort of thing I find other organisms to be, even though I can never examine myself fully in the way that I could at least in principle examine other organisms. And in the absence of uncovering in our investigations of others any evidence or reason to support the existence of immaterial entelechies, psychoids[35] (in Meehl's sense), Cartesian egos, or what not, there is every reason to suppose that physicalism will do. If any kind of dualism is to show its mettle, it must now do so from a third-person standpoint. It will have to be solely from an investigation of other people or things that we find reason to suppose the existence of Cartesian egos, entelechies, or psychoids.

Furthermore, once it is realized why it is we are never in a position fully to investigate ourselves, it should seem less counterintuitive to suppose that as we find out more and more about the neurophysiology of other people we will be really finding out more about the nature of their (and hence our) subjective minds. Let us suppose that at any given time we can only investigate ourselves up to a certain point before we, as investigators, are unable to treat ourselves as the object of our investigation; where, say, some information-processing center in the brain, some subregion of the cortex, is unable to process information about its own information processing. Let us call this point P. Let us further suppose that we are able to investigate others beyond point P, to point BP. And let us assume that what we find out at BP is similar in kind to what we find at P. What might at first sight seem odd is that what we find out by advancing to BP in the case of others should in effect be an indirect explanation of the nature of whatever there is to our own minds which we seem utterly unable to investigate in the way in which we can investigate ourselves up to P. It is easy to assimilate the rest of our mental life to this seemingly intractable residue of self and then comment on the amalgam by saying, "But I have knowledge of my self which consists of sensations, of thoughts, and of feelings—simply by having thoughts, feelings, and sensations." And what we find when we advance to point BP in the case of others will intuitively seem to have nothing to do with the clarification of our own self and what we take to be its various aspects, namely thoughts, feelings, and sensations. But the answer to the person who feels the necessity for saying something like this is simply to point out that all he knows about thoughts, sensations, and feelings is that he knows what it is to have them, what it is to have a sensation, or a thought, or a feeling. He does not thereby know how to sketch a complete picture of the nature of whatever it is he is having. To be an item which is having experiences does not guarantee a knowledge of their nature anymore than to be an item with an anatomy guarantees an awareness of the nature of that anatomy. (Compare the defect in "I know what a roller-coaster ride consists in by having a ride on a roller coaster.")

VI

The initial plausibility of nonphysicalism according to my story turns out to derive in large part from the fact that I cannot be in two places at the same time, and the tendency to wish to be in as good a position to investigate myself (scientifically) as I am in (at least potentially) with respect to others. Curiously, the failure to be able to be in two places at once in this case forces us to feel that we, as minds, or consciousnesses, are not in any place at all. As Schopenhauer was to write:

> . . .the body is an object among objects, and is conditioned by the laws of objects, although it is an immediate object. Like all objects of perception, it lies within the universal forms of knowledge, time and space, which are the conditions of multiplicity. The subject, on the contrary, which is always the knower, never the known, does not come under these forms, but is presupposed by them; it has therefore neither multiplicity nor its opposite unity. We never know it, but it is always the knower wherever there is knowledge.

So then the world as idea, the only aspect in which we consider it at present, has two fundamental, necessary, and inseparable halves. The one half is the object, the forms of which are space and time, and through these multiplicity. The other half is the subject, which is not in space and time, for it is present, entire and undivided, in every percipient being.[36]

And it is this sense of nonlocation which tends to reinforce the view that the mind is only contingently connected with the physical. But the foregoing arguments, if correct, should rid us of any temptation to adopt either view.

So too, if I am really never in a position to exhaustively inspect the self which I am, to include it in my inventory of physical facts garnered through physical investigations, since I would have to be investigator and object of investigation simultaneously, we might expect this fact to reflect itself in our language. And this, I believe, is precisely what underlies the odd referential status of the indexical "I." (Recall Professor Ryle's discussion of the "systematic elusiveness" of "I"[37] where part of his strategy was to show that the evasive reference of the indexical did not foist Cartesianism upon us.) What I have, in effect, tried to show is that the puzzle surrounding "I" is a manifestation of a deep dissatisfaction with either physicalism or any monism, a dissatisfaction which is rooted in the seeming unpublicness of our self. That "I" when used in an utterance refers only to the user and not to anyone else and is in the sense for each token occurrence private, or nonpublic, is parallel to the fact that I cannot make myself an object for public inspection by me and still remain myself. That I cannot refer wholly "outward" by using "I" reflects the fact that I cannot investigate myself as a wholly public object. By saying that the use of "I" in an utterance is restricted in that it can never be used to refer wholly "outward," I wish to call attention to the fact that even in cases where I use "I" in an utterance to specify a certain person (obviously myself) who was or will be, "I" will necessarily specify as well the person I am at the moment of utterance. Consider: I say (while looking at an old photograph) "Here I was in 1950." In such cases the "I" still serves to specify the speaker (whatever else it might do). (Note: It is precisely this fact that "I" is in any utterance token speaker-specifying which leads to the oddity Hintikka[38] points out in the case where a person attempts to convince someone he doesn't exist by saying "I don't exist.")

This feature of the first-person pronoun indexicals is the linguistic frosting on the factual cake: the ingredients of the latter being my (or anyone's) inability to treat myself (himself) wholly as another person or thing. If I were able on occasion to treat myself wholly as another person or thing, then "I" would not be, could not be, restricted in the manner specified above. The reflection of this fact underlying this restriction on "I" would, of course, be plowed under were we to imagine our language sans egocentric particulars (following Russell). Yet in agreement with Russell we can see why in one sense "I" is not needed in our descriptions of the world. For once we are aware that the unpublic nature of my self vis-à-vis me does not show my self to be unpublic simpliciter, each of us is then in a position to see and describe himself by way of an acceptance of how others see and describe us—and others do not (cannot), of course, utilize "I" in their descriptions of us.

The solution to stage one of the mind-body question, on the analysis above, turns out to be nothing more than coming to accept that we will never be in as good a position to investigate ourselves as we are to investigate others, and seeing why this makes no more difference (ontologically) than the fact that a submarine's periscope cannot locate itself in its own crosshairs makes an ontological difference between the nature of the periscope doing the sighting and the things it can sight. If this is true, then what remains to the mind-body is working out the details of characterization which so far, at least, seems snugly confined to the province of biology, chemistry, and physics.

The Schopenhauerian self which could not locate itself as just another member in the sprawly family of physical objects is comparable to a periscope which is safe from the torpedoes of its own submarine because it can never locate itself in its own crosshairs. But just as such a periscope is only safe from its own torpedoes and not the torpedoes of others, so too a Schopenhauerian self (or Cartesian ego) is only safe from spotting itself in the physical world. It is not safe from being spotted there by others.

VII

Finally, I wish to sketch the way in which I believe it possible to derive from the foregoing solution to the problem of the unpublic self a corollary solution to the problem of other minds insofar as that problem has seemed to place a stumbling block in the path leading to a consistently formulated physicalism. This corollary seems to me to deserve more elaboration than I can give it here, but at least the strategy involved can be adumbrated.

It was claimed earlier that the "My Eyes" problem is (1) exactly parallel to the problem of the self as herein described; and (2) exactly the reverse of the other-minds problem. In the one case I lack a kind of knowledge of my self which I possess with respect to others. In the other case I lack a kind of knowledge of others which I seem to have with respect to myself. Now if I have shown that the asymmetry involved in the case of the unpublic self does not constitute a threat to physicalism, or to any other monism, there is hope that the asymmetry involved in the case of other minds does not constitute a threat to physicalism either. That is, if the problem of "My Eyes" does not force dualism upon us, and if that problem is the reverse of the other minds problem, then perhaps the *solution* can simply be reversed and yield a solution to the other-minds problem. In other words, although the problem of the unpublic self and the problem of other minds are to some extent separate investigational asymmetries, they are similarly asymmetric. They have a common source and structure.

Let me now explain what I mean by this. I shall do this by showing in more detail how one's being limited to being in one place at one time gives rise to the other-minds problem. The best way to proceed may be to begin with a case where there is a simulation of a solution to the other-minds problem. By inspecting the simulation we may be able to uncover the conditions which would in actuality have to obtain in order to prevent an other-minds problem from arising.

The Cinematic Solution to the Problem of Other Minds

What I shall refer to as *the cinematic solution to the problem of other minds* is really a simulation of a situation in which aspects of someone else's mental life are made fully available to me in the way my own are. This epistemological shiftiness is encountered in those movies where a director wishes to provide the moviegoer with a sense of being fully acquainted with, say, the visual experience of one of the characters on the screen. Suppose, for example, the director wishes to make (or seem to make) available to me the visual experience vC of some character C as C walks down the garden path. How best to effect this? Not, surely, by simply flashing on the screen the scene of C walking down the garden path. Why not? Because what *we* seem to see or are made familiar with, come to know in such a case, is not C's visual experience vC, but our own visual experience vO which includes the view of C walking down the garden path. What is needed to avoid this, and to effect a sense of view C's vC, is some way of exporting our own perspective from the situation, and importing C's perspective into it. But how can this be done, or even appear to be brought about? The way to do this, and the way any movie director with slight cunning will do this, is to create the illusion that we are where C is. And this is most simply (and in fact necessarily) brought about by showing little or nothing of C's body as C walks down the garden path. The camera, in other words, is able to produce a sense of moving down the garden path without showing someone moving down the garden path. In brief, we are provided with C's perspective, the visual experience expected for C when walking down the garden path, by removing C's body from our own perspective. (Of course, selected parts of C's torso may remain in view without destroying the illusion.) In such a case it is not untoward to say we seem to see C's seeing. Consequently we are provided with a simulated solution of the other-minds problem as it arises for us vis-à-vis C's visual experience.

A suspiciously whimsical example perhaps, but one with a nonwhimsical aspect. The connection between the *cinematic solution to the other-minds problem* and the solution I have suggested to the problem of the unpublic self should be clear. Both demand what cannot in practice be brought about: being in two places at once. This is made even more apparent when it is pointed out that the problem of the unpublic self has a similar pseudosolution in the case of movies. The solution is, simply, to create the illusion that there is no investigational asymmetry, or that I stand to myself in the way I stand to others, by flashing my body on the screen along with the bodies of other people. Hence, it would be as if I were to seem to see myself walking down the garden path. Note: Although it does not seem possible to have one's perspectives and see them too, even this might be simulated in the case where (a) I see my body on the screen, and then (b) the *cinematic solution to the other-minds problem* is brought about for me vis-à-vis my own body as viewed on the screen! In other words, I am made to share the perspective of myself by the removal of most or all of the body from the screen with which I have identified myself. What this selected short subject suggests is that one cannot envision a situation in which the problem of the unpublic self is in practice solved for a person without the problem of other minds arising for that person vis-à-vis himself.

To encapsulate: The other-minds problem as I have been construing it is really a problem in sharing perspectives. And to share perspectives with another would entail being in two places at once. (Note: What others have called egocentric particulars, etc., William James labeled "words of perspective."[39]) We never do share perspectives, so in fact there always is, in one sense, a problem of other minds. We must in the case of coming to know the nature of someone else's visual experiences, for example, rely on reasonable inferences based on what we observe, discover, and so on with respect to that person (where he stands, whether he is an organism of such-and-such a sort, and similar matters). But once the nature of the other-minds problem is made clear, it should be easy to see why it does not constitute a threat to a consistent physicalism. For it is based on an investigational asymmetry which is as ontologically benign as the one underlying the problem of the unpublic self. Anyone else's visual experiences, for example, which include a perspective of the world, will never be made available to me through behavioral or neurological information. But from this it does not follow that there is anything nonphysical involved in, say, anyone's visual experiences. Although we will not find someone else's perspective by inspecting his brain, there need be no reason to suppose that there is some non-physical feature involved in that person's mental life.

I'm inclined to think that the so-called grain argument attributed to Sellars and recently discussed by Meehl rests on the mistaken assumption that physicalism involves commitment to the view that the (non-"gappy"-grained) perspective which someone has of the world could, in principle, be found in his ("gappy"-grained) brain. And it may well be that some physicalists have themselves thought this. But this is the same as supposing that the best way for a movie director to provide us with C's vC while walking down the garden path would be to flash on the screen a detailed cross section of C's brain as he walks down the garden path plus a (Utopian) neurophysiological interpretation of it. Such factors could never yield even a simulation of our seeing C's seeing. For C's brain, neurophysiological interpretation and all, would still remain mere items embraced in our own perspective.[40]

A Remark on ψ-ϕ Correlations

It is no doubt apparent that nothing has yet been said about correlations between psychological states and physiological states—a topic which has certainly been at the forefront of many contemporary treatments of mind-body perplexities. The reason this has not been dealt with (except indirectly) is that if my diagnosis of the mind-body problem is correct, it need not be dealt with at all in discussing the Investigational Asymmetry Problem. If, as I have contended, the temptation to reject physicalism (in the absence of reasons for hypostatizing vital forces, etc.) derives wholly from Investigational Asymmetries, then given that my foregoing arguments are correct we are freed from such temptation, for the asymmetries have been rendered harmless. Thus, in the absence of reasons for accepting vitalism or like doctrines, physicalism wins the game by forfeit.[41] So-called ψ-ϕ correlations, no doubt, have contributed and will contribute to solutions to what I have called the Problem of Characterization. But before there is a solution of the Investigational Asymmetries, these correlations cannot even with the aid of Occam's razor trim the psychic sideburns from the face of physicalism.

NOTES

1. I wish to thank Professor Feigl and Mrs. Judith Economos for encouraging me to write up the central ideas in this paper. I have also had the benefit of a number of discussions with Mischa Penn on these matters. I have no idea how happy they will be with the final result. Compare the final chapter of Mrs. Economos's "The Identity Thesis" (Ph.D. dissertation, Department of Philosophy, UCLA, 1967). I am also greatly indebted to my former colleague, Charles Chastain, with whom I have discussed this paper in detail. I owe to him the idea for describing Case III in section VI in terms of a Chomsky-like rendition of phrase structure grammar.

2. G. A. Vesey, *The Embodied Mind* (London: Allen and Unwin, 1965).

3. Cf. Paul Ziff's "The Simplicity of Other Minds," *Journal of Philosophy 72* (October 21, 1965): 575–584.

4. René Descartes, "Meditations on First Philosophy," pp. 69–70 in *Descartes' Philosophical Writings*, translated and edited by Elizabeth Anscombe and Peter Thomas Geach (London: Nelson, 1954).

5. George Berkeley, *The Principles of Human Knowledge* (New York: Meridian, 1963), pp. 65–66.

6. Immanuel Kant, *Critique of Pure Reason*, translated by Norman Kemp Smith (London: Macmillan, 1929), p. 332.

7. Herbert Feigl, "The 'Mental' and the 'Physical,'" in H. Feigl, G. Maxwell, and M. Scriven, eds., *Minnesota Studies in the Philosophy of Science*, (Minneapolis: University of Minnesota Press, 1958), pp. 370–497; see especially pp. 429–430. The utility of some version of the argument from analogy within the framework of Feigl's physicalistic theory became more apparent to me during a number of discussions with Professors Herbert Feigl, Paul Meehl, and

Grover Maxwell, during a colloquium on mind-body problems sponsored jointly by the Minnesota Center for the Philosophy of Science and the UCLA philosophy department, March 1966.

8. See P. E. Meehl and W. Sellars, "The Concept of Emergence," in H. Feigl and M. Scriven, eds., *Minnesota Studies in the Philosophy of Science*, vol. 1 (Minneapolis: University of Minnesota Press, 1956), pp. 239–252.

9. Thomas Nagel, "Physicalism," *Philosophical Review* 74 (July 1965): 354.

10. Bertrand Russell, "Egocentric Particulars," in *An Inquiry into Meaning and Truth* (New York: Norton, 1940), chap. 4.

11. Hans Reichenbach, *Elements of Symbolic Logic* (New York: Macmillan, 1960), pp. 284–287.

12. Nelson Goodman, *The Structure of Appearance* (Cambridge, Mass.: Harvard University Press, 1951), pp. 290–295.

13. Y. Bar-Hillel, "Indexical Expressions," *Mind* 63 (1954): 359–379.

14. Russell, "Egocentric Particulars," p. 115.

15. Cf. J. J. C. Smart's "Sensations and Brain Processes," in V. C. Chappell, ed., *The Philosophy of Mind* (Englewood Cliffs, N.J.: Prentice-Hall, 1962). Such analogies are, of course, scattered throughout the writings of proponents of the identity thesis.

16. Hans Driesch, *The History and Theory of Vitalism* (New York: Macmillan, 1914). Vitalistic metaphysics did not generally depend on puzzles about the self for its antimaterialistic conclusions. These conclusions were usually based upon seemingly inexplicable but publicly observable features of animals or people such as self-adaptive behavior. This is one reason why the counterexamples which cybernetic machines provided to the claim that nonmechanistic explanations (involving entelechies, etc.) were needed to account for self-adaptive behavior did not settle certain basic mind-body problems. That is to say, puzzles about the self could be utilized on behalf of a mind-body dualism whether or not cybernetic models made reference to entelechies unnecessary in explaining behavior.

17. Cf. Thomas Nagel's "Physicalism."

18. For summaries of these asymmetries and numerous references to further discussions of them, see Jerome A. Shaffer's "Recent Work on the Mind-Body Problem," *American Philosophical Quarterly* 2 (April 1965): 1–24, especially pp. 3–5 under the heading "The 'Asymmetry' of Mental Reports."

19. Paul Meehl, "The Compleat Autocerebroscopist: A Thought-Experiment on Professor Feigl's Mind-Body Identity Thesis," in Paul K. Feyerabend and Grover Maxwell, eds., *Mind, Matter, and Method: Essays in Philosophy and Science in Honor of Herbert Feigl* (Minneapolis: University of Minnesota Press, 1966). Cf. Meehl's remarks on privacy in this article, p. 134. He begins by saying: "It is agreed that no other person is the locus of my raw-feel events. This simple truth can be reformulated either epistemically or physiologically, as follows: (a) A raw-feel event x which belongs to the class C_1 of events constituting the experiential history of a knower K_1 does not belong to the class C_2 of a different knower K_2. (b) The tokening mechanism whose tokenings characterize the raw-feel events of organism K_1 is wired "directly" to K_1's visual cortex, whereas the tokening mechanism of K_2 is not directly wired to the visual

cortex of K_1." If I had chosen to phrase one of my asymmetries above explicitly in terms of privacy or privileged access, I would then have included an adumbration of Meehl's analysis from which the quotation above is excerpted. I agree with the essentials of his treatment but would simply add that seeing why it is that privileged access to our own mental state does not refute physicalism does not show us why it seems we are unable to treat ourselves as just another item of the physical world.

20. *Review of Metaphysics* 19 (September 1965):24–25.

21. "Sensations and Brain Processes"; Thomas Nagel, "Physicalism." Also see Smart's "Materialism," *Journal of Philosophy* 60 (October 24, 1963):651–662.

22. In a mimeographed outline called "Crucial Issues of Mind-Body Monism" distributed at the University of Minnesota-UCLA Joint Colloquium on Mind-Body Problems held at UCLA, March 1966.

23. Cf. my *Lockean Linguistics* (in preparation).

24. Ludwig Wittgenstein, *Tractatus Logico-Philosophicus*, translated by D. F. Pears and B. F. McGuiness (London: Routledge and Kegan Paul, 1961), 5.621–5.641.

25. R. Ruyer, *Néo-Finalisme* (Paris: Presses Universitaires de France, 1952).

26. This asymmetry was first called to my attention by Paul Ziff. Cf. Charles E. Osgood and Murray S. Miron, eds., *Approaches to the Study of Aphasia* (Urbana: University of Illinois Press, 1963), especially "A Mediation-Integration Model," by Charles Osgood, pp. 95–101.

27. J. L. Austin, *How to Do Things with Words* (Cambridge, Mass.: Harvard University Press, 1962).

28. Wittgenstein, *Tractatus*, p. 117.

29. Ibid.

30. Ibid.

31. (The Hague: Mouton, 1957); see especially pp. 26–30.

32. Cf. Noam Chomsky's *Aspects of the Theory of Syntax* (Cambridge, Mass.: MIT Press, 1966).

33. In a reading of this paper at the Rockefeller University (February 15, 1968), Professor Robert Nozick suggested that my conclusion would hold only if the mind were finite, and that if it could be represented by an infinite sentence total self-embedding would be possible. A number of us including myself found this a very interesting suggestion, though none of us seemed wholly to understand it.

34. See note 23.

35. Meehl, "The Compleat Autocerebroscopist," pp. 120–127.

36. Arthur Schopenhauer, "The World as Idea," 1, 2, pp. 5–6, in Irwin Edman, ed., *The Philosophy of Schopenhauer* (New York: Modern Library, 1928). Cf. George Pitcher's discussion of this passage in his *The Philosophy of Wittgenstein* (Englewood Cliffs, N.J.: Prentice-Hall, 1964), p. 147.

37. In his *Concept of Mind* (New York: Hutchinson's University Library, 1955), pp. 195–198.

38. Jaakko Hintikka, "Cogito, Ergo Sum: Inference or Performance?" *Philosophical Review* 71 (January 1962):3–32.

39. William James, *The Varieties of Religious Experience* (New York: Modern

Library), p. 192. In remarking on beliefs of Buddhists or Humians he writes: "For them the soul is only a succession of fields of consciousness: yet there is found in each field a part, or sub-field, which figures as focal and contains the excitement, and from which, as from a centre, the aim seems to be taken. Talking of this part, we involuntarily apply words of perspective to distinguish it from the rest, words like 'here,' 'this,' 'now,' 'mine,' or 'me'; and we ascribe to the other parts the positions 'there,' 'then,' 'that,' 'his' or 'thine,' 'it,' 'not me.' But a 'here' can change to a 'there,' and a 'there' become a 'here,' and what was 'mine' and what was 'not mine' change their places."

40. The problem of other minds, which I have tried to rephrase as a problem of sharing perspectives, was clearly construed that way by G. T. Fechner in his *Elemente der Psychophysik* (Leipzig: Breitkopf & Härtel, 1907). He worked up to this construal by first remarking: "When anyone stands inside a sphere its convex side is for him quite hidden by the concave surface; conversely, when he stands outside, the concave surface is hidden by the convex. Both sides belong together as inseparably as the psychical and the bodily sides of a human being, and these also may by way of simile (*vergleichweise*) be regarded as inner and outer sides, but it is just as impossible to see both sides of a circle from a standpoint in the plane of the circle, as to see these two sides of humanity from a standpoint in the plane of human existence." And he goes on to write: "The solar system seen from the sun presents an aspect quite other than that which it presents when viewed from the earth. There it appears as the Copernican, here as the Ptolemaic world-system. And for all time it will remain impossible for one observer to see both systems at the same time, although both belong inseparably together, and, just like the concave and convex sides of a circle, they are at bottom only two different modes of appearance of the same thing seen from different standpoints." And finally he claims: "The difference of standpoint is whether one thinks with one's brain or looks into the brain of another thinker. The appearances are then quite different; but the standpoints are very different, there an inner, here an outer standpoint; and they are indescribably more different than in the foregoing example (i.e., the circle and the solar system), and just for that reason the difference of the modes of appearance is indescribably greater. For the double mode of appearance of the circle, or of the solar system is after all only obtained from two different outer standpoints over against it; at the centre of the circle, or on the sun, the observer remains outside the line of the circle, or outside the planets. But the appearance of the spirit to itself is obtained from a truly inner standpoint of that underlying being over against itself, namely the standpoint of coincidence with itself, while the appearance of the bodily self is obtained from a standpoint truly external to it, namely, one which does not coincide with it."

41. But a question too crazy and deep for me to consider here has begun to haunt me: In the last analysis might physicalism and panpsychism turn out to be the same doctrine?

8

Russell on Perception
and Mind-Body: A Study
in Philosophical Method

Grover Maxwell

SOME OF Bertrand Russell's views on perception held during the last forty-five years of his life will be considered in this essay.[1] I shall not be concerned, except in a kind of negative way, with his earlier work on the subject, such as his brief but notorious flirtation with phenomenalism, circa 1914 (see, for example, Russell's *My Philosophical Development* [hereafter abbreviated *MPD*], pp. 104–105). This theory of perception was first given in detail by him in *The Analysis of Matter* (hereafter *AM*), published in 1927. Although he subsequently modified it somewhat and considerably augmented it in *Human Knowledge: Its Scope and Limits* (hereafter *HK*), it remained remarkably constant for the rest of his life.[2]

Russell felt that his theory was "almost universally misunderstood" (*MPD*, p. 16). My experience confirms his feeling—either misunderstood or totally neglected, I should say. And I fear he is almost, but not quite, correct when he says that nobody has accepted it, adding that be believes and hopes that this is only because it has not been understood (*MPD*, p. 15). The misunderstanding and neglect are, I believe, extremely unfortunate, for it seems to me that these later views of Russell's on perception and related matters are crucially important and, moreover, that they comprise the nearest thing to truth about these issues that has been proposed to date. For these reasons, this essay will be mainly expository, interpretative, and apologetic rather than critical, although I shall not

Reprinted, with minor editorial changes, from *Bertrand Russell: A Collection of Critical Essays*, David Pears, ed. (New York: Doubleday, Anchor Books, 1972), where it was titled "Russell on Perception: A Study in Philosophical Method."

hesitate to call attention to what appear to be deficiencies when they occur, either in the substance of the theory or in the clarity of Russell's presentation of it.

The task that I have set is a broad one, for in order to understand Russell's views on perception it is necessary, I believe, to be acquainted with his general epistemological and metaphysical outlook, including his "event ontology" and the theory of space-time that he develops from it, his interpretations of physics, physiology, and psychophysiology, and, of special importance, his later views on the foundations of nondemonstrative inference (i.e., on the so-called problem of induction or, in general, the problems of confirmation theory). This will lead us immediately into a consideration of what Russell takes the goals or methods of philosophical inquiry to be; and misunderstandings about this matter may well turn out to have been the greatest obstacles to a sympathetic understanding of Russell's views. It is only by considering his views on all of these matters and by reflection on his attempts to synthesize them into a comprehensive world view that one is able to understand and appreciate his theory of perception. (These attempts appear in detail in *HK*.) And until this is done, any critique of these views is premature.

Surely this is one reason, among several, why Russell's later views have been, as he says, "almost universally misunderstood." World views are given short shrift these days even when they consist, as Russell's does, mainly of attempts to give a systematic, consistent, and coherent summary of certain related parts of our scientific and commonsense knowledge. At any rate this paper will contain at least a brief exposition of Russell's views on each of these topics and of how they fit together, as he sees it, into a comprehensive account of the nature of knowledge and its subject matter, such as the physical world, mental events, the self, etc. In other words, I shall try to give a reasonably brief, but comprehensible, synoptic account of Russell's theories on these matters; and I shall not be concerned with extensive documentation and other such scholarly details, for such a project would require several volumes.

For similar reasons I shall omit almost altogether considerations of certain aspects of Russell's theory of perception, such as his attempt to "eliminate the subject," which amounts to an attempt to dispense with any *act-object* distinction in perception as well as questions about whether his event ontology provides him with a viable theory of space-time or whether his new "substances" such as redness (see, for example, *MPD*, p. 171) can be coherently so viewed, etc. Finally, in the interest of better comprehension, I shall, from time to time, make explicit what seem to me to be some of Russell's unstated, perhaps unconscious, assumptions that play an important role in understanding his philosophical motivation.

The crucial basic assumption made by Russell has been stated by him on numerous occasions. It is that our most reliable knowledge in certain appropriate domains is provided by physics and other natural sciences, including, I would judge, psychophysiology or neuropsychology (see, for example, *MPD*, p. 17, and also numerous places in *AM* and *HK*; for an especially good statement and defense of this assumption, see *The Philosophy of Bertrand Russell*, edited by P. A. Schilpp[3] [hereafter *PBR*], pp. 700–701). He begins by saying that he wishes "to distinguish sharply between ontology and epistemology. In ontology I start by accepting the truth of physics [and, presumably, other natural sciences, as mentioned above]; in epistemology I ask myself: Given the truth of physics, what can be meant by an organism having 'knowledge,' and what knowledge can it have?" (*PBR*, pp. 700–701.)

He goes on to explain that he has "merely a common sense basis ... for accepting the truth of physics," that almost any nonphilosopher, nonphysicist would agree that physics has a much better chance of being true than any philosophical system, and that attempts "to set up [philosophies] against physics ... have always ended in disaster." Essentially the same (brief) "justification" is given in the other references mentioned above. Now I believe that Russell has much more extensive grounds for "accepting the truth of physics" then he ever gives in these passages. He does make most of these grounds explicit in other places but perhaps does not make sufficiently clear their relevance to his starting "ontological assumption." This is unfortunate, for it contributes to the misunderstanding of his views, and, for many philosophers, it certainly raises insurmountable obstacles to their acceptance. For example, it seems reasonable to hold against Russell that the philosopher, certainly the philosopher of physics, far from merely accepting the pronouncements of physics, should subject them to severe critical scrutiny. He should ask himself what, if any, good reasons can be adduced that will furnish a foundation for such knowledge as physics purports to provide. Russell's answer to such an objection, or the one he would have given had he set out explicitly to give one, would be provided by his theory of "nondemonstrative inference." Using Russell's views as obtained from various of his works, I shall try to provide such a reply, as well as replies to other objections to his apparently almost cavalier "acceptance" of physics, but all of this in due course.

In fairness, it should be noted that, even at this point, Russell does go on to give a (partial) explanation of what he *means* by the phrase "accepting the truth of physics" (*PBR*, pp. 700–701). First, he says, "Although progressive changes are to be expected in physics, the present doctrines are likely to be nearer to the truth than any rival doctrines now before the world. ... It is, therefore, rational to accept ... [them] hypothetically" (*MPD*, p. 17). The other, much more difficult dimension of the meaning of "accepting the truth of physics" involves the question: What do we take physics to assert? In the passage mainly under consideration now (*PBR*, p. 701), he gives a partial answer, one, moreover, not argued for there. He merely expresses his adherence to a *realist* interpretation of physics, saying that "an honest acceptance of physics demands recognition of unobserved occurrences." Thus he emphatically rejects not only phenomenalism but *any* kind of instrumentalist interpretation, whatever. Regarding his early flirtation with phenomenalism, he says, "There are some who deny that physics need say anything about what *cannot* be observed [my italics]; at times I have been one of them. But I have become persuaded that such an interpretation of physics is at best an intellectual game." In view of such clear and unequivocal passages as this, as well as numerous other ones to the same effect, (see *MPD*, p. 205, and numerous places in *HK* and *AM*) it is remarkable that many philosophers of my acquaintance seem to believe that Russell remained a phenomenalist throughout his philosophical career.[4]

"Accepting the truth of physics," then, means, for Russell, accepting physical theory interpreted in a realist manner, which in turn, means interpreting physical theory as referring to unobservable things and events. Elsewhere at various places (*AM*, *HK*, *MPD*, and others), he gives, it seems to me, two kinds of (mutually complementary) grounds for this view of physical theory: (1) Those who propose and use the theories interpret them realistically, and (2) (more importantly) given Russell's theory of nondemonstrative inference (which I shall discuss later), this is the only reasonable way to interpret them.

Russell then goes on to say that the main business of physics involves *causal laws* (*PBR*, pp. 701–702). The notion of causality used here is a broad one; for example, the gas laws such as Boyle's law would be considered to express causal relations holding between changes of pressure and changes of volume, etc. Taking the concern of physics (including, as almost always for Russell, physiology and psychophysiology) to be causal relations among events (some of which are unobservable) makes acceptance of "the causal theory of perception" virtually inescapable, or so Russell contends. The "ontological assumption," thus, provides at least a partial answer to the "epistemological question." For our best grounded theories of physics, physiology, and psychophysiology tell us, at least in broad outline, how our perceptual experiences are related to the appropriate physical events that are causally connected with them. These theories, thus, tell us what kind of knowledge that perception, properly interpreted, can provide the organism. It is this component of Russell's theory of perception with which the major portion of this essay will be concerned. This is because my main purposes are to facilitate understanding of and increase the credibility of Russell's work on the matter. I believe that it is just this part of his theory that comprises the most serious obstacles to this.

But before examining the fascinating and, to many philosophers, shocking and outrageous inferences that Russell draws at this point, it is advisable to discuss his grounds for accepting the causal theory of perception in a little more detail. This, in turn, will lead us into a study of his general methods of inquiry and his views about the nature and function of philosophical activity.

Russell expresses surprise at finding "the causal theory of perception treated as something that could be questioned." He can "understand Hume's questioning of causality in general, but if causality in general is admitted," he says, "I do not see on what grounds perception should be excepted from its scope" (*PBR*, p. 702). It is interesting and important to note that at another place (and an earlier time), he anticipates and elegantly blocks the "'perception'-is-a-*success-word*"[5] maneuver: "I do not like the word 'perception' for the complete experience consisting of a sensory core supplemented by expectations, *because the word 'perception' suggests too strongly that the beliefs involved are true* [italics added]. I will therefore use the phrase 'perceptive experience'. Thus whenever I think I see a cat, I have the perceptive experience of "seeing a cat', even if, on this occasion, no physical cat is present"[6] (from *An Inquiry into Meaning and Truth*[7] [hereafter *IMT*]). Thus a *perceptive experience* is properly labeled as a *perception* only if it is veridical ("successful"). It follows that all perceptions are perceptive experiences but not all perceptive experiences are perceptions. So that, if all perceptive experiences are in the causal network (that they are is argued below), then all perceptions must be there also.

Consider Russell's favorite example—a case in which I see the sun (*PBR*, pp. 702–703). If science is right, he says, I will see the sun only when radiation of suitable frequency has traveled to me from the sun and has produced certain physiological effects (in the eye, the optic nerve, and the brain). "The waves can be stopped by a screen, [and] the [necessary] physiological effects [can be stopped] by destroying the optic nerve or excising the visual centers in the brain. If this is not to be accepted as evidence of the causal ancestry of seeing the sun, all scientific reasoning will have to be remodeled." Such arguments as well as even simpler ones from common sense (e.g., *PBR*, p. 702) are so compelling that I would share Russell's surprise if I ever encountered someone who flatly rejected the causal theory of perception. Philosophers that I know or read, however, are more cagey (and more obscure). Ryle, for example, does not deny, as I understand him, that light waves, the eye, the optic nerve, and the brain are somehow involved in vision. He argues, however, that perception is not a process, from which it obviously follows that it cannot be a physiological process but also, and more importantly for the point at issue, since it is not a process or an event it follows that it cannot be in the causal network. But as regards the latter inference, even if one grants the premise (which I do not[8]), the conclusion by no means follows. Russell's arguments, just cited, for the causal theory of perception, as well as numerous other similar arguments from science and even from pre-scientific common sense, hold with just as much force if perception is *not* process-like or eventlike as if it is so regarded. That is, even if *see* is just a "success word" (whatever this may mean) and even if there is no such thing as a process or an event of seeing, the arguments still show—if they ever showed anything—that certain physical and physiological events, processes, or states of affairs are *causally necessary* in order for us ("successfully") to *see the sun*.

Other arguments have been offered, of course, against casting the causal theory of perception in any kind of crucial epistemic (or epistemological) role—and, indeed, against allowing it *any* essential "philosophical" significance. An understanding of the philosophical motivations behind such arguments is not hard to come by, but it is well worth considering in any effort to assess their force.

The main motivation seems to be the desire to maintain a strongly empiricist epistemology. This, in turn, seems to have led a very large portion of contemporary philosophers to defend, or at the very least to hold tacitly, certain rather definite positions on the nature of logic, the nature of induction (and confirmation, in general), and the nature of philosophical inquiry itself. With one exception, these currently popular positions were rejected by Russell. It is for this reason that our attention turns toward them now.

The basic, almost exclusive epistemic priority that empiricism accords sense perception has been responsible for notorious and grave epistemological difficulties. These were clearly recognized and delineated by Hume, who quite straightforwardly acknowledged that he found them insurmountable. Since he was unwilling to abandon empiricism, he proclaimed skepticism to be the only rational remaining option. Of course he found skepticism to be psychologically impossible to maintain (as Russell puts it), so, again with his characteristic honesty, he admitted that all of his (and our) beliefs about matters beyond sense impressions of the moment are irrational. Empiricists, since the time of Hume, have generally not been so forthright.

Hume's dilemma arises for the empiricist in a quite simple way. According to empiricism, all of our (factual) knowledge is either direct, in which case it is known directly through sense perception, or it is indirect, in which case it must be confirmed by direct knowledge. Direct knowledge is usually considered to be relatively unproblematic, but the question then arises as to the nature of the confirmation relationship whereby the claims of indirect knowledge must be supported by direct knowledge. Hume argued lengthily and decisively that no such relationship can hold *necessarily*. But if it does not hold necessarily, the relation must always be a contingent (factual) one. That is, if it is ever true that a set of propositions (expressing direct knowledge) is evidence for some other proposition(s) (expressing indirect knowledge), it is only *contingently* true; and, moreover, it is not a contingent truth that can be known directly (by perception). Therefore, if empiricist principles are maintained, *any claim that one set of propositions is evidence for (confirms) another is a claim that stands in need of confirmation itself*, so that any attempt at confirmation leads either to vicious infinite regress or to vicious circularity, as was so clearly shown again by Hume.

Although empiricists have quite generally acknowledged the acuteness of Hume's insights and the poignancy of the "problem of induction" that he posed, they have seemed, almost to a person, to have assumed that he was wrong. Thus the literature still abounds in attempts to "justify induction", "vindicate" it, "pragmatically justify" it, show that it really needs no justification (e.g., because of [part of] the very meaning of the word "justification"), etc., etc.; and whether an empiricist would judge any of such attempts successful or not, he would assume, typically, that there must exist *some* solution and that the nondeductive reasoning necessary to extend our knowledge beyond perceptions of the moment is not only legitimate but consistent with empiricism. For many years Russell was no exception, but he slowly and gradually became convinced that Hume's dilemma is, indeed, inescapable. Unlike Hume, he rejected skepticism and embraced the other horn, recognizing the limitations of empiricism and the rather drastic modifications it must suffer and the exceptions it must admit in order to be justifiably maintained at all. I maintain that, even before he made these views explicit, they began to have an important effect on the development of his thought, including his views about the nature of philosophical inquiry. By way of contrast, it will be useful first to consider the development of the main strands of contemporary empiricism.

Lulled by the comfortable belief (faith?) that there must be some way of getting around Hume's dilemma—that nondeductive ("inductive") reasoning is somehow consistent with a thorough-going empiricism—empiricists, when they have thought about it at all, have usually gone on to the even more comforting belief in the existence of "inductive logic." Of course, inductive inferences were admittedly "risky" and not necessarily truth-preserving, but the word "logic' nevertheless was intended in a fairly strong and definite sense: (1) it was the *logical form* of the nondeductive inference or argument that was supposed to bestow upon it its legitimacy, and (2) reasoning by means of these legitimate, nondeductive forms was thought to be the "rational" way to reason in all possible worlds. This belief that the relationship between evidence and what is *evidenced* is a *logical* relationship is comfortable (or comforting), of course, because it allows the empiricist to maintain his empiricism—to hold that our selections of the best supported claims to indirect knowledge are based on direct knowledge and logic (in the fairly tough sense of "logic" just explained) and nothing else.[9] (The empiricist philosophy of logic, whereby its principles are "factually empty," is assumed and it is not my purpose to call it into question.) With these simple views of confirmation, in particular, and of theory of knowledge, in general, being held, it is easy to understand why the temptation to take the next step and adopt a "confirmability meaning criterion" is virtually irresistible. Any knowledge claim that is neither direct knowledge nor capable of being "confirmed" in the manner just discussed is quite naturally viewed as being beyond the pale, not worthy of serious consideration, and, indeed, "meaningless."

Empiricists, then, have found themselves left with two kinds of "meaningful" statements: those expressing direct knowledge or *confirmable* by direct knowledge on the one hand, and those that can be certified (or rejected) solely on the basis of the meaning of the language used, that is, logical truths, analytic statements, etc., on the other. Statements of the former kind make contingent statements about the world, while those of the latter are necessarily true (or false) but factually empty. This line of thought immediately raised crucial questions about the nature of philosophy. Statements of the first kind express *empirical* knowledge and thus, it was thought, belong to either simple, contingent, commonsense knowledge, or to the "empirical sciences." In neither case were they allowed to be considered properly *philosophical*. Philosophy, then, in order to avoid meaninglessness, would have to restrict its realm to statements of the second kind; it would have to deal only with matters that can be settled on logical, conceptual, or linguistic grounds.

The reason that philosophers who hold such views deny so vehemently the relevance of the causal theory of perception for philosophical problems about perception in particular and theory of knowledge in general should now be obvious. For, they hold, the causal theory is ("merely") a contingent, ("merely") a scientific theory and (thus!) cannot be used in answering philosophical questions. But someone who holds a radically different view about the nature of the confirmation relationship (about the "problem of induction"), as did Russell, may very well feel very differently about the relevance of the causal theory in particular and about the nature of philosophy in general. Unfortunately, when one looks at his explicit pronouncements on the matter, it is not easy to decide what view on the nature of philosophy Russell considered himself to hold.[10] But, I shall hold, if one examines his philosophical activity and its results, especially since *about* 1925, along with a few select statements he made in its defense, a fairly clear picture emerges. It is true that he emphasizes again and again that his method is "the method of analyzing" and unfortunately this is doubly misleading. First, "analysis" for him does not mean the currently fashionable "philosophical analysis," nor does it mean merely logical analysis, "conceptual analysis", or linguistic analysis. Second, he himself seems to use the word ambiguously. Sometimes he seems to intend it in its original sense of *analyzing* a *whole* into its parts (*IMT*, Chap. 24) and sometimes he uses it in a sense which he explains: "Every truly philosophical problem is a problem of analysis; and in problems of analysis the best method is that which sets out from results and arrives at the premises.[11] This may be an odd use of the word 'analysis', but this latter kind of method is surely the one used by Russell in his later philosophical work. For example, he explicitly endorses it and adopts it in *IMT* (chapter 9). The striking thing to note is that this is also the method used in physics and other advanced sciences; the scientist "starts" with "results," that is, experimental results, or observations, or other "facts," and he "arrives" at "premises", that is theories and/or hypotheses that explain the results. Again, Russell recognizes this explicitly. "I do not pretend that the above theory [about perception, the relation of mind and matter, etc.] can be proved. What I contend is that, like the theories of physics, it cannot be disproved, and gives an answer to many problems which older theorists have found puzzling. I do not think that any prudent person will claim more than this for any theory." (*MPD*, p. 27.)[12]

It is at this point that Russell's position concerning nondeductive reasoning sheds light on his views about the methods of philosophical (and scientific) inquiry. We have seen that here (and elsewhere) he endorses *hypothetico-deductive* reasoning, as it is called. ('Hypothetico-inferential' would be a better term, since sometimes the inferences from theories or hypotheses to evidence may be statistical.) That is, theories and/or hypotheses are proposed that explain the evidence, that is, yield the evidence as consequences. The pattern of reasoning may be outlined as follows: Suppose we have some evidence expressed by a conjunction of statements—call the conjunction E—and suppose a theory is proposed that, when conjoined with appropriate "background" theories and auxiliary theories and with appropriate hypotheses about initial conditions, *explains* the evidence. Call this latter conjunction T. We then proceed: (1) T implies E, (2) E, therefore ... Therefore what? The temptation to say, "Therefore T" is one to which we yield repeatedly, both in scientific and in commonsense reasoning. It might be more prudent to say, rather, that since T implies E and E is true, we have *some* evidence, or some reason for *tentatively* accepting T. However, this does not appreciably diminish the problematic character of the "inference." This backward "inference" in the opposite direction from deductive validity—this blatant "affirmation of the consequent"—turns out to be the cornerstone of most of our important nontrivial reasoning, by means of which most of our knowledge claims that go beyond sense experience of the moment are confirmed. It is this kind of inference that Russell should be interpreted as talking about when he discusses, for example, "inferences" from private "percepts" to the existence of physical objects and to the ("structural") properties of them that play an important causal role in the production of the percepts. (Of course we do not normally perform *any* conscious inference. The sense experience, under appropriate conditions, produces in us the belief that here is an *object with such-and-such properties.* But the "inference" refers to the kind of reasoning in which we should engage if we were called upon to justify the belief.) In such a case T would be the causal theory of perception conjoined with appropriate propositions about initial conditions, etc., for example, the "hypothesis" that *here is a chair*[13] *with such-and-such (structural) properties, etc.*, while E might be a conjunction of statements asserting that *I am visually aware of certain colored shapes, tactilely aware of certain degrees of roughness, smoothness, etc., etc.* Evidence such as E thus hypothetico-inferentially confirms not only the causal theory of perception *and* auxiliary and background theories from physics, physiology, etc., but specific singular hypotheses ("initial conditions") such as "A chair is now near," as well.

But can Russell, or anyone, seriously contend that our only legitimate reasons for accepting our nontrivial knowledge claims—our only means of confirmation—arise from repeatedly committing an elementary logic textbook fallacy? Surely, it might be objected, our old-fashioned "inductive methods" such as induction by simple enumeration, Mills Methods, etc., suspect though they may be, cannot be as logically indefensible as *affirming the consequent*! But Russell (and Hume) have a ready reply: logically, they are all on a par; hypothetico-inferential reasoning is no worse off (and no better off) logically than, for example, induction by simple enumeration. Just how badly off are they? Pretty bad; as Russell has put it, "Unfortunately, it can be proved that induction by simple enumeration, if conducted without regard to common sense, leads more often to error than to truth. And if a principle needs common sense before it can be safely used, it is not the sort of principle that can satisfy a logician." (*MPD*, p. 14). (What Russell has in mind as needed from common sense here is contingent and, thus, extralogical.) The proof of Russell's contention can be accomplished by proving that for any argument by induction by simple enumeration that has true premises and a true conclusion there can be constructed an indefinitely large number of arguments with the same logical form as the argument in question, each argument having true premises but, in each case, a conclusion that is inconsistent with the (true) original conclusion. This can be done in many ways, as I illustrated in my "Theories, Perception, and Structural Realism."

We have seen that hypothetico-inferential reasoning, although no worse off logically than other, more traditionally recognized "inductive" reasoning, is no better off either. Indeed, it is again easy to prove that, given any amount of evidence (say, any amount of direct knowledge) there will exist an indefinitely large number of mutually incompatible theories all of which *explain* the evidence and all of which, thus, are logically on a par with each other with respect to the evidence. Thus, even if theories could be falsified (say, by new evidence), which I maintain with Russell they cannot be if they are of much interest or importance,[14] there would always still remain a potentially infinite number of mutually incompatible theories that would explain the new (falsifying) evidence and the old as well.

What reasons, then, can we have for confidence in any of our nondeductive modes of reasoning and, thus, for having any confiidence in any knowledge claim that goes beyond the trivialities of momentary perception? Unlike Hume, Russell does not answer "None!" However, he insists, entirely correctly I believe, that any such reasons must be extralogical (and extraconceptual), and therefore they must be contingent. The assumption that we have nontrivial knowledge can be defended only by further assumptions about the structure of our world—the actual world as opposed to the infinite number of other possible worlds. He says, for example, "Owing to the world being such as it is, certain occurences are sometimes, in fact, evidence for certain others; and owing to animals being adapted to their environment, occurences which are, in fact, evidence of others tend to arouse expectation of those others" (*HK*, p. 496).

How, then, do we or should we go about discovering and chosing among the bewildering *embarass de richesse* of claims to indirect knowledge (theories, hypotheses, etc.) all of which, as far as logic is concerned, are equally well (or equally badly) supported by the evidence we may happen to have? In spite of the considerable amount of effort that Russell devoted to this matter, it does not seem to me that he ever got quite clear about it. His "postulates of scientific inference" (*HK*, Part Six), while perhaps true and perhaps employed by us at times, do not seem to be, as he had hoped, sufficient to allow the rest of common sense and scientific reasoning to proceed on the basis of direct knowledge and logic alone.[15] I mention this here not to argue it but to contrast it with another view that is, again, implicit in his philosophical activity, if not in his explicit pronouncements, the view that in each problem situation we must make a (risky) choice of the theory that seems to us best to solve the problems at hand (i.e., to explain the evidence in, say, an elegant, parsimonious, intuitively satisfactory, etc. manner.); to quote again from *MPD*, p. 27, "I do not pretend that the above theory [about perception, mind, matter, etc.] can be proved. What I contend is that, *like the theories of physics*, it cannot be disproved, and gives an answer to many problems which older theorists have found puzzling. *I do not think that any prudent person will claim more than this for any theory.*" (All italics added to the original.)

None of this provides an escape from Hume's dilemma, and Russell does not believe that there is any escape. He has said on numerous occasions (e.g., *HK*, xi) that skepticism (or solipsism of the moment, etc.) is logically impeccable (although psychologically impossible). He has no patience, however, with any "partial skepticism" such as phenomenalism, subjective idealism, or even, say, a direct realism that interprets statements about (putative) unobservables instrumentally. For any such partial skepticism must admit principles of inference that are no better off *logically* than those required for, say, the most rampant and speculative realism. Moreover, if logic can provide no arguments against skepticism, neither can it provide any in its favor, and it cannot provide any reasons for not adopting what we hope are contingently legitimate principles of reasoning in science and enlightened common sense. We cannot prove that (nontrivial) knowledge is possible, but there is nothing irrational about seeking for it and hoping, or even *believing* (e.g., on the basis of hunches or intuition) that our quest will be partially successful. There are no a priori reasons against believing that we have the capacity to make, fairly often, good proposals (that we can, on occasion make fairly good guesses) and the capacity to make correct choices from among the indefinitely large number of possible theories that can explain any evidence we may happen to have (that we are able to order our guesses in a manner not hopelessly out of line with their true prior probability)[16]; in fact, it is difficult, although of course by no means impossible, to explain our survival or to explain our ability to make bigger and better hydrogen bombs unless we do suppose that we have such capacities. Of course we do not *know* whether we shall continue to survive, but if we do not, we shall no longer be bothered with the problem of induction nor will there be any more need for hydrogen bombs.

Empiricists (and others) have seen correctly that experience (direct knowledge) plus logic is not sufficient to conclusively decide between, say, phenomenolism and realism, or among mind-body monism, interactionism, and psychophysical parallelism or epiphenomenalism. Because they failed to see that exactly the same difficulty exists in deciding between two or more competing theories in physics and any other reasonably advanced science they felt that they were forced to the strange conclusion that traditional philosophical issues like those just mentioned were pseudocontroversies and that, for example, both the assertion of the existence of external world (realism) and its denial (say, by subjective idealism) were meaningless "pseudoassertions,"[17] or to the even more mystifying (to me, at least) conclusion that, contrary to all appearances, they were really just controversies about the meaning of certain parts of our language or differences of opinion about which "language system" one should adopt (see, for example, Carnap, "Replies to Criticism"). Russell, however, clearly believes that such "philosophical" positions are *contingent* assertions about the world, and, since experience plus logical (or conceptual, or linguistic) analysis is not sufficient to decide conclusively among them, we must proceed exactly as we do when the same situation arises in science and select the position that seems to us to most satisfactorily explain the evidence. For example, he opts for realism (of a certain variety) as best explaining the "evidence," the evidence in this case including not only our direct knowledge gained by perception but much of our other commonsense and scientific knowledge as well.

It goes without saying that almost any other position, say phenomenalism, can be elaborated so that it too explains the evidence (provided we interpret scientific theories instrumentally, etc.), just as we can always patch up any scientific theory no matter what the evidence in its domain may be. But Russell would say that phenomenalism does not explain it *as well* as realism. Realism affords a more elegant, more coherent, and, perhaps just as importantly, a more intuitively plausible explanation. I would put it as follows: I would estimate the prior probability of realism to be much higher than the prior probability of its competitors. Are phenomenalism and realism, since they are contingent theories, to be classified as *philosophical* or *scientific*? The easy answer is that one is free to use the words "philosophical" and "scientific" in any way one chooses. For my part, I feel that the word "science" has been overworked and to an even greater extent misused, and I would just as soon given it a complete rest. However, we should note once more that if the theories of, say, physics are scientific, then, for reasons just given, theories such as realism, mind-body monism, epiphenomenalism, and so forth, seem to have almost as good a claim to the word. On the other hand, such theories have occupied a great portion of the attention of the thinkers that we traditionally classify as philosophers. If contemporary philosophers are to concern themselves with matters other than the trivialities that can be gleaned from logical, conceptual, and linguistic "analysis," it would seem that these problems must continue to be so treated. At any rate, this is Russell's view of the matter.

With the abandonment of the empiricists' forlorn hope that inductivism (or what I have called 'strict confirmationism') can somehow be salvaged and the resulting realization that the empiricist confirmability meaning criterion is not only without justification but untenable and impossible,[18] the way becomes completely open for the philosopher to treat his problems—or at least a significant subset of them—in the open, speculative manner of the best theoretical scientists; in the manner, also, of the best detectives. For a striking illustration of how hypothetico-inferential reasoning provides most of our significant commonsense knowledge, reread Sherlock Holmes or other good detective story. It is by this method of open theorizing that most of Russell's later philosophy has been produced.

We have finally come around full circle. Russell accepts physics (in the broad sense explained earlier to include physiology, psychophysiology, all of the causal theory of perception, etc.), and he accepts it because it explains the relevant facts from everyday life and from the laboratory in the most satisfactory manner—in the sense of "explain" and "satisfactory manner" that we have been discussing. Moreover, a realist interpretation of physics provides a more satisfactory explanation than does any "partial skepticism" such as instrumentalism. For example, instrumentalism leaves the fact that our theories make the (sometimes startlingly) true predictions that they do completely unexplained or explained in a contrived and intuitively unsatisfactory manner, while realism explains this very simply by saying that, since the theories make genuine assertions and are, we hope, true (or reasonably close to the truth), their consequences including their predictions must be true also.

Russell's next step is to try to come up with a theory that is consistent with physics (and with as much of common sense as is possible) and that will explain in the most satisfactory way the "facts" of perception in particular, and of our acquisition of (contingent) knowledge in general. Such a theory is needed for a number of reasons; one of these is the *prima facie* inconsistency of physics and that part of common sense that philosophers call *naïve realism*. The argument for the existence of such an inconsistency is a venerable one, germinal no later than Democritus and the Skeptics and given in one form or another by Galileo, Descartes, Locke, the American Critical Realists, and many others, including a disappointingly small number of contemporary thinkers.[19] One can do no better than read Russell himself on the matter (for example, in *HK*, *MPD*, *PBR*, *AM*), and so I shall merely summarize the argument briefly with two quotations. The first is from my "Theories, Perception and Structural Realism" (p. 19) and the second from my "Scientific Methodology and the Causal Theory of Perception" (p. 170):

> If our current theories in physics, neurophysiology, and psychophysiology are at all close to the truth or even if they are at all headed in the right direction, then a complete description, including a complete causal account, of everything that is involved in perception except the private experience itself would mention only such entities and events as submicroscopic particles, electromagnetic quanta, etc., and their relations and interactions with one another and with, for example, neural termini in the retina, afferent neural impulses, and patterns of neuronal activity in the brain. At no point in the entire, complete description and causal explanation is there mention of any first order property, such as color,

until we come to the private experience that results from the pattern of neuron firings in the brain. It seems to me that we must conclude that colors are exemplified *only* in our private experiences and there is no reason to believe that they are ever properties of the material objects of the external environment. *What holds for colors must also be true for all of the first order properties that we perceive directly.*

Here, something of crucial importance must be emphasized: the decisive point is *not*, as is sometimes held, that it is meaningless or self-contradictory to think of electrons, light quanta, etc., or atoms, molecules or even aggregates thereof as being colored; rather, it is that *even if such things were colored it would make no difference.* Even if it made sense to talk of a collection of blue colored molecules or atoms which emitted blue colored light photons, such a 'blue' aggregate could cause us to see the surface in question as a *red* one just as effectively as a collection of red colored ones emitting red colored quanta; the only relevant fact concerning the color we see is the amount of energy per quantum, or, what amounts to the same thing, the frequency of the radiation. So even if there are colored entities—even colored surfaces as we ordinarily conceive [of] them—in the physical environment, we never see them and their being colored plays no role in *any* process whereby we acquire or confirm knowledge. We thus have no more (perhaps less) reason for believing that there are instances of color in the external world than we do for believing in the existence of disembodied spirits.

As Russell acknowledges, the argument does not show that physics and naive realism are inconsistent with each other; it shows that if physics is true there can be no reason to believe naive realism. He says, for example, in a letter to A. J. Ayer,[20] "You say that from the fact that the perceived qualities of perception are causally dependent upon the state of the percipient, it does not follow that the object does not really have them. This, of course, is true. What does follow is that there is no reason to suppose that it has them. From the fact that when I wear blue spectacles, things look blue, it does not follow that they are not blue, but it does follow that I have no reason to suppose they are blue."

What I have called "first order properties" in the passages above correspond to Russell's "intrinsic properties," while second and higher order properties (properties of properties, properties of properties of properties, etc.) of a certain kind correspond to his "structural properties." The first tenet of the theory that Russell proposes, then, is that our only well-confirmed knowledge claims about the external, physical world must be about its second order or structural properties and that we must remain ignorant about its first order or intrinsic properties. However, this manner of putting his thesis, which is unfortunately the manner he employs, is misleading and not, I believe, exactly what he intended. For if physics and certain reformulated parts of common sense are true, we *do* know *something* about the first order (or intrinsic) properties of the physical world; we know that there *are* such things and we know *some*thing about them—we know *what* some of their properties are; in fact, the latter assertion is exactly equivalent to the assertion that we know *what* (some of) the *structural properties* of the physical world *are*, for structural properties *are* properties of *intrinsic* properties (and properties of other structural properties). The difference is that, while we have this kind of knowledge about some of the intrinsic properties of the external world, we do not know *what* they are, while we do know what some of its structural properties are.[21] We *do* know what the intrinsic (first order) properties exemplified in our sense experience are; they are properties such as redness, warmth (as felt), being warmer than, etc. And, of course, we know some of the structural properties as well; we know, for example, that the property of being to the left of in the (experienced) visual field has the structural properties of transitivity and asymmetry. Since we know *what* structural properties such as transitivity and asymmetry *are* (or, in Russell's terms, *we are acquainted* with structural properties such as transitivity and asymmetry) and since transitivity, asymmetry, etc. are also exemplified in the external world, we *do* know *what* (some of) the structural properties of the external world *are*. But of the first order (intrinsic) properties of the external world we can only know *that* they are and that they have the higher order (structural) properties that our well-confirmed theories assert that they have.

The preceding considerations provide the means of understanding how Russell can maintain his "principle of acquaintance" and also defend a strong realism regarding the external world and all of the unobservables referred to by our theories. The principle forbids direct reference by any descriptive (non-logical) term to any inividual or property with which we are not acquainted. The question thus arises: How can we even talk about, much less have knowledge of, anything that is not exemplified in our direct experience? The answers are that our knowledge of such things is *knowledge by* description, and (indirect) reference to such items is accomplished by means of indefinite or definite *descriptions*, that is, by means of variables (usually existentially quantified ones) together with terms whose *direct* referents *are* items in our experience. Suppose that I assert (truly, let us suppose and on the basis of appropriate evidence) that someone stood near my window last night, someone who was tall and large. Suppose, further, that I did not see the person and do not know who it was; that is, I did not and do not have knowledge by acquaintance of him. Nevertheless, by means of terms whose direct referents are items of my acquaintance (my window, the properties of tallness, standing near, etc.) plus an implicit variable, existentially quantified (indicated by the word "someone"), I am able to refer indirectly to whomever it was and to attribute properties such as tallness to him, even though there is no descriptive term—no name—that refers directly to the suspected voyeur. Similarly we can refer to the unobservable individuals and (first order) properties of the physical world by means of quantified individual *and* predicate variables plus terms whose direct referents are observables. (Observables for Russell are, strictly speaking, always ingredients of our private experience.) This removes one of the two main traditional objections that have been offered to representative realism, a variety of which can be quite fairly attributed to Russell. (I have called it, not too felicitously I now fear, 'structural realism'.)

Once again we may ask: How do we know what the structural properties of the world are? Indeed, how do we know that such a world exists? Russell's immediate answer is that we "infer" such knowledge from our "percepts" (sense experience). But we should remember the special sense that must be given "infer" here if we are to give him a sympathetic reading; "to infer p from our percepts" must mean something like "to propose p as the theory (and/or hypothesis) that best explains our percepts." Once verificationism and inductivism are seen to be untenable and hypothetico-inferential confirmation in the manner outlined herein is adopted, the other main traditional objection to a realism of this kind is removed.

There still may linger an uneasiness about the existence of an apparent miracle. If our direct knowledge is limited to knowledge about our private experience, and given the existence of an infinite number of possible explanations of it, it is just too much to swallow, it might be objected, to suppose that we can fairly often conjure up just those *quesses* that are not too far off the mark in giving us an accurate description of the nonexperiential (external) world. And why, it might be asked, does the fact that we *feel* that a certain guess, a certain "theory," provides a satisfactory explanation of the evidence—why does this provide any reason for supposing that this guess is any closer to the truth than any of the others that we or someone else may be bright enough to dream up? But to raise such objections is to fail to appreciate the force of the earlier critique of inductivism and strict confirmationism, in particular, and of traditional and contemporary empiricism in general—the critique initiated by Hume and elaborated by Russell and others. Experience, direct knowledge, observation knowledge—call it what you may—plus logic (even when logic is taken in a broad sense to include conceptual analysis, linguistic analysis, etc.), all of these together are not sufficient to avoid skepticism. So if we are to reject the *logically unassailable* position of skepticism, the question is: What *contingent* theory best *explains* the (hoped for) existence of (nontrivial) knowledge? I should be interested in hearing a large number of such theories proposed. But until these proposals are forthcoming, the one that I have proposed and that I have claimed was held by Russell, partly explicitly, partly implicitly, seems to me to do the job better than any other of which I am aware. As Russell says, "I do not think that any prudent person will claim any more than this for any theory."

The questions raised in the preceding paragraph can be given further answers, although they will do nothing to improve the situation from a purely logical standpoint nor will they in any way assuage the misgivings of an unregenerate empiricist. We could answer, for example, that we are able to make fairly good guesses in response to our sense experiences because our brains are "wired" in an appropriate manner, and that our brains are the way they are because we adapted (not too hopelessly, we pray) to our environment, and that we are adapted to our environment because of natural selection, or because God made us that way, etc. I am not concerned to argue for such answers here; however, I would contend that whatever the answers may be, they must be contingent ones.

The questions just discussed also call attention to the epistemic priority that is accorded sense experience or "percepts" by empiricism. It might appear that Russell uncritically incorporates this into his own views. But such an appearance, if it exists, is misleading. He explicitly gives arguments on the matter in his reply to Chisholm (*PBR*, pp. 710–714). He concludes that (private) sense experience does have a kind of priority, but *that* it does is contingent, not necessary. It is true that he accords logic a role in determining some epistemic priorities but, as to the matter at hand, the essential considerations are from common sense and from physics. Here as in so many cases, Russell begins with common-sense knowledge (or commonsense putative knowledge). Then he subjects it to critical scrutiny and, by a boot-strap operation, he endeavors to improve and expand it into something that is self-consistent, that is more comprehensive, that, as he puts it, makes fewer mistakes. And when he says that he accomplishes this by "analysis," we have seen that this must mean that he proposes theories that solve the problems, remove the inconsistencies, satisfactorily explain the results, imply that certain new results should be obtained under appropriate conditions, etc. It is, then, no accident that he holds that this is precisely the way science comes into being. It evolves in this manner from common sense and differs from common sense mainly in that it makes fewer mistakes.[22] Nor is there any wonder that he has no qualms about admitting that his reason for accepting the truth of physics (again in the broad sense of "physics" already explained) as his starting point in ontology and epistemology is "merely" a commonsense reason.

Much the same arguments from common sense and especially from physics for the epistemic priority of perception are given by Russell for the *privacy* of percepts. If what science tells us about perception is correct, then the same sense experience can be produced in many ways. For example, we can be caused to see a red chair in the usual way, but the same visual experience could be produced, if neurophysiological and psychophysiological techniques were sufficiently advanced, by appropriately stimulating the optic nerve or the visual centers of the brain by, say, electrodes; or such an experience may occur in a dream. The same pattern of neuronal activity in the appropriate region of the brain is both sufficient and necessary for us to have exactly the same sense experience. Unless we were aware of the "artificial" stimulation and its effects or, in the case of a dream, that we were dreaming, we would judge in each case that we saw the same red chair. Now all of this does not *prove* in the sense of "logically entail" either the epistemic priority of percepts or their privacy. What it does do, according to Russell, is to make *unsatisfactory*, in the sense we have discussed, any account or explanation of perception and of the knowledge, direct and indirect, obtained thereby that does not assume this priority and privacy.

I have discussed other objections to Russell's appraoch to the problems of perception elsewhere in some detail,[23] for example, the argument against the possibility of a "private language," and arguments against the existence of sense data. As regard the latter, sense data are by no means necessary for the theory. In fact, Russell tells us that he "emphatically abandoned them in 1921" (*MPD*, p. 245). When he speaks of data in places like *HK*, he is referring to "percepts" or direct knowledge of them, and percepts for him are some of the events or the ingredients of events that comprise sense experience. I have argued at length against the former argument ("no private language") in the first of the two references just cited. I have contended that it is based on a naïve verficationism, that it commits the fallacy of epistemologism (i.e., it confuses "we cannot know [for certain] whether or not a case of so-and-so is a case of such-and-such" with "there is no difference between a case of so-and-so and a case of such-and-such"), and it takes as a premise that we cannot know anything unless we can know it with absolute certainty.

I have sometimes been told in informal discussions that theories like Russell's are crucially dependent upon a "reference theory of meaning," and that when a *correct* (i.e., a *use*) theory of meaning is operative such a theory cannot get off the ground. No doubt my failure to understand this objection is partially due to my not understanding the "use" theory of meaning very well. I cheerfully grant that, if one knows the use of an expression, one knows its meaning. It seems to me howevere, that the main use of most descriptive terms is to refer to things, qualities, relations, etc. Be that as it may, since Russell's theory can be stated entirely in the object language without talking about *meanings* at all—although perhaps with some inconvenience— this objection does not seem to have much sting.

One of the "many problems which older theorists have found puzzling" to which Russell thinks his theory "gives an answer" (*MPD*, p. 27) is the "problem of the relation of mind and matter" (*MPD*, p. 15), the traditional mind–body problem. This involves his *event ontology* and his theory of space-time. I shall summarize these in a manner which is sketchy and inaccurate but which, I trust, will not do violence to his views. He rejects *substance* metaphysics altogether and replaces *things*—clumps of matter (physical objects) and the like—with classes or families of *events*. Examples of events are a twinge of pain, the occurrence of a patch of red in the visual field, etc. These examples are events such that we know *what* they are. This is *not* true of the events that comprise the vast bulk of the physical (external) world. We do not know what these events are; we do not know their intrinsic nature; we do not know what the first order properties are that are exemplified in them. What we do know, if our theories from physics and refined common sense are true or close to the truth, are some of the structural properties (mostly relational) of these events. The most prominent of such properties are the causal relations that hold among the events. Russell's theory of space-time amounts to "constructing" space-time out of events and their causal relationships to each other—a truly *relational* theory of space-time. Thus, as he puts it, "when the causal relations of an event are known, its position in space-time follows tautologically" (*PBR*, p. 705). Since we have already located mental events (the occurrence of perceptive experiences, etc.) in the causal network, they thereby acquire a spatio-temporal location, and a kind of mind–body "identity theory" automatically follows as a consequence of the theory. I believe that the matter can be made more clear if we adopt definitions of "mental" and "physical" slightly different from Russell's. Let us call anything "a physical event" that is in the causal (and, thus, in the spatio-temporal) network, and something will be called "a mental event" if and only if it is an event in our direct experience (as Russell puts it, if it [or its ingredients] can be known otherwise than by inference—in Russell's special sense of "inference" already discussed).[24] Now, since mental events are in space-time—that is, they play a causal role—it follows that all mental events are physical events. Since there *are* such things as mental events, it also follows that some physical events are mental events; of what other physical events are like, or what their intrinsic nature is, we are ignorant, so ignorant, Russell says, that we do not know whether they are similar to (in their first order or intrinsic properties) or totally different from the events in our experience (whose first order or intrinsic properties we do know by acquaintance). What we do know about physical events (including those that are mental, although about these we know more besides) are (some of) their structural or higher order properties, the more important of which give their spatio-temporal (or causal) structure.

At the risk of repetition, I must stress a point of crucial importance. The mental events that comprise our experience, that we live through and know in all of their qualitative richness, *really are physical events* (they *really are* mental events too, of course). As with other physical events, each has its own position in the spatio-temporal—causal—network and is *not* an epiphenomenal or parallelistic correlate of some other "truly physical" event that is supposed to play the "real" spatio-temporal or causal role. There *is* no such *other* physical event at the spatio-temporal locus in question. Every "truly mental" event is also "truly physical" (although not conversely so far as we know). We regard them differently than we do other physical events because they comprise our experience and, thus, we know their intrinsic properties as well as their structural ones.

Since the brain, like all portions of matter, consists of a family or families of events, causally related in appropriate ways, and since neurophysiology and psychophysiology gives us the causal locus that it does for the events that comprise our experience (our thoughts, feelings, etc.), it follows that our thoughts and feelings are quite literally among the constituents of our brains.

As Russell says, this theory may seem fantastic, but he clearly believes it is true or close to the truth and, at any rate, that it is the theory best supported by the evidence from science and enlightened common sense. Not the least component of its support comes from the fact that contemporary physics seems much better formulable using an event ontology than with using a substance one. In physics today, the "dematerialization of matter" is virtually complete. Be that as it may, I do not believe that there are any insurmountable obstacles to *understanding* the theory, especially if we remember the commonplace from the history of science that, when novel theories are proposed, old words take on meanings that, while they are quite similar to the old meanings in many respects, are sometimes bewilderingly different from them in others. And Russell's famous statement which, he says, profoundly shocked Ernest Nagel and others as well (*PBR*, p. 705) is seen to be an unexceptionable consequence of the theory. The statement is to the effect that when a physiologist examines another man's brain, what he sees is a portion of his own brain. Of course, the word 'see' here has a somewhat different meaning from its ordinary one. For the ordinary one is a naïve realist one (with possibly some of its uses excepted). To say that we see something ordinarily implies that we perceive something external. But according to Russell we never see *anything* in this ordinary sense of 'see'. All that we ever perceive visually are ingredients of the events that comprise our experience and are, thus, literally in (or are constituents of) our own brains. Russell provides for avoidance of misunderstanding here by his distinction between physical space and perceptual space, for example, visual space. Physical space, we recall, is constructed out of events and their causal interrelationships, but my visual space, in which I am aware of qualitative extension, shapes, locations of color patches, and other visual "percepts," is an ingredient of events in my experience. Thus all of my visual space, no matter how many miles common sense may indicate that it spreads over, is located at a point or within a small volume in physical space in, as a matter of fact, my (physical) brain. Let us call the physiologist's percept that common sense mistakenly identifies with the other man's brain, which is really located in the physiologist's (private) visual space, and which the other man's brain does play a crucial causal role in producing—let us refer to this percept as the physiologist's percept of the other man's brain. Then it is quite clear that the physiologist's percept of the other man's brain is *external to the physiologist's percept of his own body* (in the physiologist's visual space), while both percepts are *in the physiologist's brain in physical space.*

The difference between this kind of mind-body monism and traditional materialistic mind-body theories is extreme. Traditional materialism took our conception and knowledge of matter, of the physical, to be straightforward and unproblematic. The mental, on the other hand, was held to be not only problematic but metaphysically and epistemologically undesirable, what with its alleged privacy or subjectivity, ineffability, etc. Therefore it was something best got shut of, or at any rate swept under a rug such as epiphenomenalism or psychophysical parallelism. Traditional materialism's conception of matter was one that resulted from naïve realism or from not-too-pervasive modification thereof. Matter was something good and solid. One could see and feel that it was good and solid; as Russell says, it was bumpable into. Modern science, however, according to Russell, makes necessary the drastic revision of our conception of matter that has been discussed in this paper. It turns out that we cannot see or feel matter at all, except for those events in our visual and tactile experience that comprise a small portion of our brains. Our traditional notions of matter, rather than those of mind, turn out to be the problematic ones. Traditional materialism, by accepting commonsense naïve realism, fell into the error of identifying visual and tactile percepts with the physical objects that are merely (one crucial part of) their causes. Thus, contrary to what traditional materialism seemed to want, the mental remains every bit as mental as anyone could hope for, in spite of the fact that it is also physical. However, the portion of physical events that are mental, as far as we know today, is subject to the same principles and laws of nature as the rest of the physical world. Russell's mind-body monism retains this much in common with materialism. Whether or not further investigation will reveal that additional laws are required remains an open question.

I have discussed some of the aspects of Russell's theory of perception and of his philosophical method, theory of knowledge, and world view that evolved while he was developing the theory. I have selected those aspects that seemed to me to have the greatest importance or the greatest difficulties, or both. Of necessity, I have had to omit even mention of large portions of his theory. By far the best source on Russell is still Russell himself, and probably the best single source on these matters is *HK*. However, *AM* (a sort of early version of *HK*, although he develops his theory of space-time in much more detail in it than is done in *HK*), *PBR*—especially Russell's replies to Nagel, Stace, and Chisholm—*IMT*, and portions of *MPD* are highly recommended.

I believe that Russell's later philosophy has provided solutions, in the sense that science provides solutions—tentative ones—for which many contemporary philosophers and scientists (e.g., psychologists, neurophysiologists, and, especially, psychophysiologists) are still groping. But whether I am right about this or not, I have absolutely no doubt that his later philosophy deserves immeasurably more study than it has received and that our knowledge will be extensively enriched when this is forthcoming.

NOTES

1. Some of the research that provided material for this essay was supported by the National Science Foundation, the Carnegie Corporation, and the Minnesota Center for Philosophy of Science of the University of Minnesota.

2. Bertrand Russell, *My Philosophical Development* (New York: Simon and Schuster, 1959); *The Analysis of Matter* (London: Allen and Unwin, 1927); *Human Knowledge: Its Scope and Limits* (New York: Simon and Schuster, 1948).

3. P. A. Schillp, ed., *The Philosophy of Bertrand Russell*, The Library of Living Philosophers (LaSalle, Ill.: Open Court, 1944).

4. It is true that Russell stoutly maintained, throughout his career, his "principle of acquaintance," which may be put thus: If we can understand what a sentence means, all of its nonlogical (i.e., descriptive) terms must either directly denote items with which we are acquainted or be definable in terms of terms that denote only such items. But it is a grave misreading of the principle to take it to be incompatible with a strong realism or to suppose that it gives any support to phenomenalism, instrumentalism or related views. For Russell's own theory of descriptions, *definite and indefinite* descriptions, provides a method of *denoting* and, thus, making assertions about, holding beliefs about, having knowledge about, etc., items with which we are *not* acquainted (including items that are unobservable). Such denotation is accomplished *indirectly* by means of logical terms (usually existential quantifiers or their natural language equivalents) plus descriptive terms that do denote items of acquaintance. For a detailed discussion of these matters, including a discussion of how Russell's theory of descriptions may be extended to unobservable properties using the Ramsey Sentence, see my "Structural Realism and the Meaning of Theoretical Terms," in M. Radner and S. Winokur, eds., *Minnesota Studies in the Philosophy of Science*, vol. IV (Minneapolis: University of Minnesota Press, 1971).

5. See Gilbert Ryle, *Dilemmas* (Cambridge: At the University Press, 1954).

6. The inverted commas here are crucial, for there is the same difficulty with the word "see" as there is with the word "perception" (see, for example, *PBR*, pp. 704–705). I may "see a cat" without seeing a cat. I will accomplish the latter only if the perceptual experience of "seeing a cat" is veridical.

7. Bertrand Russell, *An Inquiry into Meaning and Truth* (London: Allen and Unwin, 1940).

8. For more detailed arguments against Ryle's position, see my "Theories, Perception and Structural Realism," in R. Colodny, ed., *The Nature and Function of Scientific Theories: Essays in Contemporary Science and Philosophy*, vol. 4, University of Pittsburgh Series in the Philosophy of Science (Pittsburgh: University of Pittsburgh Press, 1970).

9. See my "Theories, Perception and Structural Realism"; "Corroboration without Demarcation," in P. A. Schilpp, ed., *The Philosophy of Karl Popper* (La Salle, Ill.: Open Court, 1973); and "Induction and Empiricism...," in G. Maxwell and R. Anderson, eds., *Minnesota Studies in the Philosophy of Science*, vol. 6 (Minneapolis: University of Minnesota Press, 1975).

10. See, for example, Alan Wood, "Russell's Philosophy," in *MPD*, p. 276.

11. "Philosophical Importance of Mathematical Logic," *Monist*, October 1913; quoted by Alan Wood.

12. Russell says earlier (*MPD*, p. 15) that he arrived at the part of the theory that "[solves] the problem of the relation of mind and matter by analyzing physics and perception." Surely "analyzing" here must mean something like "proposing a theory that *explains* the relevant portions of physics and perception."

13. More accurately: *there is a certain collection of electrons, protons, etc., having certain (structural) properties and certain relations to each other and to certain other collections such as the one commonly called "my body," etc.* Or, still more accurately: *there is a certain family of events, having certain structural properties and relations, etc., etc.*

14. See the quotation from Russell, page 138, and my "Theories, Perception, and Structural Realism," "Corroboration without Demarcation," and "Induction and Empiricism. . . ."

15. For alternative accounts of nondeductive reasoning, see my "Corroboration without Demarcation," "Theories, Perception and Structural Realism," and "Induction and Empiricism. . . ."

16. See references in note 15, above.

17. See R. Carnap's "Replies to Criticism," in P. A. Schilpp, ed., *The Philosophy of Rudolf Carnap* (La Salle, Ill.: Open Court, 1963), p. 868.

18. See my "Theories, Perception and Structural Realism."

19. For fuller discussion and more references, see my "Scientific Methodology and the Causal Theory of Perception," and "Reply [to Professors Quine, Ayer, Popper, and Kneale]," both in I. Lakatos and Alan Musgrave, eds., *Problems in the Philosophy of Science* (Amsterdam: North Holland Publishing Co., 1968), pp. 148–177; "Structural Realism and the Meaning of Theoretical Terms"; and "Theories, Perception and Structural Realism."

20. Bertrand Russell, *Autobiography*, vol. 3 (New York: Simon and Schuster, 1969), p. 179.

21. For a fuller discussion of this point, see my "Structural Realism and the Meaning of Theoretical Terms."

22. I clearly remember this assertion of his about fewer mistakes, but I have not been able to relocate the reference.

23. For example, in "Theories, Perception and Structural Realism" and "Scientific Methodology and the Causal Theory of Perception."

24. Russell first defines "mental event" in this manner and then defines "a physical event" as one not known (or not known to be known) except by inference.

9

Identity and "the Difference"

Judith J. Economos

IN HIS ADMIRABLE book *The Difference of Man and the Difference It Makes*[1] Professor Mortimer J. Adler has considered two related topics, each of major importance in its own right: certain aspects of the mind-body problem and the moral consequences of possible settlements of the mind-body problem. (All of the source notes in this paper refer to Adler's book.)

In the interests of a relatively brief and unified discussion I shall here consider only the "Difference of Man," reluctantly postponing "the Difference It Makes" for another time. Moreover I shall consider Professor Adler's views on the mind-body problem primarily with respect to the Identity Thesis.

Professor Adler has organized his work with such care and honesty that inspection of his presuppositions is easy. I shall begin by describing and discussing them; their importance for the force of his argument is considerable. Next I shall very briefly indicate the logical structure of the argument as it leads to the consideration of the Identity Thesis; again, this task is made easy by Professor Adler's conscientious exposition. My main effort will be expended on explaining Professor Adler's views on the scope and validity of the Identity Thesis, and evaluating his challenge to it.

Foundations: Kinds of difference

Description

Since Adler poses his question in terms of the difference of man from other animals, he begins by distinguishing ways in which things may differ. Three important ways emerging from this discussion are: (a) difference in degree, (b) superficial difference in kind, (c) radical difference in kind.[2]

Differences in degree are relatively easy to understand: x *differs in degree from* y *with respect to* P, if and only if there is some feature P, capable of gradation into degrees, such that P(x) and P(y), but x possesses a greater degree of P than does y (p. 20).[3] *Warm, bright, strange,* and *fast* are instances of properties susceptible of gradation.

A difference in kind obtains when of two things x and y, for some P insusceptible of gradation, P(x) and ~P(y), obtain. Examples of properties insusceptible of gradation are *located in space, prime, odd, left-handed.*[4]

There can be merely apparent differences in kind. These are differences in degree, where the measure of difference between instances is large and no instances of intermediates are available. Since intermediates are possible, however, such a state of affairs is *not* a real difference in kind (pp. 23, 24).

The distinction of vital importance for us is between "superficial" and "radical" differences in kind. A superficial difference in kind is one "based on and explained by an underlying difference in degree, in which one degree is above and the other is below *a critical threshold* in a continuum of degrees" (p. 24). That is, for some x and y, for some properties P and Q, for some values of P: P_a, P_b and P_θ ,

'$P_a(x)$ and $P_b(y)$ and $P_a \geqslant P_\theta$ and $P_b < P_\theta$'

explains '$Q(x)$ and ~ $Q(y)$.' Adler adduces as example the critical thesholds of temperature (and pressure) for which rigid ice becomes flowing water, and for which liquid water becomes gaseous vapor. Ice, water, and water vapor differ in kind, but only superficially, since the difference is explained by critical thresholds in the continuum of degrees of molecular activity.

I do not find that the assertion that there are properties with respect to which things differ superficially in kind amounts to emergentism, because a superficial difference in kind is by definition adequately[5] explained by a difference in degree in which there are thresholds.

"Radical differences in kind" are differences in kind not adequately explained by thresholds in an underlying continuum of degrees (pp. 25 ff.), although an underlying continuum of degrees may be a necessary condition for a radical difference in kind. The assertion that there is a property P such that there are things x and y differing radically in kind with respect to P is emergentism with respect to P.

Discussion

Given that x and y differ in kind because for some nongraded P, P(x) and ~ P(y), I cannot discover whether Professor Adler would maintain a real difference in kind between x and y with respect to P if it were possible that P(y). Since paradigm cases of real differences in kind involve properties rather precisely defined, so that if ~ P(y) then necessarily not P(y) (e.g., odd and even, left and right, etc.) the question fails to arise until we have seen Adler's application of the concept. In his applications, things differ in kind with respect to properties not, prima facie, necessarily lacked by one of the differing items (or, for that matter, necessarily possessed by the other). There is nothing logically wrong here; but it is well to be warned that the concept of a difference in kind is not as strong as at first sight it might appear to be. A man with two whole arms differs in kind from a man with only one.

A more serious question concerns specifically the notion of a radical difference in kind: it appears to be a universal relation as it stands. Every individual differs radically in kind from every other, by virtue simply of its individuality (cf. Leibniz' law); and, moreover, every physical thing will differ radically from every other by virtue of its spatio-temporal coordinates (which, although graduated, are uniquely possessable, and intermediates between possessing a given set and *not* possessing a given set of them are impossible).

This consequence can probably be avoided by suitably restricting the kind of property to be considered relevant to differences in kind. With such restrictions, we may still find apparent instances of radical differences in kind; for example, atoms possess chemical identity and (more or less approximately) simultaneously certifiable position and momentum, whereas the particles of which atoms are made cannot be said to possess either. Aggregates of molecules possess temperature and color, and the molecules of which they are aggregates cannot be said to possess either. In these generally acceptable instances, however, there is a semantic factor; it is not so much that a single molecule lacks temperature, for example, as that the concept of temperature simply is not defined for single molecules. Hence we return to the question whether differences in kind, particularly radical ones, are not peculiarly dependent on a model. I cannot resolve this question within the framework of Adler's views. I can only repeat that his applications of the notion of differences in kind generally lack the flavor of necessity possessed by generally accepted examples.

Structure of the Argument

Adler's avowed intent is to discover whether there is a radical, or only a superficial, difference in kind between men and other animals. However, I shall describe his strategy as though his aim were to show that there is a radical difference in kind. This will simplify the exposition and is not altogether unfair.

The steps of the argument are, in outline, as follows (they will be examined in more detail in the following section).

1. There is a manifest (observed) difference in kind between man and other animals, due to man's use of propositional languages, totally lacking in any degree in other animals.[6]

2. This manifest difference must be explained by a psychological difference. The question now becomes: Is the psychological difference a difference in degree; and if it is a difference in kind, is it radical, or only superficial? If it is superficial,

then it is to be explained by reference to a critical threshold in a continuum of degrees of neurophysiological difference.

3. In order to answer the question in (2), Adler distinguishes between "perceptual abstractions" and "concepts." He wishes to show that the explanation of animal behavior requires positing only perceptual abstractions, not concepts, whereas the explanation of human behavior requires both. If this is true, it will constitute a psychological difference in kind.

4. To show (3), Adler distinguishes "signals" from "designators." The use of signals is tantamount to inference making of the form 'if p, then q'; signals are like cues. Designators, by contrast, have meanings existentially independent of what they may denote, and understanding them is not like making an inference, but rather consists in grasping their meaning. Some signals are natural, but all designators are conventional.[7] The only way, it appears, to ascertain whether a sign is functioning as a designator is through linguistic behavior (pp. 156, 177, 179). Consequently, the principle of parsimony denies to nonlinguistic animals the use of designators. Since concepts are the meanings of designators (p. 186), the explanation of human behavior requires positing concepts. Hence (3) is answered, and there is a psychological difference in kind, not in degree.

5. Now the second question in (2), whether the psychological difference in kind between man and other animals is radical or superficial, may be addressed. If the difference in kind is superficial, it must be fully explicable by reference to a threshold in an underlying continuum of degrees of some property—presumably neurophysiological complexity. In order to show that the psychological difference in kind is radical, not superficial, Adler must find reason to believe that it *cannot* be adequately explained in neurophysiological terms. He sets out to show something even stronger: that the psychological difference in kind cannot be explained in material terms at all.

This brings him to the issue of materialism and hence to the Identity Thesis. In the next section we shall examine his views on the Identity Thesis and, in so doing, see in somewhat greater detail his reasoning on the four steps outlined above.

Professor Adler and the Identity Thesis

The Identity Thesis, in asserting the identity of psychological and neurophysiological processes, denies that there is a radical difference in kind between man and other animals. Supposing that Adler desires to establish such a radical difference,[8] he would find some fault in the Identity Thesis. It is astonishing that he finds so little. He is willing to concede without argument the probable truth of the Identity Thesis for what has been called sentience—a staggering gift, leaving one as nonplussed as a man who has charged an unlocked door. Adler's view on sentience is:

 . . . all the phenomena of the perceptual order—sensations and sensory

affects, sensitive memories and memory images, perceptions and perceptual abstractions—can be adequately explained by reference to neurological factors and processes and, therefore, need no supplementary immaterial factor to complete the explanation.... [P. 196; see also pp. 197,
201, 202, 205]

It is, then, on the issue of sapience that Professor Adler sees trouble for the
Identity Thesis; specifically, on the issue of the explanation of conceptual thought
in neurological terms.

The "difference of man" which causes Adler to suspect a radical difference
in kind between man and other animals is the capacity for propositional speech,
requiring the notion of concepts for its explanation. We can best understand
concepts in contrast to perceptual abstractions, which Adler has said do not
require to be explained by immaterial factors. A *perceptual abstraction* is

> a disposition to perceive a number of sensible particulars (or, in laboratory
> parlance, stimuli) as the same in kind, or as sufficiently similar to be
> reacted to the same.... [P. 153]

He adds,

> This disposition is only operative in the presence of an appropriate
> sensory stimulus, and never in its absence, i.e., the animal does not exercise
> its acquired disposition to recognize certain shapes as triangles or certain
> colors as red when a triangular shape or a red patch is not perceptually
> present and actually perceived. [P. 153][9]

Contrasting with perceptual abstractions are concepts:

> If we restrict ourselves for the moment to concepts that relate to
> perceived or perceptible objects, a concept can be defined as an acquired
> disposition to recognize the kind of thing a perceived object is and to
> understand what that kind of thing is like. [P. 157]

He adds,

> The disposition to understand what dogs are like can be exercised
> when dogs are not actually perceived as well as when they are; whereas
> perceptual abstractions, as dispositions to discriminate between sensible
> similars and dissimilars, function only when sensible particulars are being
> perceived. [P. 157][10]

Both concepts and perceptual abstractions are unobservable; concepts are
no more introspectable than are perceptual abstractions (p. 156; see also pp.
148–149). Both are viewed as theoretical constructs required to explain behavior.
Perceptual abstractions are all that is needed to explain animal behavior;[11] we
must add concepts in order to explain human linguistic behavior.

Concepts, for Adler, are meanings in the sense of connotations, intensions, or universals: "... the source of all meanings possessed by anything which has, gets, loses, and changes its meaning lies in concepts, for concepts *are* meanings" (p. 186).

The source, then, of Adler's doubts about the identity thesis lies in intentionality—but not in intentionality per se. He allows that perceptual abstractions (which he takes as neurophysiologically explicable) have a kind of intentionality (cf. pp. 214–220). But they do not have the kind of intentionality which concepts have. The important difference, for him, is that the reference of perceptual abstractions never transcends particulars;[12] concepts, in contrast, are universal; they "consist in meanings or intentions that are universal" (p. 220). But everything that exists physically is particular. As Adler puts it:

> The argument in its bare bones hinges on two propositions. The first proposition asserts that the concepts whereby we understand what different kinds or classes of things are like consist in meanings or intentions that are universal. The second proposition asserts that nothing that exists physically is universal; anything that is embodied in matter exists as a particular instance of this class or that. From these two propositions it follows that our concepts are immaterial. [Pp. 220–221]

If I construe Professor Adler correctly, he does not think that there is a problem for materialism in intentionality or reference per se—which some of us have thought—but only in intentionality or reference involving universals. He says that if concepts "were acts of a bodily organ, such as the brain, they would exist in matter, and so would be individual. But they are universal. Hence, they do not and cannot exist in matter ..." (p. 221).

Again,

> Our concepts are universal in the character of their intentionality. Hence they do not exist physically; they are not embodied in matter. Since our concepts are acts of our power of conceptual thought, that power must itself be an immaterial power, one not embodied in a physical organ such as the brain. [P. 222][13]

In contrast,

> Since, unlike concepts, perceptual abstractions do not have an intentionality that is universal in character, immateriality need not be attributed to the power of which they are acts. ... It is *only* an intentionality which is universal in character and that is characteristic of conceptual acts but not of perceptual acts, which warrants attributing immateriality to a cognitive power. [P. 226; emphasis added]

Although I am not entirely satisfied with the reasoning that leads to the assertion that men have concepts,[14] I agree with the conclusion that they have;

and moreover I agree that universals, whatever they are, and in whatever sense they may be said to exist, are not material objects and do not exist in the sense in which material objects exist. However, I do not think it is necessary for universals to exist materially in order for brains to have concepts. When a man thinks of a universal, it would be odd to suppose the universal itself is somehow entering the causal order; and I do not think so, any more than I think that the abstract types of words are the wherewithal of individual utterances. I utter particular, material *tokens* of words; I think with particular, material *tokens* of universals, which are presumably individual processes or states in my material brain.

If intentionality per se is not a problem for Professor Adler, then neither, I should think, are universals.

Indeed, he does not seem altogether convinced of the soundness of his argument for an immaterial power in men, for he is willing to countenance the possibility of an empirical test[15] that would falsify his conclusion, and obligate him "to re-examine the premises and reasoning to discover the source of the error" (p. 246).

Summary and Conclusions

Professor Adler granted three major points in favor of the Identity Thesis: (1) It is probably true for sentience; (2) intentionality *per se* is not a problem; and (3) if the Identity Thesis is true, then the mind-body problem (for sentience and sapience) is solved (p. 198).

Furthermore, he is willing to submit the validity of his one objection to an empirical test, the success of which would, in his opinion, conclusively establish the Identity Thesis, and the failure of which would not conclusively falsify it. This is no small gift.

In the face of such unexpected generosity, one is hardly inclined to quibble. I can say only that I am troubled by problems that do not trouble Professor Adler, and the problem that troubles him—the immateriality of concepts—does not appear to me as a problem for the Identity Thesis at all.

NOTES

1. Mortimer J. Adler, *The Difference of Man and the Difference It Makes* (New York: Holt, Rinehart and Winston, 1967).
2. His scheme of differences is more elaborate, but these are the relevant ones. See his chapter 2, especially pages 30 and 31.
3. Adler specifies, indeed, that the property be susceptible of *continuous* gradation.
4. It is worth noticing that the properties of this sort tend to be formal properties (odd vs. even, prime vs. composite). One has to cast about for physical ones (e.g., right-handed vs. left-handed), and even these are faintly formal. By contrast, gradated properties abound in everyday experience.

5. An "adequate" explanation is a statement of sufficient condition.

6. Cf. chapter 8, "The Pivotal Fact: Human Speech." I have obviously condensed Adler's patient, cautious discussion considerably.

7. Since I found no definition or very concise characterization of signals and designators, I have perforce given an interpretation of Adler's distinction, drawn from the discussion and illustrations on pages 165–173 and elsewhere in the book.

8. A supposition indeed, but one that I think is justified by his opinions about the consequences of not establishing such a difference.

9. I am a little puzzled how an animal *could* exercise a disposition, so defined, in the absence of the stimulus.

10. The "exercise" of a non-occasional disposition, like understanding what something is like, is a touch mysterious to me; I assume he simply means that the disposition *is* non-occasional.

11. The reason apparently being that only linguistic behavior, which other animals do not evince, requires concepts to be explained (see p. 156 ff. and pp. 177–179). Since my mission is not to stand up for animal conceptualizing, I do not care to debate whether there is, or is not, a radical difference in kind between man and other animals, in that men do, and other animals do not, possess concepts.

12. Or, perhaps, that it is to universals only as they are immanent in particulars —which seems more likely to me. He is not altogether clear on the point.

13. I find the last inference a *non sequitur*. If an immaterial cause (e.g., conceptual thought) can have material effects (e.g., utterances of a physical body), I see no reason why a material cause or agent might not have immaterial effects or acts such as the production of concepts!

14. The "exercise" of a disposition to understand, the notion of a concept as an "act," and so on, bother me.

15. The "Turing test," in which a robot shows the capacity to converse in a natural language as plausibly as a man. See chapter 14, "The Third Prong: From Descartes to Turing."

10

Logic of the Empirical World, with Reference to the Identity Theory and Reductionism

Satosi Watanabe

1. Man, World, Science[1]

Let us start with an elementary remark about the role of science for the man living in the world. Man's action is goal-oriented, and he chooses the means according to his scientific or pre-scientific causal knowledge that such and such means as the cause will probably bring about the desired goal as the effect. There is no doubt that the origin and the basic role of science lie in this teleology-causality reciprocity. Science tells us: "*If* you do this, *then* you will probably get that." Man is the agent, and the world is the reagent. Such is man's world of experience. Science is the guide for the man's action on his world of experience. It goes without saying that a group of men with mutual communication and working for the same goal can be considered as a single agent in the present context.

As science progresses, this if-this-action-then-that-reaction statement of science starts to give place to another type of if-then statement, namely, "if this initial state, then probably that final state." But in order that this new kind of scientific statement can fulfill the required role of science for man, it has to be augmented by two additional conditions. First, it must be postulated that we can freely create or choose the initial state within certain limitations. The author worked out elsewhere (Watanabe, 1966b, 1970) a detailed analysis of the relationship between this vital postulate (of free choice of initial condition) and the direction of time of the physical world.[2] Second, in the object-system we are talking about, the initial and final states are the objects of man's action, that is, the world from which the man as agent is absent—a world with a "hole." Such a world-reagent is the real scientific world. To make this picture possible, it is also necessary that there be no interaction between the agent and the world-reagent during the time between the initial and the final instants. This last condition of agent-reagent isolation is often violated, invalidating the usefulness of this type of scientific knowledge.

Once science is formulated in terms of the initial and final states, it can accommodate a world view entirely different from the agent-reagent point of view which is the very foundation of science. Namely, man can now be a passive spectator, and the entire world is a drama taking place on an inaccessible stage independently of the spectator. This new "scientific" view is bound to have limitations in its validity because it is a deviation from the proper role of science. Ignorance of these limitations has led in the last two centuries to dubious philosophical tendencies such as materialism, physicalism, objectivism, etc.

What, then, are the limitations of this spectator view of the world? First, we have to point out an almost analytic absurdity involved in this world view. Namely, observation by definition implies interaction, interaction implies lack of independence. Hence, if the observer wants to be an ideal noninteracting observer, he has to give up being an observer. In other words, if the world has to be independent, it has to include all possible observers; hence it ceases to be an observable world. Of course, the materialist can "talk" about the interaction between the observer and the observed and claim to explain what the observer observes, but, in order that this talk and explanation may be scientific, they must correspond to observable or observed facts. There is no guarantee that the presence of this additional observation does not alter the situation which existed in its absence. (See a later paragraph concerning the "bystander's view.")

The paradigm case of this spectator view is the notorious demon of Laplace. In this case, in addition to the above stated spectator's world view, a strict determinism is assumed. But the strict determinism is not the major cause of the difficulties for the poor demon. We now enumerate various known difficulties other than the analytic difficulty already mentioned: (1) According to computer experts, the calculation required of the demon for his prediction needs a computer at least as heavy as the Universe itself. (2) According to L. Brillouin, the observation which the demon has to carry out to determine the initial state of the Universe requires an amount of energy that is overwhelmingly larger than the total energy content of the Universe (Brillouin, 1959). (3) In order to collect the information regarding the present (initial) state of the entire Universe, the demon has to wait an infinite length of time; hence he can never predict any finitely future state of the Universe.[3] (4) Strict determinism is simply false according to quantum mechanics except with regard to the time development of the unobservable, fictitious state-function (psi-function) of the entire universe. (5) According to Wigner (1952) and Yanase (1961), there are very few physical quantities for which a nondestructive measurement exists, contrary to von Neumann's famous theory of observation (von Neumann, 1932).

It is important to note that these difficulties are not accidental ones irrelevant to the essence of the demon's task. They stem directly from the wrong philosophy about science which gave birth to this demon. Any theory which assumes that these difficulties do not exist is not a genuine scientific theory. One can, of course, say that whether or not observed, there is such a thing as the initial state from which the future is (deterministically or probabilistically) derivable in principle, independently of the feasibility of actual calculation. But this assertion is at best an unwarranted speculation, beyond the reach of observable verification. Without feasibility of observation, one cannot know which predicates to use to describe the state of the world.

To make a scientific prediction possible, it is therefore necessary to assume that the prediction refers only to a finite isolated system. But there is no way of guaranteeing in advance the isolation of the system for the future. Indeed to ascertain that the initial state of a sufficiently large portion of the world is such that there will be no violation of the isolation of the small system under consideration, we have to wait until after the future instant for which the prediction is intended. Thus the future of a finite system is, rigorously speaking, also unpredictable. In brief, in the spectator view, the world is entirely unpredictable. All it could do, even if we decide to ignore the difficulties pertaining to the observer-object interaction, is to "predict" the future event after the future event has happened. That is an ulterior "explanation." This is not entirely meaningless because it proves the validity of the theory, but it is not science as an unfailing tool of prediction.[4] A philosophical view which assumes that the stage-play of the physical world in a finite "isolated" domain is predictable is also an unwarranted metaphysics void of scientific support.[5] See Watanabe, 1970, for more details about this matter.

Starting from the agent-reagent view or the observer-observed view, we could somewhat enlarge our viewpoint by acknowledging the existence of other agents or other observers. A second observer will regard the first observer as a part of his observed world and talk about the interaction between the two parts of his world, the one being the first observer and the other being the first observer's world minus the second observer. In this case the second observer may be called the bystander. Heisenberg's famous "explanation" of the quantum-mechanical indeterminacy should be interpreted as the description by the bystander of the interaction between the first observer and the first observer's observed object. This kind of explanation presupposes a certain degree of consistency between the first observer's observation and the second observer's observation, but by no means does it presuppose or justify the validity of the spectator view of the all-including world.

An important conclusion we can draw from this discussion is that there exists no mind-body problem in the spectator view of the world, in its cosmic version or in its isolated system version, since there is no place for mind to observe or to act on. The play is going on but the mind is forbidden to observe it or act on it. It is a dead mind, or a deistic god's mind. Physicalism is a deistic god's metaphysics.

It may be noted that the agent-reagent view of the world has acquired strong support from the two major developments of the twentieth century—quantum mechanics and cybernetics. Quantum mechanics denied the possibility of making observation without changing the state of the observed system. Cybernetics is essentially an art of controlling an outside system, whereby the action of the controller is guided by information and feedbacks from the controlled system, thus emphasizing the inseparability of the agent and the reagent (Watanabe, 1968a). The recent concern about "future" among sociologists, economists, and political scientists seems to have something in common with our agent-reagent view of the world (Watanabe, 1972). It may be added that in psychology alteration of the observed state by the act of observation is a matter of common occurrence.

2. Identity Theory and Reductionism

As we pass on, step by step, from physics to biology, from biology to psychology, from psychology to sociology, we are led to introduce new concepts which we did not use at lower levels. These concepts are introduced to make it possible to formulate some empirical laws or lawlike statements. Reductionism seems to claim that all the laws of higher levels can be explained by those of the lowest level, implying also the conceptual and ontological reducibility.[6] If the self proclaimed reductionists tried to reduce everything to physics properly understood, their harm would be much less serious; but what they call physics is the metaphysical physicalism, and their ontology is the old-fashioned nineteenth century materialism (the ontology of modern physics is the indeterminate, attributeless prima materia—nothingness).

Identity Theory (Feigl, 1967) seems to assume that there are two languages or parlances so that one proposition in Language I is true if and only if one proposition in Language II is true. This assumption of one-one correspondence[7] is objectionable for many reasons. The present author mentioned some of them in a previous paper (Watanabe, 1961), but he will add four more here: (1) Even within the well-established physics, macroscopic states and microscopic states are usually related not only by one-to-many correspondence but also often many-to-many correspondence. How can a complicated and delicate thing as a mental state correspond one-to-one to a physiological state? (2) If the correspondence is defined solely by the truth values of the two propositions, any constant truth in the mental parlance becomes the counterpart of any arbitrary constant truth in the physiological parlance.[8] Thus, for instance, the mental statement that "if I am not in a bad mood, then I have no toothache" can be considered the counterpart of the physiological statement that the average body temperature is less than 120 degrees Fahrenheit. This is certainly not what the Identity Theory intended. (3) In order to avoid this difficulty, we shall have to limit ourselves to those propositions which occasionally fail to be true. And then to verify the identity we shall have to show the coincidence of the truth periods of two propositions, one mental and one physiological. If Identity Theory is an empirical assertion, and if this temporal coincidence of occurrence is the only ground for its truth, it could not mean much more than any conclusion that can be drawn from the coincidence of Emanuel Kant walking past my window and my grandfather's clock ringing five o'clock. (4) If the identity is meant to be analytical, then there is not much to argue about. Even without going so far as to argue that identity must mean an absolute undistinguishability, one would immediately start to wonder, on one hand, what significance in life the existence of two aspects could really carry if they are identical, and on the other to suspect that the nature of the difference which makes it possible to distinguish a mental proposition from a physical proposition is precisely the essence of the mind-body problem which the Identity Theory from the beginning has sealed up so that it would never raise its ugly head again. (5) If Identity Theory is taken seriously, there is really only one set of propositions and this set is completely and satisfactorily structured by a behavioral-neurophysiological theory. Hence, Identity Theory is likely, after some argument, always to be taken over by physcialist reductionism.

Why is the physicalist reductionism a false philosophy? To begin with, let us note that reductionism was not successful even within physics itself. In the chain of names of sciences starting with physics and ending with sociology, the term physics can be replaced by two successive terms, atomic physics and thermodynamics, or roughly equivalently, microphysics and macrophysics. Then it is quite natural to apply a reductionistic effort to explain macrophysics by microphysics. This reductionism motivated a whole series of works started in the latter part of the nineteenth century, particularly by Maxwell, Boltzmann, and Gibbs, which is now incorporated in the so-called statistical mechanics, an atomistic explanation of large-scale phenomena. Did they succeed to reduce the macroscopic concept and laws in toto to the microscopic concepts and laws? In other words, could they build or explain macroscopic concepts or laws by the microscopic concepts or laws without introducing anything which did not belong to the microscopic concepts or laws? The answer is definitely no.

We can mention two important points. The zero-th law of thermodynamics and the second law of thermodynamics have been found not strictly reducible to atomic physics. More precisely, as far as the zero-th law is concerned, the concept of temperature is not a reducible concept, and as far as the second law is concerned, the increase of entropy cannot be deducible from the atomic laws. It is well known that the relation between macroscopic states and microscopic states is usually described as one-to-many correspondence. In reality even here the correspondence is often many-to-many in the sense that two macroscopic states can have some fuzzy overlapping. However, the simplification in terms of one-to-many correspondence is permissible, because we do not lose any essential features of the macroscopic state by this simplification. But in the case of temperature it is different. A given value of temperature T specifies an ensemble of systems with different (kinetic) energies with gradated weight (relative frequency) proportional to the famous Boltzmann factor $\exp(-E/kT)$ times the volume in the phase space.[9] In other words, the conditional probability $p(E/T)$ is not a delta function; neither has it a constant value for certain domain but a varying value depending on E. This implies, conversely, that if you have a finite system with a given microscopically defined (kinetic) energy E, this system can belong to an ensemble with different temperatures with gradated weights. In other words, the probability or weight $p(T/E)$ has a certain spread[10] and its value is not constant. And this weight (being essentially an inverse conditional probability) has to be determined by the Bayes rule; hence it is not a function only of E and T but depends on the prior probabilities of T which can very well depend on elements other than the physical states. The many-to-many correspondence between the temperature and the (kinetic) energy is thus even not determined by the two values E and T. It is not a fixed correspondence; it changes in each experiment. Many physicists express this fact by saying that temperature is not a physical quantity. It is a parameter in an estimation. This is not surprising, because the temperature is a numerical substitute for the reflexive, symmetrical, transitive relation that exists in the so-called thermal equilibrium. Nobody can expect an exact amount of kinetic energy of gas reached by a simple diathermal contact with a thermal bath. Temperature is thus an irreducible concept.

Let us next consider the second part of the second law of thermodynamics which says that the entropy of an (adiabatically) isolated system cannot decrease with time. Proving positively this law with the help of the atomic laws and of some imported alien elements constitutes the task of the H-theorem and is, as is well known, a complicated task (Watanabe, 1966b). But to show negatively that this law is not reducible to the atomic laws is very easy. All the atomic law is reversible, that is, if a phenomenon is allowed by the atomic law, then its time-reversed phenomenon is also allowed by the atomic law. Hence, if a phenomenon which results in an increase in entropy is allowed, then a phenomenon which results in a decrease in entropy must also be allowed. If this is prohibited, there must be an additional condition which was not in the atomic physics and which has to be smuggled in from outside. Hence, the second law is irreducible.[11]

Identity Theory requires one-to-one correspondence, reductionism presupposes one-to-one or at least one-to-many correspondence. Many-to-many correspondence is irreconcilable with reductionism. Further, if the many-to-many correspondence is unfixed, dependent on alien factors, then reductionism has no hope to survive.

3. Improper Predicates

Temperature is a good example of an improper predicate-variable. Each macroscopic system x is supposed, according to the present-day physics, to be in a well-defined microscopic state, whether or not we know which. Hence it has also a well-defined energy. But if we ask its temperature T, the answer is a probability distribution, $p(T/x)$ with a finite spread, however small the width of this spread may be. This indeterminacy is not due to our ignorance about a well-defined value of temperature, but the notion of temperature is by definition such that there is no fixed value for each system x. Yet, it is false to say that the predicate, "has temperature θ degrees", is inapplicable to the system.

In general, a predicate is said to be improper if at each time instant,[12] we cannot consistently assume the existence of a fixed (well-defined) set of objects which make the predicate true. The predicates which are not improper are proper predicates and they satisfy the "postulate of fixed truth set" which is violated by improper predicates. It should be noted that we use the phrase "we cannot consistently assume the existence of" instead of just saying, "there do not exist." The purpose of this expression is to make sure that we mean the nonexistence in principle and do not mean our ignorance about an existing exact extension.

The discovery of the existence of improper predicates is actually nothing new. When the philosophers made a distinction between a primary quality and a secondary quality, they noticed the dependence of the truth set of a secondary quality on other factors than the predicate itself and the objects involved. In fact the yes-or-no determination of the predicate "red" depends on the illumination and the state of the observer. But this type of improper predicate did not cause much trouble because by a small modification of the predicate we could make it look like a proper predicate. For instance, we could add to the definition of red based on sensation a certain condition about the illumination and a certain physical and mental condition of the observer; then the redness can become apparently a proper predicate. (Substitution of wavelength for redness is not an honest way of solving the problem.) But recent developments of science seem to indicate a widespread necessity and existence of improper predicates, in particular those improper predicates which cannot be converted to proper predicates as was assumed to be the case with secondary qualities.

Insofar as we are dealing with a proper predicate Q, we can introduce a characteristic function $f(Q/x)$ which is 0 or 1, and Q defines a subset of the set of objects X to which x belongs by the condition $f(Q/x) = 1$. For the improper predicate we cannot guarantee the existence of anything like the characteristic function. However, in order not to abandon everything, we may first try a natural generalization of the characteristic function $f(Q/x)$, by allowing it to take any value in the domain [0, 1]. For the time being, we do not even say whether or not $f(Q/x)$ is a probability of some sort.

This generalization is suggested by many newer trends in different fields of science. I shall enumerate five of them. First, we should mention a new outlook in the field of biocybernetics. About twenty years ago, people were fascinated by the triple coincidence that the neuron can take only two states, "fired" or "not-fired," that the best digital computation can be done by the binary number system, and that the logic is nothing but a handling of binary functions of a binary argument which is true or false. This gave rise to the McCulloch-Pitts theory (McCulloch and Pitts, 1943) which in spite of its stimulating nature misled many people for many years, giving the impression that the nervous system is sending and processing information on a binary basis. But in reality a neuron has also hidden continuous parameters such as dendric potential, etc. Further, the information sent by a neuron is not only coded on a discrete binary basis, but is also coded in terms of continuously valued intervals between consecutive spikes or "firings." Also, there are about 10^{10} neurons in a human nervous system, but there is every evidence that a man can store many times more than 10^{10} bits in his memory, showing that the binary theory of neurons is entirely inadequate in explaining memory. This may be partly explained by molecular memory, but between the molecular structure and the binary states of neurons there must be at different levels many other continuous variables which contribute to the memory. The new trend in brain-model-making is to use elements with continuous instead of binary states (Watanabe, 1968b, Dreyfus, 1965; Inomata, 1967). This seems to suggest that in logic, too, we should start from a continuously valued characteristic function rather than from the usual binary-valued characteristic function.

The second source of inspiration may not be called a new trend in science. But, it seems to this author that the usual way of defining probability after we have defined logic is entirely against the real nature of the matter (Watanabe, 1969a). According to the present-day theory, we have to define first a Borel field or more simply a Boolean lattice and thereupon introduce a σ-additive measure or a probability function according to Kolmogoroff's prescription. The former has its root in the binary characteristic function, that is, a true-or-false logic. But if we reflect a little on our daily experience, this must be found to be all wrong. We have first a vague probabilistic causal knowledge, and the logic emerges as a special case. First, there is a conditional probability of the type $p(A|B)$, and then $B \to A$ emerges as a special case $p(A|B) = 1$.[13] We can give an example showing how the notion of conditional probability $p(A|B)$ is more natural than the material implication $B \to A$. Everybody who has taught elementary logic knows how it is difficult for the human brain to understand the relation, $\phi \to A$ for all A, where ϕ is absurdity. There is a reason for that, because $B \to A$ with $B \neq \phi$ can be characterized by the fact $p(A|B) = 1$, but $\phi \to A$ cannot, because $p(A|\phi) = p(A \cap \phi)/p(\phi) = 0/0 =$ indeterminate. For this and many other reasons, it seems much more natural to start with some probability-like quantity such as the continuously valued characteristic function with an expectation that the usual black-and-white logic will emerge as a special case at a later stage.

The third source of encouragement comes from quantum mechanics. It is well-known by now that the quantum mechanics states that if we measure a physical quantity q on a system x, then there is no black-and-white certitude whether we get a particular value q_o; there is only a probability $p(Q/x)$ where Q stands for "obtain the value q_o on the measurement of the quantity q." This probabilistic nature is not due to our ignorance or to an imperfection of the measurement, but is due to the very nature of the physical world. It is true that occasionally $p(Q/x)$ can become unity. However, if x is in such a state, there exists another proposition R for which $p(R/x)$ is neither 0 nor 1. In such a case, R is said to be incompatible with Q.

As a fourth argument supporting our continuous characteristic function, we may mention the notion of "fuzzy set" advocated by L. Zadeh (1965). According to him, practically every notion has fuzzy membership. Who is, and who is not tall? Who is, and who is not bald? etc. He introduces what he calls membership function $\mu(Q, x)$ which measures the degree to which an object x can be considered as a member of class Q. $0 \leqslant \mu \leqslant 1$. He further postulates

$$\mu(Q \cap R, x) = \underset{Q, R}{\text{Min}} \left[\mu(Q, x), \mu(R, x) \right]$$
$$\text{and } \mu(Q \cup R, x) = \underset{Q, R}{\text{Max}} \left[\mu(Q, x), \mu(R, x) \right].$$

This certainly satisfies the probability axiom: $p(Q) + p(R) = p(Q \cap R) + p(Q \cup R)$, but this definition of $p(Q \cap R, x)$ and $p(Q \cup R, x)$ seems to be too narrow to allow him to derive many interesting results. But it is obvious that we can consider his membership function as a variant of our characteristic function.

As the fifth argument, we shall mention the method used in modern mathematical psychology. It is essential to this new science that the state of a subject be characterized by the probability distribution $p(R_i | x)$ where R_i is one of the possible responses when the subject x is placed under a certain stimulus (let us assume for simplicity that we are interested only in one kind of stimulus). Even when the mathematical psychologists talk about a Markov chain, we should not imagine that an individual subject is a single chain following the Markov transitive probability. We should consider each subject as incorporating the entire ensemble of all possible individual chains. From a behavioral point of view, R_i is the predicate or state description of the subject and it is very significant that the psychologist has to assume that each individual has to be characterized by the probability on R_i.[14]

In the framework of thought of reductionism, each individual case must have a precise description in terms of lower-level concepts and a higher-level concept corresponding to a well-defined truth set consisting of a fixed collection of individual cases. If the higher-level concept is an improper predicate, this scheme will not work. In the case of reductionism, the correspondence between two levels is one-to-many. In the case of Identity Theory, the correspondence between two parlances is one-to-one. If concepts are improper, however, an individual case can belong to more than one concept of the same parlance. As a result, there cannot be such a thing as one-to-one correspondence of concepts. Thus the necessary existence of improper predicates destroys the very foundation of reductionism as well as that of Identity Theory.

4. Two Sources of Logic

It is obvious that if the characteristic functions are all binary, that is, if $f(Q/x) = 0$ or 1 for all x and all Q under consideration, then $f(Q/x) = 1$ determines a subset of X, and the entire logic can be derived from the set theory.[15] This logic is isomorphic with the set theory including its distributive law. This is our usual Boolean logic. Note $f(P \cap Q/x) = f(P/x) \cdot f(Q/x)$; $f(\neg Q/x) = 1 - f(Q/x)$.

But if $f(Q/x)$ is not necessarily 0 or 1, how should we come around to reconstruct a logic? To answer any basic question, we have to go back to the elementary starting point. As we have seen, the prototype of scientific thinking lies in the teleology-causality reciprocity connecting two interactions or two observations, earlier and later. Hence, we may take "if-this-then-that" as the most basic form of our rational thinking. So we should first try to define this "if-then" relation or implication with the help of the continuously valued characteristic function $f(Q/x)$, and then see what we can produce out of it.

Charles S. Peirce (1960) considered also what he calls illation as the basis of logic. He writes: "I have maintained since 1867 that there is one primary and fundamental logical relation, that is illation.... A proposition, for me, is but an argument divested of the assertoriness of its premises and conclusion. That makes every proposition a conditional at bottom" (vol. 3, p. 279). Thus the proposition "a is Q" should be reformulated as meaning that "if we take an indeterminate object and find it to be a, then it is Q." This mode of reinterpretation has a salutary effect on other problems. For instance, the notorious sentence: "The King of France is bald" will become "If we take an indeterminate person and find it to be the King of France, then he is bald." In this last formulation, all the trickiness of the original sentence has disappeared.

With the idea of implication or illation, how far can we go? Actually, with the help of a few more minor assumptions we can fairly easily show that the set P of predicates constitutes a lattice, which guarantees most of the axioms of logic. I shall now enumerate the basic assumptions to make P a lattice.

1. Between some pairs A, B of the set P there exists a reflexive, non-symmetric and transitive relation $A \to B$, which we read A implies B. Transitivity means, of course, that if $A \to B$ and $B \to C$, then $A \to C$. Further, if $A \to B$ and $B \to A$, then $A = B$.

2. *P* contains a member ϕ which implies all the members of *P*. *P* contains a member $\square$ which is implied by all the members of *P*.

3. For any given pair *A*, *B* of *P* there exists another member *C* of *P* which is the conjunction $A \cap B$ of *A* and *B*. The definition: For the given pair *A*, *B* consider the subset *Y* of all those members of *P* which imply both *A* and *B*. That member of *Y* which is implied by all the members of *Y* is called the conjunction of *A* and *B*.

4. For any given pair *A*, *B* of *P* there exists another member *C* of *P* which is the disjunction $A \cup B$ of *A* and *B*. The definition: Interchange "implies" and "is implied by" in the above definition.

In order to be able to use the negation in our logic, we have to show that our lattice is a complemented lattice. In order to introduce the negation in a lattice which is not necessarily Boolean, the following three properties of negation are suitable and sufficient.

5. If *A* is a member of *P* then there is another member, denoted $\neg A$, in *P* such that

(5a) If $B = \neg A$, then $A = \neg B$ (double negation)
(5b) If $A \rightarrow B$, then $\neg B \rightarrow \neg A$ (contraposition)
(5c) If $A \rightarrow \neg A$, then $A = \phi$ (self-contradiction)

If axioms (1) through (5) are satisfied then the *P* is a complemented lattice which guarantees the following basic laws:

I.   Idempotent Law: $(A \cap A = A, A \cup A = A)$

II.   Associative Law: $[(A \cap B) \cap C = A \cap (B \cap C), (A \cup B) \cup C = A \cup (B \cup C)]$

III. Commutative Law: $[A \cap B = B \cap A, A \cup B = B \cup A]$

IV.   Absorptive Law: $[A \cap (A \cup B) = A, A \cup (A \cap B) = A]$

V.   De Morgan's Law: $[\neg(A \cap B) = \neg A \cup \neg B, \neg(A \cup B) = \neg A \cap \neg B]$

VI.   Implication: $A \rightarrow B$ is equivalent to $A = A \cap B$ or $B = A \cup B$

VII. Constant Absurdity and Constant Truth: $\neg\phi = \square, \neg\square = \phi, \phi \cap A = \phi, \phi \cup A = A, \square \cap A = A, \square \cup A = \square$

VIII. Contradiction and Excluded Middle: $A \cap \neg A = \phi, A \cup \neg A = \square$.[16]
In a word, the complemented lattice provides everything we need in logic except for the distributive law. For details see Watanabe, 1961, 1966a, 1969a, and 1969c.)

Now we shall show informally and briefly without proof how we can derive the basic axioms (1) through (5) from our nonbinary characteristic functions $f(Q/x)$.

We said that the predicate *Q* is an applicable predicate to an object *x*. We interpret this as meaning that there is a method of observation to determine whether or not Q is true on x. Hence, the outcome of the observation is always binary, but the state of the object is described by a probability (or relative frequency) $f(Q/x)$. This is precisely the case in quantum mechanics as well as mathematical psychology. If $f(A/x) = f(B/x)$ for all x, we write $A = B$.

First, we have to define a compound predicate AB from a pair of predicates. AB is true if and only if both test of A and test of B give affirmative results, whereby the test of A is done immediately after the test of B. We say that A is a simple predicate if $f(AA/x) = f(A/x)$ for all x, that is, $AA = A$. If $f(AA/x) \neq f(A/x)$ for some x, we say that A is a complex predicate. A predicate that is specified to be neither simple nor complex means generally a simple predicate. If A and B are such that $f(AB/x) = f(BA/x)$ for all x, or simply $AB = BA$, we say that A and B are compatible and write $A \sim B$. This compatibility relation is reflexive, symmetric but nontransitive.

The implication $A \rightarrow B$ is defined by the conditions: $A \sim B$ and $AB = A$. We can easily prove the transitivity: if $A \rightarrow B$ and $B \rightarrow C$, then $A \rightarrow C$. We can also easily define ϕ and $\square$ by $\phi \sim A$, $\square \sim A$, for all A and $f(\square/x) = 1$, $f(\phi/x) = 0$ for all x. The existence of a conjunction (and disjunction) is guaranteed. In fact, if we consider an infinitely long sequence $\dots ABABAB \dots$, we can show this corresponds exactly to $A \cap B$. If $A \sim B$, this long sequence becomes AB, provided A and B are simple predicates. As far as the negation is concerned, we can satisfy all the axioms involving the negation by the definition that $f(\square A/x) = 1 - f(A/x)$ for all x.

Thus, we can retrieve a large portion of logic even in the case of a continuously valued characteristic function. The only thing we cannot obtain is the distributive laws, $A \cup (B \cap C) = (A \cup B) \cap (A \cup C)$, $A \cap (B \cup C) = (A \cap B) \cup (A \cap C)$. We cannot give the mathematical proof here because of its length, but we can further show that if P consists only of mutually compatible predicates $(A \sim B)$, then we can again prove the general validity of the distributive laws, in spite of the continuous values of the characteristic function. (For details see Watanabe, 1966a and 1969c.)

5. Indescribable Object

We have introduced the class of improper predicates by the condition that the characteristic function $f(A/x)$ is not 0 or 1 for at least some x. Of course, if we could eliminate just those objects for which the characteristic functions of some predicates are neither 0 or 1 from the set of objects under consideration, then the predicates would become again proper predicates. But generally we cannot do this, and even if we could that would artificially impoverish the actual world. In this section, we shall show the existence of two distinct cases of x which make the characteristic functions take on a value other than 0 and 1. In one case, the inbetween value of characteristic functions is due to an insufficient specification of (the state of) the object. In the other case, the object cannot be properly described in terms of the available predicates.

To do this analysis, we have to introduce two characterizations of our set P of predicates. In one case, all the predicates in the set P commute with one another, that is, for any two predicates A and B of P we have $f(AB/x) = f(BA/x)$ for all x, i.e., $A \sim B$. [This entails also $AB = A \cap B$.] In this case we shall speak of s commutative set of predicates. In the other case, that is, where there exists at least one pair (A, B) in P such that $f(AB/x) \neq f(BA/x)$ for some x, we shall speak of a noncommutative set of predicates. [This entails also $AB \neq A \cap B \neq BA$.]

What we can show is that in the commutative case, we can improve the specification of each x in such a way that with the improved specification all the available predicates become proper predicates. Without this improvement, x specifies only a mixture of different cases (object types), each of which, however, makes all the characteristic functions 0 or 1. This would guarantee the Postulate of Fixed Truth Set, hence also the distributive law. This is the kind of world we are accustomed to, with the usual logic and classical physics.

At the opposite end, we have a case of noncommutative P. In this case, we cannot make improper predicates disappear by improving the specification of x. In other words, there are some x for which not all characteristic functions can become 0 or 1. In such a case, we cannot say that x is in reality either in a state affirming the predicate or in a state negating the predicate. We cannot say either that x is in a mixture of affirmative and negative cases as we could in the commutative case. We have to say that x is in a latent state which is neither affirmative nor negative, nor a mixture of the two. It is simply indescribable by the predicate unless the observation is made. This destroys the Postulate of Fixed Truth Set, depriving the logic of the distributive law.

We have no space in this paper to demonstrate in detail what has been said above, but we can at least mention without proof some important points which constitute the gist of a rigorous proof. When the set (lattice) P of predicates is commutative, we can show that the characteristic function satisfies the basic axiom of probability

$$f(A/x) + f(B/x) = f(A \cap B/x) + f(A \cup B/x) \tag{1}$$

for all A, $B \in P$, and all x. Together with $f(\Box/x) = 1 - f(\phi/x) = 1$ for all x, this axiom (1) guarantees that for any given x the function $f(A/x)$ can be considered as a probability (defined on the distributive lattice P). The formula shows that we can assign arbitrary values (between 0 and 1) to three out of four terms in (1), say, $f(A/x) = a$, $f(B/x) = b$ and $f(A \cap B/x) = c$, provided $c \leqslant a$, $c \leqslant b$, $a + b - c \leqslant 1$. The last three restrictions are derived also from (1) respectively by substituting $A \cap \ulcorner B$ and $A \cap B$ for A and B, substituting $\ulcorner A \cap B$ and $A \cap B$ for A and B, and noticing $f(A \cup B/x) \leqslant 1$. This probability distribution can be explained by assuming that the object x is actually a mixture of four types of objects, x_1, x_2, x_3 and x_4, such that if $f(A/x_1) = 1, f(B/x_1) = 1; f(A/x_2) = 1$, $f(B/x_2) = 0; f(A/x_3) = 0, f(B/x_3) = 1; f(A/x_4) = 0, f(B/x_4) = 0$. Indeed if we mix these four in the ratio, $\rho_1 : \rho_2 : \rho_3 : \rho_4$ (with $\rho_1 + \rho_2 + \rho_3 + \rho_4 = 1$), we shall get the probability $a = f(A/x) = \rho_1 + \rho_2, b = f(B/x) = \rho_1 + \rho_3, c = f(A \cap B/x)$ $= \rho_1$. Thanks to the restrictions mentioned above, the solutions of these equations $\rho_1 = c, \rho_2 = a - c, \rho_3 = b - c, \rho_4 = 1 - a - b + c$ are all between 0 and 1 and satisfy $\rho_1 + \rho_2 + \rho_3 + \rho_4 = 1$. It is important to notice that each of the four types makes the characteristic function either 0 or 1 for any logical combinations made out of A and B. For instance, object type x_1 will make the characteristic function 1 for eight logical functions, $A \cap B, A, B, (A \cap B) \cup (\neg A \cap \neg B), A \cup B, A \cup \neg B, \neg A \cup B, \square$. Similarly, object type x_1 makes the characteristic function 0 for the remaining eight logical functions that can be made out of A and B.

What we have just done can be described more simply by saying that the entire possibility ($\square$) is divided into four disjoint elementary (atomic) propositions: $A \cap B, A \cap \neg B, \neg A \cap B, \neg A \cap \neg B$, which correspond to the four types x_1, x_2, x_3, x_4 and the probability of these four elementary propositions are precisely the required mixing proportion of these four object types. The characteristic function of an object type for a predicate is 1 if that predicate is implied by the elementary proposition corresponding to the object type, and is 0 otherwise. This description shows immediately how we can demonstrate a similar theorem when there are more than two predicates involved. We take the elementary (atomic) propositions of the given lattice P, which correspond to elementary object types, and consider the probabilities of these elementary propositions as the mixing ratio of the object types. These object-types are "pure states" in the sense that their characteristic functions are either 0 or 1 for any predicate belonging to P.

In a noncommutative case, the axiom (1) breaks down for some A, B and some x. For instance, under some conditions available in an example in physics, we obtain, $f(A/x) = 1, f(B/x) = 1/2, f(A \cap B/x) = 0$ and $f(A \cup B/x) = 1$. In a case like this, we see that what we have done above cannot be applied, and the decomposition of x into a mixture of pure state cannot be achieved.

Within a noncommutative lattice P, we can always select a subset of predicates which constitute a commutative sublattice P'. Thus, restricting our language we can again reestablish the distributive law and the concept of proper predicates. But this language is a deficient one in the sense that we are depriving ourselves of certain perfectly allowable utterances.

The so-called modular logic (which is more restrictive than the general nondistributive logic but less restrictive than the distributive logic) can be obtained by requiring the following two additional conditions of a nondistributive logic. In a nondistributive lattice, the axiom (1) breaks down as a general rule, but we may still require (i) that there exists at least one x for which the relation (1) holds for the entire P. In addition to this we require (ii) that for this particular

x, if A, B are such that $A \rightarrow B$ but not $B \rightarrow A$, then $f(B/x) > f(A/x)$. If these two requirements are satisfied, we can prove that if $A \rightarrow C$, then $A \cup (B \cap C) = (A \cup B) \cap (A \cup C) = (A \cup B) \cap C$. This law is called the modular law and amounts to admitting the distributive law under a restricted circumstance $(A \rightarrow C)$.

It is instructive to examine the effect of observation on the mixture of pure states. Coming back to the example mentioned above, suppose we have a mixture of x_1, x_2, x_3 and x_4. If we observe A first and get the affirmative result, the possibility of object types x_3 and x_4 is eliminated, because these two would have given a negative result by the observation of A. Suppose we carry out a second observation with respect to B right after the first observation of A, and get also an affirmative result. This eliminates the possibility of the object being x_2, leaving x_1 as the only possibility. This result will be the same if we interchange the order of A and B. This means that in the commutative case, the observation is just selecting well-fixed object types. But this interpretation would not work in the noncommutative case, because the result of AB and the result of BA are not the same. This means that in the noncommutative case, the observation not only selects the object, but also alters it. This point becomes more obvious by the following fact. In the commutative case, if $f(B/x) = 0$ then always $f(BA/x) = 0$ for any A. This is understandable because if x does not contain an object type which makes B affirmative, the result of observation of B will be always negative even if we do some other observation (A) before testing B. On the other hand, in the noncommutative case, $f(B/x) = 0$ and $f(BA/x) \neq 0$ are perfectly compatible. This shows that the observation of A changes the nature of x in the second case.

6. Implications on Reductionism and Mind-Body Problem

It was already indicated that the biological and psychological predicates are mostly improper predicates. Furthermore, we can reasonably suspect that most of them are noncommutative. In an extreme case, a microscopic physiological description of an organ will probably all but destroy the function of that organ. Hence, it will be noncommutative with another predicate which presupposes the normal function of the organ.[17] In psychology, the dependence of answers on the order of two questions is daily experience. We may then safely conclude that the description in terms of biological and psychological predicates does not satisfy the Postulate of Fixed Truth Set, invalidating the usual distributive logic. This, in turn, will deprive any attempt at identity theory or at reductionism of the basic assumption that there is such a thing as proper description of a person by biological and psychological predicates. See the last paragraph of Section 3 above. It should be noted that in the present context, "biological predicates" mean physiological tests and "psychological predicates" mean behavioral tests such as observation of responses and questionnaires. A person is indescribable by these predicates.

It is extremely interesting that we can come to this conclusion without referring to the introspective observation.[18] Hence we do not need to talk about the asymmetry to which K. Gunderson refers (Chapter 7 in this volume). In the present author's earlier paper (Watanabe, 1961), he referred to both the introspective description and the behavioral-neurophysiological description, each of which was assumed to be separately distributive. In this picture, if a person is in a pure state or a mixture in terms of the introspective description, he is neither a pure state nor a mixture in terms of the behavioral-neurophysiological description. The conclusion is not so different. The external psychological description is improper.

The mind-body problem is most typical when it refers to my mind and my body. The peculiarity of this case is that the interaction which is the cause of the breakdown of the concept of class is so intimately built in that there is no hope of avoiding it by any kind of approximation. If I observe or somebody else observes my body behaviorally or physiologically, my body is affected by being observed and this change in body is bound according to any reasonable mind-body theory to be accompanied by a change in my mind-observer. This is a kind of feedback of mind's own action. Furthermore, an opposite circular feedback exists in the mind-body problem: the very fact that I get physiological information about my brain, either through my own observation or through somebody else's observation of my brain, changes my mind in some way and this change must be accompanied by a change in my physiological state of brains, invalidating possibly the earlier observation (if it refers to the instant before my reception of the information). This second circular change has to be acknowledged even by a hard-headed materialist and makes his theory further difficult. The most ingenious theory of freedom put forward by Donald MacKay uses this second kind of circular interaction as the starting point of his argument (MacKay, 1967). Under these strong interactions no behavioral-physiological predicates can be "proper" in describing the mental state, and no mental predicates can be expected to be proper in describing the physiological state.

Returning to the general problem of loss of truth set and of the usual logic, we should repeat that this is due to the fact that the observation changes the observed system. In other words, this is due to the fact that we separated a mutually interacting whole into two portions, one observer, the other observed. This interaction is exceptionally weak in the case of classical physics of macroscopic objects, and for that reason we are accustomed to the notion of fixed truth set and the distributive logic. But it is absolutely unfounded to assume that the notion of truth set and distributive logic works also in the description of objects with which our interaction is strong. In microscopic physics, it is natural that the interaction is of the same order of strength as the observed microscopic phenomena, hence the interaction is appreciable. In the case of a biological problem the reason seems to be somewhat different. Namely, similar phenomena here are due to the extremely sensitive nature of the system under any external influence. In the mental problem, the interaction is characteristically amplified by the built-in feedback system.

In summary, the origin of the trouble is now obvious. It is due to separation of the inseparable: agent and reagent, observer and observed, life and physiology, mind and body. Wittgenstein will agree with oriental philosophers in refusing to create a new problem by separating the inseparable. But we should not just stop there. We should have the courage to separate the inseparable. But we must be prepared for the price we have to pay in so doing. The price we pay is a loss of a usual logic and the concept of class. If somebody lacks the courage to pay the due price, he is intellectually a coward. If he does not see this inevitable consequence, he is intellectually dishonest. The oriental philosophers were at least honest, if they were not very courageous. From this viewpoint of separation of the inseparable, it is easy to understand why the words "I", "now," and "here" are lacking in the physicalistic language. For it is precisely at the point of interaction between the agent and the reagent, between the observer and the observed, that "I" am "here" and "now." In the language which ignores this basic interaction, there cannot be a place for "I" or "here" or "now."

The author is grateful to J. J. C. Smart who read this manuscript carefully and raised many meaningful objections. The author allowed himself to include some of his answers to Smart's objections in the text as well as in the footnotes of this manuscript.

The work connected with the logical problem treated in this paper was partly supported by U.S. government research grant AF-AFOSR-68-1466.

NOTES

1. Those readers who are interested only in the problem of logic can skip the first two sections and start from Section 3. The purpose of the first two sections is to prepare the background from which our central problem of logical nature arises. Our analysis of this logical problem inversely is bound to alter drastically the whole aspect of this background.

2. See Watanabe, 1968c, for the newest result regarding the connection between the possibility of prediction (retrodiction) and the entropy increase (decrease).

3. This point has been raised by the author (Watanabe, 1966a). He mentioned that this difficulty is alleviated by Tomonaga's "flying saucer theory," because the information can be collected within a finite time, yet the prediction can be made only after the predicted event has happened.

4. This is another example of the basic asymmetry between prediction and explanation, which many philosophers of science have failed to notice.

5. In the agent-reagent view, the claim of science is much more modest than in the spectator view. It need not be an unfailing predictor to be a useful guide in choosing an appropriate means which probably leads to the desired end.

6. Hence ontological irreducibility implies nomological irreducibility. The author should point out a fundamental ontological irreducibility of biology to

physics which seems to be universally unnoticed. The essence of life does not reside in a living "matter," but in the very process of entrance and exit of matter. This is true not only of the ordinary functions accompanied by metabolism but also of the formation of proteins by the template action of DNA. The function of thinking cannot be an exception.

7. If Identity Theory literally implies a strict "identity" rather than equivalence or correspondence, how can the two descriptions be differentiated? If two can be identical, then why can three or four or one hundred not be identical? Why two?

8. Identity Theory may claim a correspondence between two structures or two networks of propositions instead of between two isolated propositions. But, how can such a structural correspondence be guaranteed to be unique?

9. When the degrees of freedom are very high, this volume increases very fast with energy. As a result, the spread of probability in energy is very sharp. Yet it is not a true delta function.

10. Small as it may be, it can vanish only in the limit of an infinitely large system.

11. Some reductionists would say that *strictly speaking* the second law is false. This means that the second law can be correct only in an inexact, approximate sense. Note the use of negative modifier "inexact" or "approximate" here. The most important point is that the second law is correct in a positively definable frame of concepts. These concepts are precisely what is irreducible. (See Watanabe, 1966b.)

12. It is understood that the object at each instant is in a certain state which may change with time. By specifying an instant, we fix the state.

13. In our notation, we do not bother to make distinction between a proposition and its name, A and "A". If two symbols are connected by a relation ($=$ or $\rightarrow$) we should understand that each of them is in quotation marks. If they are connected by a connective ($\cap$ or $\cup$) or if they are following the negation ($\neg$), they are not in quotation marks. In other words, $=$ and $\rightarrow$ belong to the metalanguage while $\cap$, $\cup$, and $\neg$ belong to the object language. In the distributive case, "A" $\rightarrow$ "B" is equivalent to saying that "$A \supset B$" is true. In the nondistributive case the former implies the latter, but the latter does not imply the former. In both distributive and nondistributive cases, "A" $\rightarrow$ "B" is equivalent to "$A \cap B$" $=$ "A". Any proposition A can be made to correspond one-to-one to a predicate by converting it into the form: The case is "such that A is true."

14. In the five arguments mentioned above, except the fourth, the capitalized Latin symbols, such as Q, R, A, B, can be considered as predicates whose truth-value can be determined by some observational procedure. In the fourth case, Q is meant to be a set, but Zadeh often states that belonging or not belonging to Q can be determined only by asking the opinion of persons, hence it is reducible to an observation. In the second case, the symbol is the name of a proposition, hence some of them can be verified directly by observation and some others are only indirectly connected to observations. But, even so, they can be reduced to predicates.

15. Q is a predicate and x is an object (in a certain state).

16. Conversely, two propositions that satisfy the laws of contradiction and of excluded middle are not necessarily the negation of each other in the non-distributive complemented lattice.

17. This argument may be crudely operationistic. But, a strategic operationism has often a salutary effect in destroying old realistic idola theatri.

18. This fact can perhaps be used to distinguish a robot from a man without entering into the problem of consciousness.

REFERENCES

Brillouin, L. 1959. *Life, Matter and Observation*. Paris: Albin Michel.

Dreyfus, H. L. 1965. "Alchemy and Artificial Intelligence." Internal publication, Rand Corporation.

Feigl, H. 1967. *The "Mental" and the "Physical": The Essay and a Postscript*. Minneapolis: University of Minnesota Press.

Inomata, S. 1967. "Panel Discussion on Pattern Recognition, Language and Artificial Intelligence," moderated by S. Inomata. In *Information Science and Cybernetics*, vol. 2, edited by AVIRG. (In Japanese.) Tokyo: Maruzen.

MacKay, D. 1967. "Freedom of Action in a Mechanistic Universe." A. S. Eddington Memorial Lecture, Cambridge University.

McCulloch, W. S., and Pitts, W. 1943. "A Logical Calculus of the Ideas Immanent in Nervous Activity." *Bulletin of Mathematical Biophysics* 5:115.

Peirce, C. S. 1960. *Collected Papers of Charles Sanders Peirce*. Edited by Charles Hartshorne and Paul Weiss. Vol. 3. Cambridge, Mass.: Harvard University Press.

Neumann, J. von. 1932. *Mathematische Grundlagen der Quantenmechanik*. Berlin: Julius Springer.

Watanabe, S. 1961. "A Model of Mind-Body Relation in Terms of Modular Logic." *Synthèse* 13 (4):261.

―――― 1966a. "Algebra of Observation." In *Progress of Theoretical Physics*, supplements 37 and 38 (dedicated to Professor Tomonaga), p. 350.

―――― 1966b. "Time and the Probabilistic View of the World." In J. T. Fraser, ed., *The Voices of Time*, p. 527. New York: Braziller.

―――― 1968a. "Epistemological Implications of Cybernetics." In *Proceedings of the XIV International Congress of Philosophy*, vol. 2, p. 594. University of Vienna.

―――― 1968b. "La simulation mutuelle de l'homme et de la machine." In S. Dockx, ed., *Civilisation Technique et Humanisme*, vol. 6, p. 19. Paris: Beauchesne.

―――― 1968c. "'Teleological' Explanation in Biophysics," *Progress of Theoretical Physics*, Supplement Extra Number (dedicated to Professor M. Kobayashi), p. 495.

―――― 1969a. *Knowing and Guessing*. New York: John Wiley and Sons.

―――― 1969b. "Modified Concepts of Logic, Probability and Information Based on Generalized Continuous Characteristic Function." *Information and Control* 15(1):1.

―――― 1970. "Creative Time." *Studium Generale* 23:1057.

——— 1972. "La futurologie et le concept du temps." In *La Méthode Prospective*, vol. 17, des Archives de l'Institut des Sciences Théoriques, p. 35.

Wigner, E. P. 1952. "Die Messung quantenmechanischer Operatoren." *Zeitschrift für Physik* 133:101.

Yanase, M. M. 1961. "Optimal Measuring Apparatus." *Physical Review* 123:666.

Zadeh, L. A. 1965. "Fuzzy Sets." *Information and Control* 8(3):338.

11

Can the
Cognitive Process Be
Totally Mechanized?

Satosi Watanabe

A MAN IS NOT a machine. A machine is not a man. If these two statements were both false, man and machine would be synonymous, and it would become meaningless to discuss the similarity and the difference between man and machine. We know there are some differences. The human body and the physical structure of a machine are not the same. Many people will agree also that the aesthetic, ethical and religious functions of a human being can not be simulated by a machine (Watanabe, 1959, 1968, 1969c). But, at least in the domain of cognitive processes, a legitimate doubt can be raised whether there is anything human intelligence can do and machine intelligence cannot, although the machine undoubtedly can carry out most of the known cognitive functions better and faster than the man. Thus, we ask ourselves in this paper the question: Can the cognitive process be totally mechanized?

This question by itself is interesting in the age of electronic computers and of wholesale mechanization of human beings in the society. But, beyond that, the question could be expected to shed new light on many age-old epistemological problems. Whatever has been taken for granted in human intelligence may acquire new importance if it is found to be lacking in machine intelligence. For this reason, we shall try to select topics which are closely related to traditional epistemological problems, rather than blindly following current hot topics in computer technology.

We shall first take up (Section 1) the problem of deduction which should be the strongest field for machine intelligence. We shall examine whether this area at least can be wholly mechanized. Next, we shall discuss induction (Section 2), which is not a purely logical process and hence could be beyond the capability of a machine. This brings up a difficult problem of the relationship between the aesthetic and the cognitive (Section 3), since induction involves the aesthetic. Any cognitive process presupposes the universal, and we should ask whether a machine is capable of forming concepts and universals on its own (Section 4). This question takes us to the controversial problem of pattern recognition (Section 5). This is important because a myth about human superiority in this domain is widespread. The computer is essentially an information "processor," and so is the human brain in some respects. But where is the information "producer"? (Section 6). This problem is intimately bound up with learning process and adaptation (Section 7). Adaptation, however, is not a monopoly of human intelligence; there are adaptive programmings for a computer, too. Then, what are the characteristically human aspects of adaptation? These are the questions we raise and seek to answer.

1. Deduction

Deduction is a logical process, and the computing machine is supposed to be capable of doing all logical processes correctly and efficiently. As a consequence, one might think that the computer is equally competent or superior to human intelligence, at least in the domain of deduction. This is not entirely the case.

The machine is an artifact which is capable of carrying out all logical operations (such as conjunction formation, etc.) and arithmetic operations, and which is furnished with sufficient memory space not only for the execution of the logical and arithmetic operations but also for keeping the rules of deduction, the assumed postulates, and the data. If we define the machine this way, it should be capable of carrying out logical deduction within the framework of formalized logic (which may be even non-Boolean), but it excludes automatically two kinds of informal deductive reasoning. One is the nonnumerical probabilistic deduction and the other is the so-called metalogic.

An example of nonnumerical probabilistic deduction runs somewhat like this: "If the sunset glow is beautiful, tomorrow is likely to be fair. The evening sky is as red as a tomato today. We may hope to have fine weather tomorrow." It is undeniable that this sequence of sentences is a deduction in a broad sense because a particular proposition is derived as likely to be true from a general proposition. It is noteworthy that on the one hand there is no necessity or certainly involved, and on the other it is impossible to express the degree of uncertainty as any numerical value like a probability. Furthermore, the conclusion depends considerably on feeling rather than reason, expressible in such terms as beautiful, red as a tomato, hope, etc. This kind of nonnumeric probabilistic deduction is very common in everyday life, but it is of course outside the scope of formalized deductive logic, hence outside the reach of a machine.

The fact that there exists a valid theorem in arithmetic for which the machine cannot produce a demonstration is a conclusion derivable from Gödel's theorem and the definition of machine given above, and by itself it is nothing interesting. But what is interesting is the coexistence in human mind of the two layers of reasoning, informal (metalanguage) and formal (object language), and it seems to be precisely in virtue of the coexistence of the two-layer structure that Gödel's theorem can be proven (Lucas, 1961, p. 112). In other words, the machine is incapable not only of producing a demonstration to a certain valid theorem but also of producing the general theorem underlying this incapability. It is granted that metalanguages can be formalized step by step, but there seems to be necessarily one term left out of this infinite regression.

During the development of human civilization, there must have been at first a stage at which men recognized the existence of types of reasoning which everybody agreed to be valid, and the logical rules must then have been extracted from these valid types of reasoning by a kind of inductive process. As we shall see later, induction is a kind of operation the machine is incapable of executing in its entirety. The formulation of a formal logic on the basis of the vaguely conceived rules of logic is again a product of a process which is inductive in nature, hence this, too, is outside the reach of a machine. What is feasible by the machine is only execution of demonstrative processes within the given formal system.

The above-mentioned two kinds of impossibilities derive directly from the fact that the tasks involved lie overtly outside the legitimate domain of a formal deductive system, and in that sense, they are not interesting. I shall now mention three more types of impossibilities which involve tasks apparently within the legitimate domain of a deductive system. An interesting fact in these cases is that man circumvents the difficulties with the help of certain techniques of which the machine seems to be incapable.

One form of typical deduction is theorem proving. We are given a theorem in addition to all the axioms, definitions, rules of inference. The machine is required to produce a sequence of propositions logically derivable from the axioms terminating with the given theorem. In principle, one might think that the machine needs only to generate all true propositions derivable from the axioms and one of them will turn out to be the given theorem, provided that the theorem is "provable." If the machine keeps the record of all the logical operations used in the derivation, that record will be the required proof. But in practice this is impossible, because the number of possible theorems will increase enormously fast with the number of steps the demonstration takes. The human mind uses special techniques of narrowing down this fanning-out process of the derivation, some of which can be formulated as machine-legible algorithms and fed into the machines. These machine-legible algorithms indeed tend to decrease the number of steps but do not eliminate the fanning-out search trees entirely (Gelernter, 1959; Wang, 1960). More important, these algorithms are man-made and it is doubtful, whether they can ever be produced by machines only. One possible algorithm is to start from both ends, that is, from the axioms down and from the theorem up.* The first way is deductive but the second is inductive, because one has to produce a true proposition(s) from which the desired theorem is derivable. The inductive process is not logical and it cannot guarantee to hit the right answer. In usual programming of this kind, some man-made inductive heuristic algorithm is fed into the machine. In summary we can say that a purely deductive machine is in practice incapable of proving not only unprovable theorems but also some provable theorems.

So much for theorem proving. Another important aspect of deductive inference is the process of prediction, which consists in deriving the future (final) state of a system from the present (initial) state of the system with the help of a dynamical law governing the system. In order to deal properly with the problem of prediction, we have to clarify two widespread misunderstandings. First, the process of prediction cannot be completed at the "initial" instant unless the system is finite and is guaranteed to be isolated from the time at which the initial data are collected (this time instant has to be earlier than the "initial" instant) to the "final" time to which the prediction refers. If we feed the machine with this assumption of isolation, the machine can deductively derive the final state, but the machine itself cannot guarantee the correctness of the assumption. In human predictive process, this assumption is made on a vast empirical knowledge of the surrounding world which cannot be deductively derived from a set of postulates. See Watanabe, 1970, for a detailed discussion of this problem.

Second, neither human predictor nor machine predictor can take every detail of the initial state into account in an actual prediction, because that would take too long to have the prediction completed at the time when it is needed. Only a limited number of salient features of the initial state is taken into account in prediction with the hope that the final state is not appreciably affected by the neglected items in the initial state. This is the cause of the basic asymmetry between (anterior) prediction and (ulterior) explanation, because the latter has the privilege of calling in some apparently insignificant initial features which would have been ignored in prediction. That means that there is no foolproof criterion for importance as to which features have relevance in determining the future. The judgment of importance usually has to be left to human hunch, which is by no means a mechanical process governed by a set of rules.

We have shown in this section that practically every aspect of deductive process presupposes certain functions of human mind which are not only non-deductive but also often nonrational. For this reason, the machine will not be able to perform deductive functions without human assistance.

---

*This differs from the method of starting from the negation of the given theorem and showing that this leads to an absurdity or a contradiction with the axioms. This contrapositional method may in some cases become shorter, but it is a deductive algorithm and does not result in an essential change in the nature of difficulties.

2. Induction

Induction consists of two phases. In phase one, which may be called abduction according to Charles Peirce, we have to produce worthwhile hypotheses. In phase two, which may be called induction proper, we have to evaluate the relative merits of existing hypotheses in the presence of evidential facts. It is possible to assume abduction itself as consisting again of two stages, one of randomly producing as many candidate hypotheses as possible and one of quickly evaluating them without paying much attention to their exact correspondence with the evidential facts. Thus, a mechanical model of abduction would involve a blind mechanism which grinds out all possible hypotheses and a monitoring mechanism which rejects worthless hypotheses. But this model is utterly impossible, first because there is no such thing as a fixed knowable set of possible hypotheses, and there seems to be an endlessly growing number of possibilities for new hypotheses. Second, we cannot think of any mechanical way of evaluating hypotheses without reference to logic and evidence. In human abduction, it is certain that not "all possible" hypotheses are "ground out"; hypotheses are somehow created in very much the same fashion as art objects are produced. The merit of each hypothesis, before it is placed before the tribunal of induction proper, is appraised mainly according to an aesthetic sense of the human creator. This seems to indicate that the abductive part of induction is entirely outside the realm of mechanical simulation, in the same way as true creation of art objects cannot be mechanized. So much for abduction; now for induction proper.

I cannot forget a brief conversation I had with Professor Carnap in 1951, right after he gave his lecture on probability and induction at one of the American Physical Society meetings in Chicago. To my question: "Do you mean that induction can be done by a machine?" he answered in essence (if my memory is correct), "I do not predict the actual appearance of an inductive machine in the near future, but insofar as a machine is defined as capable of carrying out all *necessary* inference, induction in principle is machine-feasible." I felt immediately that this conclusion was wrong, and now, after seventeen years, I know why Carnap was misled and where he made a mistake.

The source of Carnap's misconception can be located in his belief in the Keynesian (necessary) view of probability which maintains that given any arbitrary pair of propositions A and B, the value of conditional probability of A given B, $p(A|B)$ is necessarily determined by the nature of the two propositions A and B, independently of human evaluation. This necessity should be understood in a certain analogy to logical implication between two propositions. Thus, if a hypothesis h and a set of particular events e are given, not only the probability $p(e|h)$ of the occurrence of e on the ground of h but also the probability (credibility) $p(h|e)$ of the hypothesis h on the ground of evidence e would be determined by the necessary relationship existing between h and e. The latter probability is the famous c-function, $c(h, e)$ of Carnap (1950). The evaluation of the quantity $p(h|e)$ should constitute the process of induction proper.

I have shown elsewhere (Watanabe, 1965b, 1969a) that for a given pair of propositions A and B, if the conditional probability $p(A|B)$ is determined by the definitions of A and B, then the inverse conditional probability $p(B|A)$ is not determined by the definitions of A and B, except in the case where the unconditional probability $p(B)$ also is determined by the definitions. This is so because $p(B|A)$ is proportional to $p(A|B)$ times $p(B)$. Applied to the present case, this theorem tells us that since $p(e|h)$ is determined by the nature of h and e (in fact, that is the content of the hypothesis), the inductive credibility $p(h|e)$ is not determined by the nature of h and e except in the case the (prior) credibility $p(h)$ of hypothesis, apart from any evidence, is determined solely by h itself. This last condition is never satisfied (see below), hence the credibility $p(h|e)$ is not determined by h and e alone.

What are the extra-evidential factors in determining the credibility of hypotheses? That is, what factors other than the relationship between evidence e and hypothesis h affect the value of $p(h|e)$? The relationship between e and h is the degree to which the hypothesis h is supported or confirmed by the evidence e. As a consequence, the extra-evidential factors in question can be characterized also as those which affect the credibility of h for reasons other than confirmation. The existence of these extra-evidential factors refutes the basic assumption of Carnap's theory. We shall mention some of the extra-evidential factors that are obviously at work when a scientist is evaluating a hypothesis.

(i) Other Hypotheses. Suppose we have a hypothesis which is confirmed to a satisfactory degree by the evidence. If, however, we suddenly hit upon another hypothesis which agrees with the evidence to a still better degree, then the credibility of the first hypothesis has to decrease although its degree of confirmation remains the same. In general, the credibility of a hypothesis depends on other competitive hypotheses. This is inevitable because, we think, if one hypothesis is true the others must be false.

(ii) Theory Making. A hypothesis governing one domain of experience and another hypothesis governing a related but different domain of experience must be united harmoniously by a higher level hypothesis in a theoretical structure. The ease and beauty with which such a unifying theory is possible affect inversely the measure of credibility of lower level hypotheses.

(iii) Deductive Influence. As explained above, a lower level hypothesis h' plays the role of evidence for a high level hypothesis h''. It often happens that a higher level hypothesis h'' is modified due to some reason found in a domain different from the domain of h'. But, since h' is deductively affiliated to h'', the modification of h'' entails a modification of h' (or modification of credibility distribution among the set of competitive hypotheses to which h' belongs).

(iv) Aesthetic Evaluation. There are usually many (often infinitely many) hypotheses which are equally confirmed by the available evidence and the choice made by scientists is based mainly on an aesthetic preference. Elegance, simplicity and compactness, etc., are usually sought after in formulating and choosing hypotheses.

Among the four extra-evidential factors mentioned above, (i) is introduced through the normalization condition of the inductive credibility $p(h|e)$ with respect to the h's. The remaining three have to be introduced through the evaluation of the prior credibility $p(h)$. Some of the extra-evidential factors may be calculated by a computer, but the aesthetic elements cannot be entirely carried out by a machine.

The basic issue here is the necessary concurrence of the two conflicting factors: the a posteriori reflected in the evidential confirmation and the a priori reflected in the extra-evidential evaluation. Should one ask which of the two is stronger in determining our judgment with regard to induction, we have to say that, insofar as the volume of our experience is finite, the a priori judgment could overrule the a posteriori, but at the limit of infinite experience, the a posteriori will defeat any a priori prejudgment (Watanabe, 1965b). As beings with finite experience, we have to learn to harmonize the two. The establishment of this harmony is hopelessly beyond the capability of a computer. Carnap's theory considers only what is called the a posteriori in the present context.

3. The Aesthetic and Knowledge

In connection with abduction, and again in connection with the extra-evidential evaluation of hypotheses, I mentioned the essential role played by the aesthetic and stated that this cannot be performed by a machine. Let us now explain why it is so.

First, one may think that we can formulate different aesthetic criteria in a machine-legible language and let the machine select those which pass the criteria. It is true that such an attempt succeeds apparently to some extent, but the selection by a *codified* criterion is never a true aesthetic selection. The basic reason for this is that primarily there are individual beautiful things, but there has never been an exhaustive set of codes by which these beautiful things can be defined. For instance, the moment we set up a rule of beauty, there occurs immediately a desire to break this rule. This is inevitable because the true aesthetic judgment is a living and moving thing, while the codified criteria are dead and fixed. Besides, the aesthetically valuable is not a synonym of the beautiful.

Second, we could supply the machine with some kind of codes of beauty as stated above, but the machine cannot produce these codes by itself. The fundamental reason for this impossibility stems from the fact that the aesthetic in a human is intimately related to his entire unified system of internal values. It has its root in his physiological chemistry and its ultimate height blends with his religious or religion-like ideals. Unless the machine acquires a unified system of internal values, it cannot produce an aesthetic judgment of its own.

Third, as stated above, the value of an artistic creation lies in its individuality, and not in its membership in the class of beautiful or aesthetically valuable things. Seen from the nomological point of view, each individual object is nothing but a stochastic instantiation. The difference between the attitude of regarding an object as an individual carrying a special meaning and the attitude of regarding an object as a mere stochastic instantiation divides the scientific-universalistic language and the aesthetic-existentialistic language. The machine can understand only the scientific-universalistic language.

It cannot be overemphasized that the statistical-nomological approach can never fully characterize an individual object and discover its meaning. Taking the simplest case of a sequence of Bernouilli trials, the rule can produce an infinite variety of sequences. From the point of view of probability rules, each sequence is nothing but a stochastic sample, but one of them may be carrying a special message for a particular person.

Creation cannot be a product of a set of rigid rules. Hence, any simulation of art creation by computer utilizes somewhere in the program the so-called random-number-producing subroutine or something equivalent, in addition to certain rules of composition. One might object that the so-called random-number-producing program is in reality a fixed rule of producing numbers, hence its product is not a true random number. We can, however, overcome this objection, for instance by coupling the computer to a Geiger tube measuring high-energy particles emitted by some radioactive substance. The truly crucial point is that the product is just a stochastic sample devoid of individuality with meaning. It is true that by some accident a particular listener (in the case of computer-produced music) might attach a special meaning to a particular stochastic sample. But the computer-composer has no content to express by its creation. Hence, it is not creation.

4. Concept Formation

We do not usually raise the slightest doubt about the existence of a class of animals called swans, a class of ducks, a class of objects called desks, a class of objects called chairs. This implies that two swans are more alike than one swan and one duck. By "more alike," everybody would agree, we mean "sharing more predicates." Two swans share more predicates than a swan and a duck. But is this all true?

The negative answer is given by the following Theorem of the Ugly Duckling (Watanabe, 1965a, 1969a). Insofar as the total number of available predicates is finite and all the predicates considered can be meaningfully applied to (that is, either affirmed or negated by) all the objects considered, the number of predicates shared by any pair of two nonidentical objects is the same. By nonidentical is meant distinguishable by some of the predicates under consideration. When we enumerate the shared predicates, we consider all possible logical functions of the predicates available.

This theorem shows that from a purely logical point of view, there exist no such things as classes of similar objects if two members should be more similar than one member and one nonmember. In other words, any arbitrary grouping of objects can be claimed to be a class of similar objects if a member and a nonmember should not be more similar than two members. For each of such groupings, there exists a predicate which is affirmed by all the members and negated by all the nonmembers. This predicate is the intension of the concept corresponding to the extension represented by the objects included in the grouping. But such an arbitrary grouping is obviously not what is usually meant by a class and a concept.

What went wrong in our statement at the beginning of this section about the undoubtable existence of certain classes? The error was lurking in defining similiarity by enumeration of shared predicates. From the logical point of view, there is no such thing as "importance" of a predicate, but in the empirical life there are more important and less important predicates. By similarity, then we mean sharing of more important predicates. A class of objects is a grouping of objects such that the number of important predicates shared by two members is larger than that shared by a member and a nonmember. The concept formation therefore depends on the scale of importance we attach to available predicates. So does the "universal."

The crucial question concerns then the source of this preferential importance placed on certain predicates. In simple daily life, predicates which are directly connected with our sensory organs are usually given more importance than complicated logical functions formed from them. Thus, redness and heaviness will be more important than the combinations "red and nonheavy" or "heavy exclusive or nonred." We may roughly say that, by the development of sensory organs during the process of evolution, those predicates which have close relations to survival and other goals of life have come to be detected directly. Thus, a frog's eyes sense directly the predicate bug-likeness, and the nose of every animal discriminates foul food.

The scale of importance of predicates therefore actually originates from the purpose which the resulting concepts and classification can serve. The distinction between edible and nonedible objects is vital for any animal, although such a distinction may be a very complicated notion from the chemical point of view. This value-dependence of concept does not stop at the animal level. All our concepts in life are strongly dependent on our value system.

A corollary to the value-dependence of concepts is the nonuniqueness of concepts. For formation of a classificatory zoology, it is more convenient to place the whale with the elephant in a class, but there should be no hesitation, for a certain industrial purpose, in placing the whale with the tuna in a class. To make an elegant physical theory, the concept of absolute temperature is very appropriate, but for the purpose of characterizing our comfort, the concept of THI (temperature-humidity index, which is a special function of physical temperature and humidity) is more appropriate. Neither the absolute temperature nor the THI can claim to be the "correct concept."

Let us now try to relegate the function of concept formation to a machine. We can do that by feeding the machine with a certain scale of importance of predicates. What we cannot do is to make the machine produce the scale of importance of its own, in particular, a scale which is intimately coupled with the unified personal value system of the person (machine).

5. Pattern Recognition

There is a common misunderstanding with regard to the true nature of the inherent limitations of mechanical method of pattern recognition. These limitations are essentially of the same nature as those we saw in connection with induction and concept formation. To make our argument concrete, let us define the problem of pattern recognition as follows: We are shown during the so-called training period a certain number of objects of Class I and a certain number of objects of Class II. We are told the properties of each object and its class-belongings. They are class-samples, or "paradigms." After the training period, we enter the so-called recognition period, during which we are shown new objects whose properties are known but whose class-belonging is not. We are required to place each of these new objects into either Class I or Class II in simulation of the paradigms. For instance, we may be shown during the training period ten photos of Mr. A and ten photos of Mr. B. During the recognition period, we are shown a new photo known to be of either Mr. A or Mr. B but not which. Our task is to determine whether it is Mr. A or Mr. B.

The usual story about mechanical pattern recognition is that no machine can detect such subtle and Gestalt-like features as those which distinguish the face of Mr. A from that of Mr. B. I maintain that if the machine by itself cannot distinguish Mr. A from Mr. B, it is not because the features are too subtle or Gestalt-like. It is only because there is no logical and necessary ground according to the Theorem of the Ugly Duckling to place the new picture together with the sample pictures of Mr. A or with those of Mr. B. If we decompose the picture into a large number n of meshes and measure the grayness of each mesh, we can represent the whole picture by an n-component vector. Even a subtle or Gestalt-like property is a function, complicated as it may be, of these n variables, and the machine would be able to detect it if we gave this function to the machine. The only thing is that we are incapable of formulating such a mathematical function.

A machine with its logical mind devoid of an inherent value-system of its own cannot recognize simple patterns any better than complicated patterns. The only difference is that in the case of simple patterns we men can indoctrinate the machine with our scale of importance of predicate-variables, whereas in the case of complicated or subtle patterns, we men have some difficulty in translating our scale of importance into the machine-legible language.

The key point is that there exists no such thing as similarity or nearness or distance between two objects in the pure world of logic. In our human or animal world of perception, we have a certain scale of similarity, which implies that some special predicate variables are more important than some others. This preferential weighing is intimately related to our internal system of values. The reason why we succeed in making machines carry out the task of pattern recognition in simpler cases is that we can tell the machine a special way of calculating the degree of similarity or distance. For instance, we often let the machine use the Euclidean distance between two vectors as the measure of dissimilarity between the two objects represented by these vectors. This may seem natural and innocuous, but this is a typical case of "cheating," in the sense that we are passing our sense of importance to the machine in a clandestine fashion. In simpler cases we often succeed in cheating, but in more complicated cases we fail. As a matter of fact, the Euclidean distance is not an invariant for unorthogonal or nonlinear transformations of variables, hence it is contingent on the accidental way in which the variables are measured and expressed. Unless this last is specified, the distance remains an undefined quantity.

All these troubles originate from the simple fact that pattern recognition is a logically unsolvable problem. Everybody senses that pattern recognition is a special case of induction. But, except for one paper by myself, (Watanabe, 1969b) no serious effort has been made to clarify the relationship between induction and pattern recognition. I shall now briefly explain why I call pattern recognition a double induction.

In pattern recognition, three types of propositions are involved. A "hypothesis," H_j, is a statement of the type "An object of Class I has such and such properties and an object of Class II has such and such properties." A "classificatory proposition," A_k ($k =$ I, II), states that "the object belongs to Class I (or II)." A "descriptive proposition," D_i, states that "the object has such and such properties." The basic deduction of classification is of the type: $H_j \cap A_k \to D_i$. If hypothesis H_j is true and if the object is of class k, then it should have properties as described by D_i. During the training period we are given A_k and D_i, and we try to guess the right hypothesis H_j. This is a partial inversion of the deduction and is a typical induction. During the recognition period, we are given a D_i and we try to guess A_k on the basis of an adopted hypothesis H_j. This is a second type of inversion of $H_j \cap A_k \to D_i$ and constitutes a second kind of induction.

In probabilistic language, the basic deduction consists in evaluation of probability $p(D_i|H_j \cap A_k)$. The task of the training period is evaluation of probability $p(H_j|A_k \cap D_i)$, and the task of the recognition period is evaluation of ability $p(A_k|H_j \cap D_i)$.

Whether one prefers the nonprobabilistic version or the probabilistic version, it is clear that each step of induction involves inductive ambiguities. Our judgment has to mobilize an extra-evidential, extra-logical evaluation which is inseparable from our internal sense of value. This is the reason why pattern recognition cannot be done by a machine alone.

6. Source and Storage of Information

It is basic to the problem of mechanization of cognitive processes to note the difference between what is meant by source and storage of information in communication and machine computation, and what is meant by the same terms in reference to human mind.

The most simple-minded concept of source of information is defined as the choice of an alternative from among many available alternatives. Suppose that there are n letters L_i, i = 1, 2, ..., n available and that the probability of occurrence of letter L_i is p_i, and assume for simplicity that there is no correlation among the letters. Each time, before a letter is chosen, the ambiguity as to which one will be chosen is expressible numerically as

$$- \sum_{i=1}^{n} p_i \log p_i,$$

and after the letter is chosen this ambiguity vanishes. Hence the amount of information, which may be equated to the amount of decrease in ambiguity, is

$$0 - (- \sum_{i=1}^{n} p_i \log p_i) = - \sum_{i=1}^{n} p_i \log p_i.$$

Thus, the choice is said to have "created" information in the amount

$$- \sum_{i=1}^{n} p_i \log p_i.$$

Now the question is whether this process of creation of information can be carried out by a machine. The answer is obviously in the affirmative. You can connect a piece of radioactive substance and a Geiger tube to a computer in such a way that letter L_i will be produced with probability p_i. But can you call this stochastic process a creation of information in the true sense? The answer is obviously in the negative, simply because it does not carry any content. This is a stochastic accident devoid of meaning. If an apparently similar stochastic situation is observed in a real communication channel connecting two human beings, each symbol is carrying some meaningful message. This shows clearly that the mathematical notion of information has nothing to do with meaningful information in the sense of human cognitive process.

A little more sophisticated type of argument with regard to source and storage of information runs somewhat as follows: The human mind is an information transducer. According to Shannon's information theory, information can only decrease through transduction. Hence the total information in human civilization can only decrease with time, and at the end there won't be any information left. This argument also refers only to the meaningless mathematical notion of information. For the sake of argument, however, let us for the moment place ourselves in the framework of the mathematical information theory. Even then, there are several misconceptions involved in this argument (see Watanabe, 1969a for details). Most important of all, there is no such thing as total amount of information possessed by a civilization or, for that matter, the amount of information possessed by a book.

The mathematical information is actually definable only at the moment of transfer and cannot be defined as a quantity possessed by an object or a system. This implies two important facts. First, the amount of information depends on the concepts or categories which the information receiver uses in classifying possible events. The concept in general, as explained earlier, is dependent on the internal value system of the one that forms it. Second, the amount of information depends on the subjective probability placed by the information receiver on each of the possible events. This must be so because the less the expectation, the larger the information amount received. We can make a model of information reception by a computer by furnishing the machine with the man-made concepts and the man-conceived probabilities. But the machine itself cannot produce the concept system because it has no internal value system and it cannot itself produce probabilities because it cannot expect different events with different degrees of certainty. Therefore, the machine cannot receive information in the sense of mathematical notion of information either.

It is instructive to examine the way the so-called subjective probability is defined by such proponents of this concept as Ramsay, de Finetti, and Toda. One assumption is common in all of these theories: man behaves in such a way as to maximize the expected utility, which is essentially the product of probability and utility. Without a concept of utility or its equivalent, we cannot define subjective probability. Utility is the numerical expression of desirability which is intimately based on the internal sense of value of a person. Since the machine does not have such an internal sense of value, we cannot define the subjective probability of a machine by its behavior.

Coming back to the problem of storage of information, one should first notice that the ordinary memory device of a computer has no resemblance whatsoever to human or animal memory. The machine memory is an array of yes or no. The machine does not even "know" what is affirmed and what is negated. It is again meaningless information. In the human mind, memory is inseparable from its content, its context, and its sensorial and emotional background. There is an engineering effort to produce what is presumptuously called associative memory, but there is absolutely no hope at present of reproducing the amazing function of mental association by a machine. Human memory is so intimately related to sensory and emotional experience that it cannot be mechanically simulated by a system which is devoid of sensation and emotion. (Watanabe, 1974.)

A further, and probably the deepest, gap between animal (and human) memory and mechanical memory lies in the fact that memory storage in animals seems to be spread over the entire body and to penetrate into not only the cells but also the molecules constituting the body. This seems to entail not only an immensely large memory capacity but also an entirely different quality of information storage. For one thing, we animals seem to have a memory system like an iceberg whose small visible part appears in the conscious and whose large invisible part is buried in the unconscious. Second, we must be born, somewhat in the fashion suggested in Menon, with a tremendous amount of knowledge accumulated in earlier generations ("reincarnations"). This inborn and latent knowledge is not limited to the a priori or the analytic, but it includes a large number of "empirical" facts. This is the only way by which we may explain the fantastic "knowledge" possessed by newly born animals, for example, by migrating birds. This kind of memory is so entirely different from the memory device of a computer that it is ludicrous to compare them. (See also Watanabe, 1969a, pp. 252–253.)

This type of latent knowledge is certainly not formulated or stored in any language. It is my conviction that the nonlingual nature of knowledge goes far beyond latent knowledge, and that most of our conscious process of thinking is done also in a nonlingual mode. I am perfectly aware that I am opposing the majority of contemporary philosophers who still follow the once-fashionable language-oriented approaches. I have come to my conclusion from an entirely different starting point. I have often been asked whether I think of a new theory in science in English or in Japanese. I tried hard to answer this question and soon discovered that the question was nonsensical. Even with a problem of a mathematical or logical nature, what is going on in my mind is a kind of "abstract" motion picture, some kind of changing relations among images, consisting often in color patches and lines.

There are two meanings of the word "symbol," one in the sense of mathematical notation and the other in the sense of symbolism in literature. In the former, the symbol is devoid of any physical existence and stands for an abstract concept defined without ambiguity. In the latter, the symbol is a particular concrete object, standing for an undefined vast domain of association of ideas which it can elicit. The mechanical mind can handle only the first kind of symbols. The human mind can handle both kinds of symbols. But the greatest part of human intelligence, I submit, is carried out in terms of the "poetical" or "paradigmatic" symbols. (Watanabe, 1974.)

Many years ago, Masanao Toda said half-jokingly, "You may succeed in simulating human intelligence by a computer but not the intelligence of lower animals." I interpret this as saying that that infinitesimally thin layer of human intelligence which is expressible by abstract symbols subject to logical rules can be mechanized, but the greater part of human intelligence, which is shared by lower fellow-creatures, is entirely outside the realm of language, abstraction, and logic, and hence inimitable by machines. The intelligence of lower animals is by no means lower intelligence, if judged by effectiveness in achieving goals. I may be accused of confusing knowledge and instinct. It is also true that our conscious effort sometimes disturbs or inhibits otherwise smooth and effective instinctive performance. Yet it is undeniable that there exists a constant and active trade between the conscious and the unconscious types of knowledge, and that such a trade makes human intelligence what it is—rich, profound, and superbly adaptive.

7. Adaptation and Learning

Adaptation is not just a gradual change of response pattern. The change involved in adaptation has at least two remarkable features. One is its inverse H-theoremic (Watanabe, 1960, 1962) character, and the other is its value-orientedness. In this section, I want to explain these two features in connection with the cognitive type of adaptation and show why they cannot be duplicated by a machine.

The inverse H-theoremic trend can be easily understood if one envisions a student trying to answer a multiple-choice question. When he does not have much knowledge about the subject, every alternative choice in the question will look equally probable (plausible). As he learns about the subject, the probability distribution will become more and more sharply concentrated on fewer and fewer alternatives, until finally one becomes the only possible choice. This trend can be conveniently formulated if one defines an entropy function with the help of the probability distribution, because a uniform distribution of probability means a large value of entropy and a sharply concentrated distribution of probability means a small value of entropy. Learning means an entropy descrease in this sense. This is the meaning of the inverse H-theorem.

The same thing can be said of the process of induction. As our experience grows, the credibility distribution over competing hypotheses becomes more and more sharply concentrated on fewer and fewer hypotheses. This is also expressible as an inverse H-theorem by defining the entropy by credibilities.

Historically, there have been many thinkers who felt that the behaviors of living beings are going in the opposite direction to that indicated by the second law of thermodynamics (law of entropy increase). Bergson is one of them. (Bergson, 1944). Since a living system is an open system, its physical entropy can increase as well as descrease with time. But the "anti-entropic" tendency of living beings to create structure, to produce difference, to organize, to concentrate, to select seems to go beyond the physical level. The inverse H-theorem of inductive process which I introduced and mathematically demonstrated is the first rigorous formulation of such anti-entropic tendency, although it does not cover all the aspects of the anti-entropic tendency.

I have also demonstrated that this inverse H-theoremic tendency of induction can be simulated by a computer. The computer calculates the credibilities according to the Bayes formula and shows that the entropy defined by these credibilities in fact decreases if we continue to increase the experimental data. But is the machine really learning by this inductive process? The answer is no. The credibilities are just numbers in the machine while they mean degree of belief or credence in a human being. A machine does not have the functions of believing or placing confidence. Believing something, translated behaviorally, may mean using it as a guide of action and as such may be simulated by a machine. But, mentally speaking, believing cannot exist in the absence of the sense of reliance and security, and this last is missing in a machine. Consequently, all my experiments on machines of the inverse H-theorem are not true simulations; in fact, they are not handling the actual credibilities, but just the numbers which the mathematical theorem of Bayes would recommend to use. As a result, the convergence in the sense of the inverse H-theorem does not leave any lasting change in the machine. It can be completely deleted simply by erasing the memory device. On the other hand, such a convergence in a man means an irreversible change, small as it may be, in the very person.

This computer simulation of inductive learning may be compared to simulating heat conduction by computer. The computer may produce the exact temperature distribution and its temporal change, if any, according to a set of well-established physical laws, but there is an essential difference from the real situation: there is no heat or temperature in the computer. Heat conduction is usually accompanied by an entropy increase, and this, too, may be calculated by the computer. But this entropy has nothing to do with the entropy of the computer. The same is true of computer simulation of learning.

Starting with the cognitive type of learning, I showed that the applicability of the inverse H-theorem can be extended to the behavioral type of learning, such as T-maze experiments, and Solomon-Wynn's avoidance tests (Watanabe, 1962, 1969a). The result was that in each case, if we define an entropy by the response probabilities, the learning process can be characterized by a decrease of entropy. In some cases, this learning period of entropy decrease is preceded by an unlearning period of entropy increase, during which the earlier bias is gradually destroyed.

From the descriptive point of view, learning implies an entropy decrease. But from the point of view of the subject, there is more to learning. In the cognitive case, the subject is searching for truth. In the behavioral case with animal experiments, the subjects are trying, consciously or unconsciously, to get food pellets or to avoid bodily discomfort. This can be seen also by noticing that an arbitrary entropy-decreasing change does not necessarily imply learning. In the cognitive case, a student could choose a wrong alternative and a scientist could finish his task, believing in a wrong hypothesis. That this is usually not the case means that there is a special guiding principle of selection. The man and animal are guided by their internal sense of value during this process of adaptation or learning. This is the second important feature of adaptation which cannot be simulated by a machine.

In the cognitive case, the machine can be programmed to search for truth as well as untruth, because the machine itself does not "want" truth or untruth. The machine can also simulate the behavioral learning of animals, and we can even incorporate "reinforcement" in the program. But what is called reinforcement is simply a change in the existing response pattern in the direction of either increasing or decreasing the present tendency. We can very easily exchange the negative and positive reinforcements in the program. The machine does not care. With animals it is not so. There are things animals want and things they do not. You cannot change this fact.

What is most important is that this internal sense of value guiding adaptation and learning is somehow harmoniously unified with the entire existence of the animal. This unity of an individual is the fundamental of life and precisely what is missing in a machine. It is easy to build a robot with purposive behavior, that is, a robot with a goal. But the programmed goal is not integrated with other functions and the "life" of the robot (Watanabe, 1956). I have mentioned various other reasons why animal or human cognitive processes cannot be totally carried out by a machine. If we try to summarize these various reasons in a word, we may say that they, too, are in essence attributable to the absence of all-pervading, value-oriented unity in the machine.

REFERENCES

Bergson, H., 1944. *Creative Evolution*. New York: Random House.

Carnap, R., 1950. *Logical Foundations of Probability*. Chicago: University of Chicago Press.

Gelernter, H.L., 1959. "Realization of a Geometry-Theorem Proving Machine." *Proceedings of an International Conference on Information Processing*, p. 273. Paris: UNESCO House. Reprinted in E. Feigenbaum and J. Feldman, eds., *Computer and Thought*, p. 134. New York: McGraw-Hill, 1963.

Lucas, J., 1961. "Minds, Machines and Gödel," *Philosophy* 36 (137): 112.

Wang, H., 1960. "Toward Mechanical Mathematics," *IBM Journal of Research and Development* 4 (1): 2.

Watanabe, S., 1959. "Civilization and Science (Man and Machine)." *Annals of the Japan Association for Philosophy of Science* 1 (4): 216.

Watanabe, S., 1960. "Information-Theoretical Aspects of Inductive and Deductive Inference." *IBM Journal of Research and Development* 4 (2): 208.

Watanabe, S., 1962. "Learning Process and Inverse H-Theorem." *IRE Transactions Information Theory, PGIT Transactions*, IT-8, p. 246.

Watanabe, S., 1965a. "Une explication mathématique du classement d'objets," p. 39. In S. Dockx and P. Bernays, eds., *Information and Prediction in Science* p. 39. New York: Academic Press.

Watanabe, S., 1965b. "A Mathematical Explication of Inductive Inference." In *Proceedings of the International Colloquium on the Foundations of Mathematics, Mathematical Machines and their Applications*, p. 67. Budapest: Akadémiai Kiado.

Watanabe, S., 1968. "Epistemological Implications of Cybernetics." In *Proceedings of the XIV International Congress of Philosophy*, vol. 2, p. 594. University of Vienna.

Watanabe, S., 1969a. *Knowing and Guessing*. New York: John Wiley and Sons.

Watanabe, S., 1969b. "Pattern Recognition as an Inductive Process." In S. Watanabe, ed., *Methodologies of Pattern Recognition*, p. 521. New York: Academic Press.

Watanabe, S., 1969c. "La simulation mutuelle de l'homme et de la machine." In S. Dockx, ed., *Civilisation, Technique et Humanisme*, vol. 6, p. 19. Paris: Beauchesne.

Watanabe, S., 1970. "Creative Time," *Studium Generale* 23 : 1057.

Watanabe, S., 1974. "Paradigmatic Symbol." In IEEE Transactions on Systems, Man, and Cybernetics, SMC-4, no. 1, p. 100.

12

The Mind-Body
Equation Revisited

James T. Townsend

GUSTAV FECHNER believed in the fundamental mind–body unity of man. In fact, his monism formed the motivating philosophy which led to the two tomes of *Elemente der Psychophysik* first published in 1860. It was his hope that this work would influence philosophical thought concerning the mind–body problem. Nevertheless, he was quite adamant in stressing the firm empirical basis for his experiments and theoretical conclusions. Fechner felt that whatever the outcome of the mind-body controversy (assuming eventual resolution), his empirically derived laws would stand in their own right.

The late Edwin G. Boring remarks that Fechner "was never accepted as a philosopher" (Boring, 1950, p. 281), and in another place "Fechner's fame is as a psychophysicist and not as a philosopher with a mission" (Boring, 1950, p. 279). Thus, although there was some reference to Fechner at the Honolulu conference, in general we must accept the fact that Fechner's goal of proselytization within the realm of philosophy, via his psychophysics, was never attained. Nevertheless, Fechner undoubtedly had an enormous impact on the emerging experimental psychology. Indeed, as we shall see, the ramifications of his "solution" to the mind-body problem are still giving rise to empirical and theoretical research and controversy in psychology, which in turn create some eventual feedback to the parent tree of philosophy.

In this context, it seems quite manifest that fundamental contributions to science have often depended on or interacted with the contributor's philosophy. Newton's conception of space apparently was related to his acceptance of Euclid's axioms as empirical statements, as Kant's belief in an absolute space was to Newton's great Principia. Developments by nineteenth-century mathematicians in non-Euclidean geometry and empirical models for these constructions provided a philosophical base for Einstein's contributions to a new model of the universe (see, for example, Jammer, 1954). Recent interaction goes in reverse also, as witness the influence of scientific advance on the development of logical positivism or the (sometimes spurious) theological and philosophical interpretations of Heisenberg's principle. Even rejection of a point or a problem on one or the other side is, of course, additional comment on the mutual influences. Behavioristic psychology's eschewing of the mind-body problem helped determine content of experiment and theory especially in the area of "learning" for many years. We are apparently still seeing a backswing of experimental psychology to more "mentalistic" approaches which gained impetus with the innovation of the intervening variable and has gathered further acceptance with the advent of artifical intelligence, and communications and systems theory. With this apologia it will perhaps be clear that this exposition rests on the assumption tersely stated by Herbert Feigl, " ... that there is no sharp demarcation between (good) science and (clearheaded) philosophy" (Feigl, 1967).

From this point of view, it may be of interest to the philosophically minded to obtain a glimpse of where Fechner's contributions stand today, as well as to engage in some side excursions to a few related areas and issues. Our tour will be in no way exhaustive. I will attempt to introduce some novel thoughts on some of the topics rather than simply provide reviews, which would be severely limited by time and space. Interested readers are referred to the appended references. Hopefully, the intellectual diversions will help compensate for the somewhat desultory presentation.

We first briefly consider modern interpretation of Fechner's derivation of his mind-body equation, especially with respect to the mathematical principles involved. Next, the role of degree of precision in falsifiability will be encountered in remarks on (1) number of free variables in mathematical statements, (2) Meehl's recent article on a "methodological paradox," (3) a possibility for taking the importance of any given magnitude of "significance," in tests of the null hypothesis, into consideration when selecting the number of subjects to run, and (4) Fechner's logarithmic law versus an alternative proposed by S. S. Stevens. Following this, an apparent difficulty in applying Duncan Luce's (1959) findings that relate scale types and psychophysical functions to Stevens' power law will be noted. Finally, we will discuss the influence of experimental contexts on the form of psychophysical functions and methods of incorporating these effects into a mathematical theory of these functions.

Essentially, Fechner trichotomized the state of affairs into the external world, the body (the physical), and the mind. Excitation in the body was, he thought, related in a proportional manner to the magnitude of a stimulus and he endeavored to support this notion with several arguments, most of which appear irrelevant now. Given this relation, he assumed that an obtained curve relating the stimulus to sensation, and therefore to mind, must reveal the functional relationship that holds between mind and body. His contribution to this problem, resulting in the establishment of a function that maps stimulus values on numbers representing sensation magnitudes, is accepted as a rather monumental scientific effort, although current perspective now emphasizes his influence on other investigators and on psychophysical methodology rather than his final conclusions regarding the psychophysical law (which we shall use as equivalent to mind-body equation).

Fechner employed as a hub assumption Weber's law, which states that resolving power of a sensory system is inversely proportional to the magnitude of the stimulus, that is, $\frac{\Delta X}{X} = k$, where X is the stimulus magnitude, ΔX the stimulus increment necessary for a 50 percent correct discrimination rate, (a just noticeable difference or JND), and k is (Weber's) constant. Fechner next assumed that just as one may measure material by matching equal intervals of one substance (e.g., the wood of a yardstick) to equal intervals of another, one can use the (equal) ascending Weber ratios as building blocks which correspond at each increment to equal sensation steps. Thus, he believed in the equality of sensation JNDs and further that a sensation value corresponding to a particular stimulus magnitude could be determined by summing the component JNDs. If Fechner had paused here and employed the finite calculus (for an elementary treatment, see Goldberg, 1958) to establish a functional relation between stimulus and response, he would have obtained the equation,

$$X_n = (kh + 1)^n X_o,$$

where k is Weber's constant, h is the (constant) sensation increment for each stimulus JND, X_o is the absolute threshold stimulus and X_n is the stimulus magnitude in JNDs above threshold. Hence, this equation shows that for (n) equal steps in sensation one obtains a geometric increase in stimulus magnitude. We can also solve the difference equation in terms of equal stimulus increments (h') to obtain an expression structurally similar to Fechner's continuous solution:

$$Y_n = \sum_{i=1}^{n} [\frac{1}{X_o + ih'}] \frac{h'}{k},$$

in which Weber's law is implicit, or using direct summation, obtain

$$Y_n = \frac{1}{k} \sum_{i=1}^{n} \frac{X_i - X_{i-1}}{X_{i-1}}, \quad (Y_n = \text{sensation valve})$$

in which Weber's law is explicit. The latter can be verified by observing

$$Y_n - Y_{n-1} = \frac{1}{k} \frac{X_n - X_{n-1}}{X_{n-1}} = 1 \text{ (letting } h = 1).$$

Fechner, however, using his mathematical auxiliary principle, solved a continuous approximation to the difference equation, namely,

$$\frac{dX}{X} = kdY,$$

from which he obtained

$$Y = k' \ln \left(\frac{X}{X_o}\right), k' = \frac{1}{k}.$$

This expression also implies Weber's law, since $\Delta Y = k' \ln \left(\frac{X + \Delta X}{X_o}\right) -$

$k' \ln \left(\frac{X}{X_o}\right) = k' \ln \left(1 + \frac{\Delta X}{X}\right) = k' \ln (1 + k)$, a constant, but we now know that

the continuous approximation will not in general imply a result found with finite differences (Luce and Edwards, 1958). To illustrate this point, suppose the empirical relation

$$\frac{\Delta X}{X(X - 1)} = k, (X_o > 1),$$

were discovered. Using Fechner's first assumptions we find the difference equation

$$X_n = k\Delta Y X_{n-1} (X_{n-1} - 1) + X_{n-1}.$$

Direct summation, which corresponds to simply graphing equal sensation increments against cumulative stimulus JNDs, gives

$$Y_n = \frac{1}{k} \sum_{i=1}^{n} \frac{X_i - X_{i-1}}{X_{i-1} (X_{i-1} - 1)}$$

Similarly, it is easy to see how the stimulus values change in the special case where we set the (constant) sensation increments to $\Delta Y = \frac{1}{k}$; for this yields the difference equation solution,

$$X_n = X_o^{2^n}.$$

This expression shows, as we might expect, that for an equal sensation step the stimulus magnitude changes much faster than geometrically, in fact as a power of 2^n of absolute threshold. (Compare this with the consequence of letting

$h = \frac{1}{k}$ in $X_n = (kh + 1)^n X_o$ which yields $X_n = 2^n X_o$). On the other hand, the associated differential equation would, according to Fechner's auxiliary principle, presumably be

$$\frac{dX}{X(X - 1)} = kdY,$$

and the solution to this expression is

$$Y = \frac{1}{k} \ln(1 - \frac{1}{X}).$$

Testing to see if this expression yields Weber's law, we derive

$$\Delta Y = \frac{1}{k} [\ln(1 - \frac{1}{X + \Delta X}) - \ln(1 - \frac{1}{X})]$$

$$= \frac{1}{k} [\ln(1 - \frac{1}{X + X(X - 1)k}) - \ln(1 - \frac{1}{X})]$$

which we easily see is not constant by letting $k = 1$, for then

$$\Delta Y = \ln(1 + \frac{1}{X}).$$

In fact, the only value for which constancy is attained is the degenerate, experimentally uninteresting $k = 0$.

The above question of correct derivation procedures does not appear to be of trivial importance, since expressions that are more complex than Weber's law seem to be required at stimulus extremes and under certain background conditions. Luce and Edwards (1958), taking a functional equations approach, have shown how one can obtain continuous solutions that are compatible with a general JND relationship. Recently, Levine (1970), Falmagne (1971), and Krantz (1971), have made further contributions to the understanding of scales derived from discrimination measures in general and JND functions in particular.

Fechner's logarithmic law seems to hold rather well for a number of what the late S.S. Stevens (1957) referred to as methathetic continua, but to be largely inappropriate for prothetic continua, these adjectives corresponding roughly to "qualitative" and "quantitative" respectively. An example of a prothetic stimulus continuum is energy in a sound wave and an example of a methathetic stimulus continuum is frequency in a sound wave. Fechner's first nonempirical assumption seems to be false for prothetic continua; namely sensation JNDs are not subjectively equal. It is not clear precisely why Fechner chose to define his sensation units in terms of resolving power of the sensory channel, but part of the explanation may be that he was overly impressed with the logarithmic relationship suggested by Laplace and others to hold for such "psychological" quantities as the subjective value of money (see for example, Fechner, 1966, pp. 197–198). The subjective value of an increment of money was taken to be inversely proportional to the wealth already accrued.

The greatest and most successful empirical assault launched against Fechner's law has been that of S. S. Stevens (see for example, Stevens, 1959; 1957). In contrast to Fechner's theoretically based approach, Stevens proceeded in a more experimentally direct manner. His experimental tasks involve the observer with making one of various estimates or productions related to his perception of the magnitude of the stimulus. Most of these methods rest on the rather strong and apparently implicit assumption that sensations lie on a ratio or log-interval scale (corresponding to a power function) and, further, that an observer can meaningfully report these sensations in terms of ratios. However, Stevens attempted to show, not without success, that the form of the psychophysical function is constant across these methods. A method fairly typical of Stevens' approach is that of magnitude estimation, and I will base most of my later remarks on this method. For later reference we note here that Stevens' basic obtained relationship reads: $Y = AX^B$ where A corresponds to the unit and B governs the curvature of the relation.

Apart from questions of validity of assumptions and correctness of mathematical derivations, one may ask about the ease with which one can test a theory. The concepts concerned with this latter problem are often subsumed under the general heading of "falsifiability."

Falsifiability of Psychological Laws

Before taking up the question of falsifiability for the psychophysical function, we will discuss problems of falsifiability within psychology and statistical decision making. This discussion will include some comments on a recent article by Paul Meehl (1967) and some suggestions for dealing with scientific meaningfulness of hypotheses alternative to the null hypothesis and selecting the proper sample size. It will conclude with a remark on the falsifiability of a logarithmic function versus a power function.

The aspects of falsifiability with which we begin refer to what Popper (1959) has called degree of universality and degree of precision. Popper uses an example of the orbits of heavenly bodies (more universal) or planets (less universal) being posited to be either circles (more precision) or ellipses (less precision) to illustrate the concepts. It is difficult to say how much such considerations play a subconscious role in the theoretical undertakings of psychologists; unfortunately it is quite rare to see them overtly used either in theory formation or, for that matter, in theory evaluation.

It is not always easy to tie down exactly what we should mean by degree of precision. In psychology, when testing two models, it is common to attempt to equate the number of parameters in each to give each an equal opportunity to fit the data. But the complexity of the resulting theoretical curves is often related to the way in which the parameters enter the functions of each model. (Straight lines are said to be less complex than curves, and curves with an inflection point more complex than those always positively or negatively accelerated.) So this rather simplistic criterion seems to go away in certain areas, such as signal detection. A typical simple yes-no detection experiment involves the presentation on each trial of a signal plus noise, or of noise alone, the observer's task being to report as best he can whether the signal was present. The observer's hit frequency, P(HIT), is defined as the probability of his making a correct response,

P(yes|signal + noise). The observer's false alarm frequency, P(FALSE ALARM), is defined as the probability of his reporting the presence of a signal when only noise is presented, P(yes|noise alone). These two probabilities completely describe his performance frequencies. As the experimenter manipulates the pay-off structure and the intensity of the signal relative to the noise, the observer's hit and false alarm frequencies change. A theoretical or empirical function relating P(HIT) to P(FALSE ALARM) as the experimenter manipulates the situation is called an ROC (receiver-operating-characteristic) curve. This type of experiment can be viewed as the study of discrimination behavior where physical and motivational variables are manipulated.

There exist theories that are sufficiently complex to make predictions for several dependent variables but which predict straight-line ROC curves (e.g., Townsend, 1966) with slope 1; similarly, there are theories of rather astonishing simplicity that predict curvilinear ROC curves (see for example, the exponential model of Green and Swets, 1966, pp. 78–81). Furthermore, it is usually easy to equate number of parameters in testing ROC predictions against the data in these diverse models. However, note that a model that posits that P(HIT) = A P^2(FALSE ALARM) + B P(FALSE ALARM) + C, that is, that the probability of a hit is a quadratic function of the probability of a false alarm, implies the coefficients:

$$-1 \leqslant A \leqslant 0, B = 1 - A, C = 0.$$

These coefficients guarantee that the ROC curve will look familiar (roughly similar to the curvilinear ROC function predicted by signal detectability theory), but there are no values of the coefficients that make the curve symmetric about the antidiagonal except for the limiting trivial case of A = 0. Thus, most of the parametric freedom was used in simply obeying rather general constraints of a reasonable ROC function and the generality given by two-parameter signal defectability theory (Green and Swets, 1966, pp. 62–64) does not accompany the quadratic function. It might be remarked peripherally that a strict interpretation of Fechner's threshold views implied a straight-line ROC curve and that, although strict threshold theories appear to be negated for yes-no signal detection experiments, they can on occasion account quite well for data obtained in forced-choice detection situations (see for example, Atkinson and Kinchla, 1965; Kinchla, Townsend, Yellot, and Atkinson, 1966).

Meehl (1967) has discussed what he refers to as a methodological paradox. The idea seems to be that an increase in experimental precision or in number of subjects run (tested, etc.) results in increased falsifiability for physical theories but in decreased falsifiability for psychological and other social science theories. The main contributing factors are (1) the tendency to formulate hypotheses which predict only that a difference exists or that a difference in one direction should exist, and (2) because of the high degree of intercorrelation of psychological variables, groups differing on almost any independent variable will be almost certain to differ in a positive or negative direction on the dependent variable. In contrast, physical theories are more likely to predict (point) numerical values; so, although a purist might object that everything pretty much affects everything else in physics, too, in the sense of various measurable characteristics or events being correlated, this is largely ameliorated by the point predictions. In fact, it is probably the case that the impossibility of eliminating all "irrelevant" variables in physical experiments would lead ultimately to the falsification of any (point prediction) theory, due to the concomitant constant errors. This is because the empirical mean would converge in probability to the incorrect value.

Meehl's critique must relate to the modal state of affairs rather than to theorizing dilemmas that arise by necessity; for example, there is nothing that prevents even a low-level theory (i.e., not involving a high degree of theoretical structure) from predicting the null hypothesis, in which case falsifiability increases with increased precision or sample size. Occasionally a neophyte in psychology is taken to task for attempting to "prove the null hypothesis. However, it is the centention here that the obverse aspect of Meehl's criticism is that the null hypothesis is a point prediction and hence in some ways more justifiable than predicting that a difference exists.

Meehl also scores psychologists for failure to appreciate the difference between

$$\{[T \Rightarrow O] \& \sim O\} \Rightarrow \sim T \text{ and } \{[T \Rightarrow O] \& O\} \rightarrow T,$$

where "$\Rightarrow$" is logical implication and "$\rightarrow$" is inductive inference.

There are two asymmetries between these two modes of inference. One is that the first rules out all theories that imply O, including T, but the second (excluding the second problem, to be discussed shortly) offers unique support for T if and only if T is the only theory that predicts O; therefore the larger the class of theories that predicts O, the less the support offered T by $[(T \Rightarrow O) \& O] \rightarrow T$. The second asymmetry, somewhat weaker than the first, is associated with the typical universal quantification of theoretical predictions. Thus, within the classical hypotheticdeductive framework, O must occur in empirical test every time, if the theory is true. One failure of O to evidence itself and T is falsified forever, but T is never quite verified completely since it is always possible that the "next" test will discover $\sim O$ and hence $\sim T$.

Although the above reasoning is compelling as far as it goes, it would be more pertinent for modern science if both asymmetries were discussed within the context of statistical decision theory. For example, suppose a theory T predicts a significant one-tail difference, and the prediction is confirmed at some given α level (i.e., probability of a Type I error, the probability that significance is obtained when, in fact, no difference exists). Then if one is willing to posit an a priori probability distribution over the set of possible theories, including theory T and the null hypothesis, he can compute the a posteriori probability that T is true. This approach allows us to handle the first asymmetry in a more rigorous manner. The Baysians argue (fairly convincingly, it seems to me) that when we (even non-Baysians) interpret scientific results we informally or intuitively assign a priori values or ranges of values to the set of possible theories and make some rough estimate in our heads concerning the likelihood it is, in fact, our own theory that is true (it is not necessary to know all other possible theories, only some probability for our theory versus all other theories); and that therefore we may as well perform some actual computations. The Baysian point of view, of course, prescribes the setting of the decision cut point, and therefore the α level, by maximizing expected value of the experiment.

For the second asymmetry also, we can employ statistical thinking. Errors of measurement and inextricable "irrelevant" random variables greatly reduce our expectation of obtaining a predicted result on every test, even though the theory is correct and predicts logically that a certain result should occur all the time. The statistical aspects seem to largely outweigh the strictly logical aspect. For instance, suppose that (now) T predicts that a difference between two groups of 4 exists and that the standard error of the mean is 1. Suppose also that it is about equally likely, a priori, that T is true as that the null hypothesis T_n is true, and that either one or the other must be true. If we let $\alpha = .0001$ and a significant result is obtained, it follows that the probability that T is true, *given* significance, is very, very close to 1 (on the order of $0.99984+$). It would therefore seem that, here, the verification induction problem (closely connected with the second asymmetry) would not ordinarily cause a scientist much concern. Although this example is extreme and contrived, it does suggest that the logical asymmetries can be ameliorated or possibly exacerbated (for the latter, suppose one's theory predicted the T_n in this example) by the laws of chance.

A similar problem, intimately related to theory testing, concerns the practical or scientific importance of a (true) difference. Although the larger the sample size (N) we employ, the more probable that statistical significance will be attained if *any* difference exists, in practice differences below some point may be useless or uninteresting. Furthermore, it is easy to construct simple but reasonable examples where not only does the a posteriori expected (i.e., mean) difference conditionalized on statistical significance *increase* with *decreasing* N, but also the a posteriori probabilities that the various possible alternative hypotheses gave rise to the significant difference shift toward the larger alternatives as N decreases.

Table 1 gives such an example (slide rule accuracy) in the case where the possible (true) means are m = 0, 1, or 4, where m = 0 with probability 1/4, m = 1 with probability 1/2, and m = 4 with probability 1/4. It is assumed that the population standard deviation, σ, is 1, that $\alpha = 0.10$ (constant) and that the distributions for each m are normal. The table then shows for N = 1, 9, 100, + ∞: (1) the values of the overall probability that statistical significance is obtained, (2) the conditional or a posteriori probabilities that the null hypothesis (m = 0) or either of the alternatives (m = 1, m = 4) is true given significance, and (3) the overall a posteriori expectation. The case where the a priori probabilities are uniform (1/3 for each, rather than 1/4, 1/2, 1/4) turns out to give the same types of changes with manipulations of N. Thus, if one is not so much interested in obtaining significance per se as being assured that, if it is obtained, it is a meaningful result, it may behoove him to refrain from acquiring a very large sample size. This antinomy does not, of course, actually contradict such other laws as that, for a fixed level of confidence, the interval corresponding to that confidence increases in width as N decreases or that the likelihood of a correct decision increases as N increases (as some quick calculations with the above example will show). Hence, these remarks should not be interpreted as a claim that small N is better than large N, but only that the frequently heard admonition to acquire as large a sample size as time and cost permits may not always be justified.

TABLE 1   *Probability of Significance, A-Posteriori Probabilities, and A-Posteriori Expectation (Conditional on Statistical Significance) as Functions of Sample Size N*

	N			
	1	9	100	∞
P (Significance)	.47	.63	.68	.78
P (M = 0|Significance)	.05	.04	.04	.03
P (M = 1|Significance)	.42	.56	.60	.65
P (M = 4|Significance)	.53	.40	.37	.32
E (M|Significance)	2.54	2.15	2.08	1.94

[M] = set of alternative means = [0, 1, 4]
E = expectation (average)
α = .10

More generally, statistical decision theory can be employed to utilize any number of variables and/or aspects to help determine not only a cut point on a decision axis, but also the best value of N. We shall develop the general mathematics of the situation here; specific distributions and functions could be inserted to fit particular cases. In order to prevent losing sight of the forest because of the trees, we assume at the outset the necessary continuity and differentiability of the various functions.

The definitions of our required symbols are given in the following list:

$\bar{x}$ ≡ observed (experimentally determined) mean
m ≡ difference of true mean from zero, m ⩾ 0
m* ≡ upper limit on true mean, 0 ⩽ m* ⩽ +∞
o ≡ no difference, m = 0, corresponds to null hypothesis

d($\cdot$|x̄) $\equiv$ probability of coming to decision $\cdot$ ($\cdot$ = o or a)

a $\equiv$ decision corresponding to rejecting the null hypothesis, i.e., conclude that m > 0

f(m|x̄) $\equiv$ conditioned probability of m given x̄

f(m) $\equiv$ a priori probability of m

N $\equiv$ sample size

c(N) $\equiv$ cost function for obtaining N samples

L(x,y) $\equiv$ loss function for deciding y when x is true

E(L|x̄) $\equiv$ expected average loss given x̄

E(L) $\equiv$ overall expected loss

The function L(x,y) tells us the importance of concluding that a difference exists (a: m > 0), L(m,a) where one does and the importance of deciding that no difference exists (o: m = 0), L(0,o) when in fact, none does. It also shows the loss involved where we incorrectly conclude that no difference exists, L(m,o), m > 0, and that occurring when the incorrect decision is made that a difference does exist, L(0,a). Typically, L(m,a) $\leqslant$ 0, (m > 0), L(0,o) $\leqslant$ 0 and L(m,o) $\geqslant$ 0, (m > 0) and L(0,a) $\geqslant$ 0. We then wish to minimize the overall expected loss E(L) for given loss (L) and cost functions (c) and for given probability distributions (f). We write integrals of f as if f is always a density function but generalizations in notation are obvious for non-Riemannian integration and without loss of generality we could make f(0) a probability mass rather than a density. One further assumption we make is that N and c(N) are independent of L,f. N is implicit in affecting, of course, f(x̄|m) by way of its standard error $\sigma_{\bar{x}}(m) = \dfrac{\sigma(m)}{\sqrt{N}}$, where $\sigma(m)$ is the standard deviation in the probability density function with mean m.

We shall first write down the expected loss for any given empirical mean x̄ and any fixed N. It will be convenient in the following to let m > 0 distinguish the possible (true) alternative means from the null mean.

$$E(L|\bar{x}) = f(0|\bar{x})\,[d(o|\bar{x})\,L(0,o) + d(a|\bar{x})\,L(0,a) + \int\limits_{\{m>0\}}^{m^*} f(m|\bar{x})\,[d(o|\bar{x})$$
$$(L(m,o) + d(a|\bar{x})\,L(m,a)]dm,$$

where {m > 0} indicates that the integrand is "summed" over all values of m that are greater than 0.

If we determine a method of minimizing this expression for any N, x̄, we can then show how to select (in principle) a value of N that will be optimized in terms of minimizing E(L) (and hence maximizing expected value).

Since d(o|x̄) = 1 − d(a|x̄), we can rewrite the foregoing expression as

$$E(L|\bar{x}) = d(a|\bar{x})\,[f(0|\bar{x})\,(L(0,a) - L(0,o)) - \int\limits_{\{m>0\}}^{m^*} f(m|\bar{x})\,(L(m,o)$$

$$- L(m,a))dm] + f(0|\bar{x}) (L(0,o) - \int\limits_{\{m>0\}}^{m^*} f(m|\bar{x}) L(m,o) dm.$$

Next, since

$$f(0|\bar{x}) (L(0,a) - L(0,o)) \text{ and } \int\limits_{\{m>0\}}^{m^*} f(m|\bar{x}) (L(m,o) - L(m,a))dm$$

give the average total weighted losses for saying o or a respectively for the given $\bar{x}$, it follows that $E(L|\bar{x})$ will be minimized by taking $d(a|\bar{x}) = 0$ (always accepting the null hypothesis) when

$$f(0|x) (L(0,a) - L(0,o)) > \int\limits_{\{m>0\}}^{m^*} f(m|\bar{x}) (L(m,o) - L(m,a))dm,$$

letting $d(a|\bar{x}) = 1$ (always rejecting the null hypothesis where the inequality is reversed) and arbitrarily picking a response when the two sides are equal. (Note that the term

$$f(0|\bar{x}) L(0,o) + \int\limits_{\{m>0\}}^{m^*} f(m|\bar{x}) L(m,o) dm$$

does not affect the decision and is a constant loss [or gain], always present.) This decision rule may be summarized as:

$$\text{If } f(0|\bar{x}) (L(0,a) - L(0,o)) \left\{ \begin{matrix} > \\ < \\ = \end{matrix} \right\} \int\limits_{\{m>0\}}^{m^*} f(m|\bar{x}) (L(m,o) - L(m,a))dm$$

$$\text{then, let } d(a|\bar{x}) = \left\{ \begin{matrix} 0 \\ 1 \\ 1/2 \end{matrix} \right\}.$$

It will be helpful in the remainder of the derivation to note that

$$f(0|\bar{x}) = \frac{f(\bar{x}|0)f(0)}{f(\bar{x})}, f(m|\bar{x}) = \frac{f(\bar{x}|m)f(m)}{f(\bar{x})}$$

and that the $f(\bar{x})$'s cancel out in the above inequality.

With this decision rule in hand, we now peruse the overall expected loss, employing again $f(\cdot|\bar{x}) = \frac{f(\bar{x}|\cdot)f(\cdot)}{f(x)}$.

$$E(L) = \int\limits_{\bar{x} = -\infty}^{\infty} \{d(a|\bar{x}) [\frac{f(\bar{x}|0)f(0)}{f(\bar{x})} (L(0,a) - L(0,o)) - \int\limits_{\{m>0\}}^{m^*} \frac{f(\bar{x}|m)f(m)}{f(\bar{x})}.$$

$$(L(m,o) - L(m,a))dm] + \frac{f(\bar{x}|0)f(0)}{f(\bar{x})} L(0,o) + \int\limits_{\{m>0\}}^{m*} \frac{f(\bar{x}|m)f(m)}{f(\bar{x})} L(m, o) dm] \cdot$$

$$f(\bar{x})d\bar{x} + c(N).$$

By our decision rule, this complicated expression devolves itself to

$$E(L) = \int\limits_{\bar{x}=-\infty}^{+\infty} f(\bar{x}|0)f(0) L(0,o)d\bar{x} + \int\limits_{\bar{x}=-\infty}^{+\infty} [\int\limits_{\{m>0\}}^{m*}$$

$$f(\bar{x}|m)f(m)L(m,o)dm]d\bar{x} + \int\limits_{\{\bar{x}|d(a|\bar{x})=1\}} [f(\bar{x}|0)f(0)(L(0,a) - L(0,o)$$

$$- \int\limits_{\{m>0\}}^{m*} f(\bar{x}|m)f(m)(L(m,o) - L(m,a))dm]d\bar{x} + c(N),$$

and assuming sufficient regularity conditions, this becomes

$$E(L) = f(0)L(0,o) + \int\limits_{\{m>0\}}^{m*} f(m)L(m,o)dm + f(0)(L(0,a)$$

$$- L(0,o)) P(d(a|\bar{x}) = 1|0) - \int\limits_{\{m>0\}}^{m*} P(d(a|\bar{x}) = 1|m)f(m)(L(m,o)$$

$$- L(m,a))dm + c(N).$$

This expression could now be differentiated with respect to N and thence investigated for values of N that will yield relative or absolute minima for E(L). We should pause here to note that without including c(N), we can expect E(L) to decrease monotonically as a function of N, and that minimizing E(L) is therefore different decision strategy than simply basing our decision, for example, on E(m|significance). Nonetheless, the importance of the difference m will affect where the decision threshold is placed.

This is about as far as we can go with no knowledge of the pertinent functions to be employed. It may be quite difficult in particular cases to carry out the above program analytically and probably represents too much labor and expense for many experiments to justify. Nevertheless, in cases where great cost of sampling is involved or when it is very important to be sure an "important" difference is "really" there if statistical significance is obtained, the present procedure can be carried out on digital computers.

From a philosophy of science point of view it might be interesting to conditionalize E(L) on subsets of the set of possible theories and investigate the a posteriori support for these subsets as functions of N, different loss functions, and the like.

From these statistical matters, we return to questions more immediately related to the mind-body problem.

With regard to degree of precision, Fechner's predicted psychophysical function makes a stronger statement about the world than does that relationship described by Stevens. Fechner's prediction is written $Y = k \log(\frac{X}{X_o})$ where X_o is the threshold stimulus value, k is the reciprocal of Weber's constant, and k and the base of the logarithm determine the unit. Stevens' curve is usually given by $Y = a(X - X_o)^b$, where again X_o is interpreted as a threshold, a corresponds to the unit, and b is a positive real number. To convince oneself of the latitude of Stevens' function relative to that of Fechner's, one need merely note that by choosing b greater than or less than 1, one can make the function positively or negatively accelerated without affecting the sign of the first derivative, whereas we are constrained to a negatively accelerated function with the logarithmic expression as long as we demand (as we must) that the function be monotonic increasing. Poulton (1968) in remarking on the scope of Stevens' power function has suggested that its usefulness be checked by trying out other functions with the same number of parameters, such as a polynomial of degree 2. The polynomials, however, suffer from a constitutional deficiency (for $X \geqslant 0$) not unlike that of the log function: namely, a polynomial cannot be both always increasing *and* negatively accelerated. This is because the leading coefficient determines, for large X, the sign of all the derivatives. For example, a quadratic function must be positively accelerated to be always increasing and $\geqslant 0$. Of course, one may fit part of a concave-down parabola to the points (as when they appear to level off) but even then the second derivative is fixed, rather than a function of X as for Stevens' function. Thus, it is seen that allowing noninteger exponents purchases an investigator a great deal of fitting power regardless of the formula's ultimate validity. One constraining factor that the power function does have is that it can possess no inflection points in a finite stimulus range.

These comments on degree of precision in psychophysical functions are especially germane in the case of Stevens' work since the form of the function seems to have been induced from data (albeit a wide range of data) rather than predicted on the basis of an underlying theory. A straight line is a straight line regardless of whether it is obtained by curve fitting or by prediction, but when more complex curves appear, one should be chary of prematurely generalizing the expression for an empirically obtained curve.

Measurement Theory and the Psychophysical Function

Measurement theory has come a substantial way since Campbell (1920) implicitly made disreputable any measurement other than that corresponding to additive numerical operations. We may ask what part, if any, measurement theory has played in the establishment of a psychophysical equation. Actually, strange though it appears, there have been few attempts to establish a scale of sensation by the accepted method (see Suppes and Zinnes, 1963) of proving a representation theorem establishing a system of measurement of sensation within a modality, and a consequent uniqueness theorem giving the admissable transformations on the numbers representing measurements of sensation.

There are conclusions that might be drawn if we know independently the scales of measurement appropriate for sensation and stimulus. Duncan Luce (1959) has shown the scale types (corresponding to the class of admissable transformations) of the dependent variable and the independent variable can, within certain limits, very strongly restrict the possible laws holding between the independent and dependent variables. If the independent variable is on a ratio scale and we assume on the basis of Stevens' indirect evidence that sensation lies on a ratio or log-interval scale, then Luce shows that the intervening function must be a power function or possibly (in the latter case) of the form $Y = \delta \exp(\alpha \chi^{\beta})$.

Luce's results hold for the general formula $Y = a(X - X_0)^b$ if the independent variable is designated as $X - X_0$ rather than X. However, to be quite precise, it is not the experimenter who subtracts the threshold value from the input; on the contrary, it is the sensory or perceptual system of the observer. Hence, it seems somewhat specious to refer to $X - X_0$ as the independent variable, although the experimenter does set the background level (except for the observer's internal noise) of the stimulus. What if the internal function is formed not by taking a power of $X - X_0$, but in some other fashion? For example, let $b = 2$. Then it might be that the first stage of processing involves subtracting X_0 from X and then squaring this difference (for $X \geqslant X_0$); this would be in consonance with the assumption that $X - X_0$ is on a ratio scale. However, it might just as well be the case that the observer's system takes X, squares it, subtracts $2XX_0$ from it and adds X_0^2 to it. The basis for $X - X_0$ being a ratio scale-independent variable then would seem rather tenuous. In fact, it is not immediately clear how one would ever test this proposition in terms of extensive scale properties (Suppes and Zinnes, 1963).

If X is indeed mapped by the observer's system onto $X - X_0$ and the latter is on a ratio scale, how does this fit in with Luce's development which says that two ratio scales must be related, if at all, by a power transformation? The quantity $X - X_0$ is, of course, a difference transformation. The rub is that $X \to X - X_0$ for *all* X is not a positive nonconstant function between 0 and X_0, which Luce assumes. In fact, a reasonable transformation which shows the ratio scale properties of X and $X - X_0$ is

$$T(kX) = \begin{cases} 0 \text{ if } X < X_0 \\ k(X - X_0) \text{ if } X \geqslant X_0, \end{cases}$$

and hence $T(kX) = k T(X)$.

Influence of Experimental Contexts and the Use of Mathematical Models

Aside from the problems associated with the threshold, the results of a magnitude estimation study depend heavily upon certain aspects of the experiment that affect the observer's use of the number system. This in turn seems rather dramatically to affect the exponent of the power function. Poulton (1968) made some very trenchant comments on these types of problems. Even apart from possible confounding factors due to the penchant for averaging across observers in these studies (Stevens does not pretend to possess a curve that will fit everyone), since the exact form of the function for magnitude estimation seems to depend on so many extraneous factors (extraneous to the transduction and transmission through sensory channels), one may well be concerned about the fruits of this great body of research.

Two comments are apposite here. First, even if we knew no more than whether an exponent for a given sensory system was greater than or less than one, we would know considerably more about the system than we did when we began. It is perhaps something of a pleasant surprise even that a sensory channel can be described behaviorally in terms of a single-signed second derivative. Second, even the knowledge of likely ranges of exponents and thresholds may prove of value for at least some aspects of communication engineering. Where it is not possible or feasible to precisely control for the observer's use of the number system, which may be discussed as a function of his response bias, one may use mathematical models which include structure both for sensory processes as well as for response bias (which depend upon experimental response-constraints, and learning and motivational variables). Indeed, in almost any circumstance, they can prove of value as "filters" to expose more cleanly the sensory characteristics. This function is partially distinct from their use as theoretical descriptions and predictors.

Luce (1959) has developed an elegant theory resting primarily upon a single axiom, and he has applied this theory to the problem of magnitude estimation. He has shown, among other things, what conditions on the response-bias function and the stimulus-generalization function must be satisfied for the arithmetic and geometric means to be proportional to the "true" psychophysical function (within his theory).

Atkinson (1963); Atkinson and Kinchla (1965); Kinchla, Townsend, Yellott, and Atkinson (1966); Luce (1963); and Krantz (1969) have suggested intuitively pleasing theories for simple signal detection situations which I have recently generalized to models of complete identification experiments (i.e., recognition of one of a finite set of signals on each trial) (Townsend, 1968, 1971a, 1971b). The ideas inherent in the model are capable of motivating a very general theory for the magnitude estimation setting. Basically, the model posits that the result of a single sensory stimulation is the activation of a hypothetical sensory state; a decision is then made by the observer on the basis of this sensory state, and it is here that his response bias may enter. Hence, we may impose a conditional probability distribution relating the presented stimulus S to the hypothetical sensory states, which we will denote by a random variable s. Similarly, we may postulate the existence of another distribution relating an activated sensory state to the set of possible responses, which we call R. Lee (1963) discussed this type of model when the set of sensory states is on a continuum, the latter probably more appropriate than a finite set of discrete states for direct scaling experiments.

Although frequently the conditional geometric mean has been employed to describe (usually to define) the psychophysical function because of skewed data, it is far from certain that this strategem "reveals" the underlying sensory functions. At any rate, we will here confine our remarks to a few simple observations about the arithmetic mean. In this case, it seems reasonable, as a first approximation, to define the psychophysical function as the expected value (mathematical arithmetic means) of the sensory state conditionalized on a particular stimulus presentation, i.e., $Y = E(s|S)$. Since what is usually obtained in a magnitude estimation experiment corresponds to

$$E(R|S) = \int_s \int_R R \, f(s|S)g(R|s)dRds = \int_s \{\int_R g(R|s)RdR\}f(s|S)ds,$$

it is immediately apparent that a sufficient condition to permit $E(R|S) = k \, E(s|S)$, is that $E(R|s) = \int g(R|s)RdR = ks$, where k is a constant. That is, if the average response given a particular sensory state, s, is proportioned to s, then the average response would be proportional to the average sensory state resulting from stimulus S. One can, of course, impose as much theoretical structure on the distributions as is consonant with one's aims.

My own bias would favor increasing utilization of mathematical models, both as possible substantive explanations, and as devices to reveal those underlying characteristics of the observer in which the investigator is interested. For instance, the effects upon responses noted by Poulton might well provide the basis for some first approximations to the response function for the above model. A purely empirical and/or purely scaling approach seems to leave many areas of ambiguity.

In summary, we have discussed the mind-body equation in reference to several points of methodology and epistemology. We have seen that Fechner, significant though he was in the establishment of an important segment of today's psychology, employed a mathematical technique that is legitimate only in a few special cases, the most noteworthy fortunately being Weber's law. We have also seen that current investigations have clarified the problems involved with this project of Fechner's considerably and brought alternative conceptions and competing theories to the mind-body scaling problem. Finally, we have tried to make the point, via somewhat discursive comments on issues related to the mind-body problem, that considerations and application of such concepts and areas of falsifiability, measurement theory and substantive mathematical models can play an important role in the delineation and explanation of psychophysical processes as well as theory testing in general.

REFERENCES

Atkinson, R. C. 1963. "A variable sensitivity theory of signal detection." *Psychological Review* 70:91–106.

Atkinson, R. C., and Kinchla, R. A. 1965. "A learning model for forced-choice detection experiments." *British Journal of Mathematical and Statistical Psychology* 18:183–206.

Boring, E. G. 1950. *A history of experimental psychology.* 2nd ed. New York: Appleton-Century-Crofts.

Campbell, N. R. 1920. *Physics: the elements.* London: Cambridge University Press.

Fechner, G. T. *Elemente der Psychophysik.* 1964. Amsterdam: E. J. Bonset. (First published in 1860.)

——— *Elements of Psychophysics.* Translated by Helmut E. Adler. New York: Holt, Rinehart and Winston.

Feigl, H. 1967. *The "Mental" and "Physical"; the Essay and a Postscript.* Minneapolis: University of Minnesota Press.

Falmagne, J. C. 1971. "The generalized Fechner problem and discrimination." *Journal of Mathematical Psychology* 8:22–43.

Goldberg, S. 1958. *Introduction to Difference Equations.* New York: John Wiley and Sons.

Green, D. M., and Swets, J. A. 1966. *Signal detection theory and psychophysics.* New York: John Wiley and Sons.

Jammer, M. 1954. *Concepts of space.* Cambridge Mass.: Harvard University Press.

Kinchla, R. A., Townsend, J. T., Yellott, J. I., and Atkinson, R. C. 1966. "Influence of correlated visual cues on auditory signal detection." *Perception and Psychophysics* 1:67–73.

Krantz, D. H. 1971. "Integration of just-noticeable differences." *Journal of Mathematical Psychology* 8:591–599.

Lee, H. 1963. Choosing among confusably distributed stimuli with specified likelihood ratios. *Perceptual and Motor Skills* 16:445–467.

Levine, M. V. 1970. "Transformations that render curves parallel." *Journal of Mathematical Psychology* 7:410–443.

Luce, R. D. 1959. "On the possible psychophysical laws." *Psychological Review* 66:81–95.

——— 1959. *Individual Choice Behavior.* New York: John Wiley and Sons.

Luce, R. D., and Edwards, W. 1958. "The derivation of subjective scales from just noticeable differences." *Psychological Review* 65:222–237.

Meehl, P. E. 1967. "Theory testing in psychology and physics: A methodological paradox." *Philosophy of Science* 34:103–115.

Popper, K. R. 1959. *The Logic of Scientific Discovery.* New York: Harper and Row.

Poulton, E. C. 1968. "The new psychophysics: Six models for magnitude estimation." *Psychological Bulletin* 69:1–19.

Stevens, S. S. 1957. "On the psychophysical law." *Psychological Review* 64:153–181.

—— 1961. "The psychophysics of sensory function." In W. A. Rosenblith, *Sensory Communication.* Cambridge, Mass.: M. I. T. Press.

Suppes, P., and Zinnes, J. L. 1963. "Basic measurement theory." In Handbook of Mathematical Psychology, vol. 1. New York: John Wiley and Sons.

Townsend, J. T. 1966. "Choice behavior in a cued recognition task." Technical Report No. 103, Institute for Mathematical Studies in the Social Sciences, Stanford University. 1966.

—— 1968. "Recognition models and metric assumptions in the identification of upper case English letters." Paper presented at the meeting of the Western Psychological Association, San Diego, March, 1968.

—— 1971a. "Theoretical analysis of an alphabetic confusion matrix." *Perception and Psychophysics* 9:40–50.

—— 1971b. "Alphabetic Confusion: A test of models for individuals." *Perception and Psychophysics* 9:449–454.

The Contributors

CHUNG-YING CHENG received his B.A. degree from National Taiwan University in 1956, his M.A. from the University of Washington in 1958, and his Ph.D. from Harvard in 1964. He is professor of philosophy at the University of Hawaii, where he has taught since 1963. He has also taught at Yale University (1968–1970), at National Taiwan University (1970–1972), and at Queens College of the City University of New York (1972–1973). He is founder and editor of the *Journal of Chinese Philosophy*. His publications include *Peirce's and Lewis's Theories of Induction* (1969), *Tai Chên's Inquiry into Goodness* (1971), and many articles on philosophy of logic and language, Chinese philosophy, and Chinese logic in well-known Eastern and Western philosophy periodicals.

JUDITH J. ECONOMOS received her B.A. from the University of Florida in 1961 and her Ph.D. from the University of California at Los Angeles in 1967. She has been a teaching assistant at UCLA (1965–1967) and an instructor at Princeton University (1969–1970). Her interests include philosophy of mind, epistemology, sculpture, and painting.

BRIAN ELLIS is professor or philosophy at La Trobe University, a position which he has held since 1966. He has also held several visiting positions in the United States. In 1962 to 1963, he was visiting associate professor at the University of Pittsburgh; in 1970, visiting professor at the University of Illinois, Chicago Circle; and in 1972, visiting professor at the Minnesota Center for the Philosophy of Science. Professor Ellis is the author of *Basic Concepts of Measurement* (1966) and many articles in philosophical journals and books, mainly on topics in or related to the philosophy of science.

HERBERT FEIGL, Regents' Professor Emeritus of Philosophy, University of Minnesota, received his Ph.D. in philosophy and physics at the University of

Vienna in 1927. He was a Rockefeller Research Fellow at Harvard Univerisity in 1930 and at Columbia and Harvard universities in 1940. In 1947 he received a Guggenheim Research Fellowship. He has taught at the State University of Iowa (1931–1939) and at the University of Minnesota (1941–1971), and was director of the Minnesota Center for Philosophy of Science from 1953 to 1971. He is a well-known philosopher and author of many important philosophical treatises.

KEITH GUNDERSON received his Ph.D. from Princeton University in 1963. He is professor of philosophy at the University of Minnesota and a research associate for the Minnesota Center for the Philosophy of Science. He is editor of Volume VII of the Minnesota Studies in the Philosophy of Science series, entitled *Language, Mind, and Knowledge*, and the author of *Mentality and Machines* (1971), two books of poetry, and numerous articles and reviews.

DAVID LEWIS, professor of philosophy at Princeton University, received his B.A. degree from Swarthmore College and his M.A. and Ph.D. degrees from Harvard University (1964 and 1967). He is the author of *Convention* (1969) and *Counterfactuals* (1973), and articles on metaphysics, semantics, and philosophy of science.

GROVER MAXWELL holds a Ph.D. in physical chemistry and has taught and done industrial research in that subject. In 1954 he began a four-year period of graduate study in the Department of Philosophy and the Minnesota Center for Philosophy of Science at the University of Minnesota; he has been associated with these units ever since. He is co-editor of and contributor to numerous volumes on philosophy and philosophy of science, including the Minnesota Studies in the Philosophy of Science series.

STEPHEN C. PEPPER (died 1972) was emeritus professor of philosophy at the University of California at Berkeley. His publications include *Esthetic Quality* (1938), *World Hypotheses* (1942), *The Basis of Criticism in Arts* (1945), *Digest of Purposive Values* (1947), *Principles of Art Appreciation* (1949), *The Work of Art* (1956), *The Sources of Value* (1958), *Ethics* (1960), and *Concept and Quality* (1967).

J. J. C. SMART is emeritus professor of philosophy at the University of Adelaide, and reader in philosophy at La Trobe University. From 1950 to 1972 he was Hughes Professor of Philosophy, University of Adelaide. He has been a visiting professor at Princeton, Harvard, and Yale universities. Since 1969 he has been a Fellow of the Australian Academy of the Humanities. His publications include books in the philosophy of science, metaphysics, and ethics, and numerous philosophical articles.

JAMES T. TOWNSEND received his B.A. degree from Fresno State College and a Ph.D. in experimental psychology from Stanford University in 1966. After teaching at the University of Hawaii for two years, he moved to Purdue

University where he is associate professor in the Department of Psychological Sciences. He was visiting associate professor at Rockefeller University during the academic year 1972–1973, engaging in theoretical and experimental research in the Mathematical Psychology Laboratory of W. K. Estes. A member of AAAS and Sigma XI, his interests center in the mathematical and experimental study of human cognition and information processing. He is the author of numerous papers on these topics appearing in *Perception and Psychophysics*, *British Journal of Mathematical and Statistical Psychology*, and *Memory and Cognition*.

SATOSI WATANABE received a B.S. in physics at the University of Tokyo in 1933, and D.Sc. degrees from the University of Paris in 1935 and from the University of Tokyo in 1940. He has taught physics at the University of Tokyo, Wayne State University, the U.S. Naval Postgraduate School, and the University of Hawaii. He has also taught applied mathematics at the University of Tokyo, electrical engineering at Yale and Columbia universities, and philosophy at Yale and Fordham universities. His publications include *Knowing and Guessing* (1969), and more than a hundred papers in various scholarly journals.

About the Editor

CHUNG-YING CHENG, the editor of this volume, is professor of philosophy at the University of Hawaii. A graduate of National Taiwan University, he studied at the University of Washington and received his Ph. D. degree from Harvard in 1964. His areas of special interest are logical theory, philosophy of language, and Chinese philosophy. Dr. Cheng has contributed numerous articles to both Western and Eastern philosophical journals. He is the author of *Peirce's and Lewis's Theories of Induction*, published in 1969, *Tai Chên's Inquiry into Goodness*, published in 1971, and *Chinese Philosophy and Chinese Culture* and *Scientific Truth and Human Values*, both published in 1974. He is also the founder and editor of the *Journal of Chinese Philosophy*.